Immigration Economics

Immigration Economics

George J. Borjas

Harvard University Press

Cambridge, Massachusetts
London, England   2014

Library of Congress Cataloging-in-Publication Data

Borjas, George J.
  Immigration economics / George J. Borjas.
    pages cm
  Includes bibliographical references and index.
  ISBN 978-0-674-04977-2 (hardcover : alk. paper)
  1. Emigration and immigration—Economic aspects.   I. Title.
  JV6217.B673 2014
  331.6'2—dc23

                                                    2013040285

To my mother

Contents

Immigration Economics

Introduction

♦

NATIONAL BORDERS SEEM increasingly porous. Nearly 215 million persons now live in a country where they were not born, so immigrants account for about 3 percent of the world's population. It is not surprising that the surge in large-scale international migration increased the foreign-born share of the population in a traditional immigrant-receiving country like the United States—from 6 to 13 percent in the past 30 years. What is surprising is that the foreign-born share now stands at record levels in countries that have little historical experience with immigration: 9 percent in Portugal, 10 percent in Norway and the United Kingdom, 13 percent in Germany, 14 percent in Spain and Sweden, and 16 percent in Austria (United Nations 2011). Much of the developed world is increasingly composed of "nations of immigrants."

Inevitably, the rise in the demographic importance of international migration has led to a parallel increase in the amount of time and effort that economists devote to studying the determinants and consequences of immigration. Part of the increasing interest undoubtedly arises because of the policy concerns raised by large migrant flows in receiving (and sending) countries. In practically all immigrant-receiving countries, the debate over immigration policy revolves around a number of politically sensitive questions that can, in principle, be addressed through economic

1

analysis. Is the country better off attracting high- or low-skill immigrants? In fact, is the country better off with *any* immigrants? Are immigrants assimilating too slowly? How can a host country ensure that the "melting pot" works across generations? What is the impact of immigration on the employment and earnings of native workers?

Each of these policy concerns is controversial, and each has surely motivated many studies in economics and other social sciences. There is, however, another set of concerns that stimulate the typical economist's interests in migration issues. The study of worker flows—across jobs, across cities, across industries, across occupations—is a core topic in labor economics. The movement of workers from a low-paying to a high-paying sector creates competitive forces that tend to equalize wages in the two sectors. A central lesson of economics is that the equalization of a worker's value of marginal product across markets yields an efficient allocation of workers to jobs, an allocation that maximizes the total value of worker product in a competitive economy. From this perspective, migration is perhaps the key tool used by the labor market to iron out inefficiencies and to ensure that workers are allocated to those jobs where they are most productive.

Given the intimate link between labor mobility and labor market efficiency, it is no surprise that the study of international migration flows raises a number of conceptual and methodological questions that are inherently interesting—even when taken outside the controversial policy context. For example: How exactly does one measure the rate of economic assimilation experienced by immigrants in a receiving country? What does the canonical model of migration as a human capital investment imply about the types of workers who choose to migrate—are the "movers" the least skilled or the most skilled from the workforce of the sending country? What does economic theory imply about the impact of immigration on the wage of native workers, and exactly how would one go about measuring this impact? Under what conditions will immigration generate a net gain for the host economy, and how can one use the available models and data to calculate those gains?

These questions inspire economists to adapt the technical tools of economic theory and econometrics in ways that are often intriguing and occasionally raise more puzzles of their own. Sometimes the empirical answers to the underlying questions depend on the methodological approach, adding to the uncertainty about how the role of immigration should be assessed. Certainly the findings in these studies can have important policy implications, but the study of immigration also can teach economists a great deal about how labor markets respond to supply shocks, about the role that labor mobility plays in equilibrating labor markets, about the process of human capital accumulation, about the link between self-selection and labor market outcomes, and about how the implications of economic models can be tested with often imperfect data. It is these issues in the *economics* of immigration, rather than the policy context, that first sparked my interest nearly three decades ago. After all, I began my exploration at a time when the "immigration problem" had little policy relevance.

The combination of the contentious policy concerns and the intrinsic interest in the economic issues raised by immigration inspired the growth of a voluminous academic literature since the 1980s. By now, a book that covers all of the topics and variations on the themes in the vast literature would require an encyclopedic treatise several times the length of this book. I have never been a fan of reading those types of treatises; I would much prefer to read a shorter volume that focuses on what is essential to get a good understanding of the question. As a result, I have had to make hard choices about which topics to cover and which topics to ignore. In the end, and not too surprisingly, I have chosen to go with the issues that I find economically most interesting. Some issues that play a central role in the policy debate, such as illegal immigration, barely make an appearance in the discussion—not because they are not interesting or important (they are!), but because their analysis does not really teach us much more about the underlying economics of the problem. In fact, I have noticed that the questions that are driven by policy concerns tend to change from year to year as the political winds shift. But the questions that make immigration economics an intellectually fruitful subject of study endure over long spans of time.

Further, I have chosen to limit the discussion to those issues that are directly related to the costs and benefits that arise from immigrant participation in the labor market. There is one other economic consequence—namely, the fiscal impact of immigration and the interaction between immigration and the modern welfare state—that is at least as important, and that itself deserves a book-length treatment. However, the issues surrounding the definition and measurement of the fiscal impact of immigration have, for some reason, received far less academic attention than the labor market issues. Even though the fiscal impact raises interesting conceptual and methodological challenges, many of these problems have not yet been addressed satisfactorily. A full study of the economic approach to examining the fiscal impact of immigration, therefore, is relegated for the future.

I would be remiss if I did not note that the frequent use of economic models throughout this book goes somewhat against the grain of the atheoretical fashion of research that has dominated the study of labor economics in the past decade. At the same time that the immigration literature was coming of age, labor economics as a field changed from one that paid close attention to theoretical insights, and where the empirical work was more often than not guided by the theory, into one where many academic papers simply attempt to measure the impact of this or that policy shift on whatever interesting outcome variable happens to be readily available. Even though the "project evaluation" approach has made the very important contribution of forcing researchers to directly confront the key question of exactly what parameter can possibly be identified by the data at hand, I also believe that the combination of theory and empirics helps to provide a much deeper understanding of the economic problem.

A theme that recurs throughout the book is that immigration has consequences, and these consequences generally imply that some people lose while others benefit. The notion that immigration has both costs and benefits is somewhat foreign in the policy arena, where the lines of demarcation between the two extreme sides are clearly delineated, and immigration is held to be almost always beneficial or almost always costly. In fact, both the theory and the data suggest repeatedly that costs and benefits matter, and the identification of these distributional consequences forms a core contribution of the economic approach.

A second theme is that the insights of the theoretical models and the findings from empirical analysis are not always robust to changes in the underlying assumptions or in econometric methods. Perhaps nowhere is this lesson clearer than in the literature that purports to estimate the impact of immigration on the wages of preexisting workers in a host country. This literature has gone through several iterations in the 30 years since the initial studies were published. Each new generation of studies has certainly increased our understanding of the *mechanics* of the labor market impact, but each has also generated new empirical methods and evidence that often contradict what came before.

So let me succinctly state the questions at the heart of this book: What does economics have to say about immigration, and what do we have to assume to get it to say what we think it says? The presentation will often be critical and emphasize the need to be cautious in interpreting the implications of the models and the evidence. Nevertheless, I strongly believe that the economic analysis of immigration makes a valuable and unique contribution. If nothing else, it forces rigorous thinking and requires the delineation of the specific assumptions used in any examination of the determinants and consequences of international migration flows.

Organization of the Book

The book begins by asking the question upon which everything else rests: Who decides to become an immigrant? Chapter 1 presents the canonical economic model of the immigration decision. The model views immigration as a human capital investment; a person migrates whenever the gains from migration (such as the expected wage gain) exceed the costs. More importantly, the discussion derives the implications of this type of behavior for the selection of the subsample of immigrants. Not everyone in a source country decides to move, so it is important to establish the conditions that describe *which* particular subset leaves. A crucial implication of the theory (supported by some of the evidence) is that the commonly held notion that immigrants are "the best and the brightest" is not necessarily an implication of the income-maximization hypothesis.

The selection process determines the stock of preexisting skills that immigrants bring to the host economy. Immigrants, however, continue to acquire new skills after the move takes place. These post-migration investments determine the rate of economic assimilation between the immigrants and the native population in the host country. Chapter 2 derives and tests the implications of a model of optimal human capital accumulation for the rate of economic assimilation. The chapter also summarizes the econometric methods that are used to measure the rate of assimilation. The discussion emphasizes the difficulty of separately identifying the rate of economic assimilation from secular changes in the preexisting skills of immigrants.

The combination of pre- and post-migration skills determines the distribution of skills that immigrants offer to employers in the host country's labor market. Chapter 3 uses neoclassical factor demand theory to show how the interaction between the skill distributions of the immigrant and native populations determines the labor market impact of immigration. A typical implication of these models is that immigration reduces the wage of competing native workers, at least in the short run. Over time the labor market adjusts and the adverse wage effect is attenuated. Even in the long run, however, after all adjustments have taken place, the theory implies that immigration has distributional consequences: the relative wage must decline for the skill groups that experienced the largest immigration-induced supply increases.

Chapters 4 and 5 summarize the empirical literature that tests the implications of factor demand theory for the wage impact of immigration. Chapter 4 discusses "descriptive" methods that typically correlate the wage of a particular group with the supply shock experienced by that group, whereas Chapter 5 discusses "structural" methods that estimate a general equilibrium model of the labor market and then use the parameter estimates to simulate the impact of immigration on the wage structure.

The empirical literature summarized in these two chapters offers something for everyone. Some of the empirical approaches lead to the conclusion that immigration has no impact on the wage of competing native workers; other approaches suggest that immigration has a negative impact; and yet other approaches suggest that immigration has a positive impact. Remarkably, it has proven surprisingly difficult to demonstrate empirically the trivial Economics 101 theoretical implication that an outward shift in labor supply lowers the wage.

The discussion in Chapter 6 attempts to explain the source of some of these discrepancies. Part of the confusion arises because the different approaches are identifying the labor market impact of immigration under different conditions. If immigration has wage consequences in the host country's labor market, the preexisting participants in that market, both firms and workers, will take stock of the changed situation and adjust accordingly. These adjustments often diffuse the impact of immigration from one market to another, even to markets that received no immigrants whatsoever. The different approaches used in the literature often control for these adjustments in different ways and inevitably lead to conflicting estimates of the wage impact.

An important insight of economic models of immigration is that the *same* parameters that determine the distributional impact of immigration on the wage structure also determine the size of the net economic benefits that accrue to the host economy. In fact, the greater the distributional pain, the greater the net economic gains. Chapter 7 presents the basic model that describes the source of the gains from immigration, and applies this model both to the U.S. context and to a global context where immigration across countries is "free." A central lesson is that it is extremely difficult (if not impossible) to construct a competitive market model where the net gains accruing from immigration to a country like the United States are large. The framework also implies that the net gain to world GDP could be substantial if people could move freely across countries *as long as* the institutional and economic infrastructure that gives the developed world its productive edge remains intact after the inflow of perhaps billions of new workers.

Because the net gains from immigration to a host country like the United States tend to be small, many studies emphasize that the benefit could be much larger if the immigrant influx consisted mainly of high-skill workers. The rationale for these large gains, however, hinges on a key departure from the canonical model. Specifically, the gains arise because high-skill immigrants impart positive externalities on the productivity of workers in the host economy. Chapter 8 presents the models that allow for these types of external effects and summarizes the empirical methods that attempt to measure the human capital externalities.

Chapter 9 concludes the journey by examining the skill composition of the children of immigrants, a factor that will determine the (very) long-run impact of immigration on a host economy. There is a strong correlation between the mean skills of national origin groups in the immigrant generation and the mean skills of the corresponding ethnic groups that make up the second generation. To explain the correlation, some studies argue that ethnicity acts as a human capital externality, so that children who grow up in advantageous ethnic environments, where "ethnic capital" is beneficial and abundant, do better after they enter the labor market than children who grow up in disadvantaged ethnic neighborhoods. The chapter summarizes both the theoretical framework and the empirical approach that examines the nature and determines the empirical relevance of the ethnic externality.

Finally, the Conclusion offers some closing thoughts, noting a number of questions that have not yet been addressed and puzzles that remain unresolved. Although the literature has traveled far, the study of the economics of immigration remains an intellectually vibrant endeavor: there is still much to learn.

1

The Selection of Immigrants

---♦---

THE ECONOMIC IMPACT of immigration ultimately depends on the differences between the skill distributions of immigrants and natives. At any point in time, the human capital stock of the foreign-born population in a host country consists of the skills that the immigrants acquired prior to migration and of the skills acquired in the post-migration period.

This chapter examines the determinants of the volume of preexisting skills. It starts my exploration of immigration economics by asking a simple question: Who moves? Immigrants are not a randomly selected sample of the population of the source countries; some people choose to migrate and some choose to stay. The skill distribution of immigrants at the time of entry depends entirely on the nature of the selection algorithm that separates the movers from the stayers. As a result, any attempt to understand the skill differentials between immigrants and natives must begin with an analysis of the factors that motivate only some persons in a source country to emigrate.

The Migration Decision

It is instructive to begin by considering a two-country framework. Residents of a source country (country 0) consider migrating to a host country

(country 1). Assume initially that the migration decision is irreversible, so that no return migration occurs. Residents of the source country face the earnings distribution:

$$\log w_0 = \mu_0 + v_0, \qquad (1.1)$$

where w_0 gives earnings in the source country; μ_0 gives the mean (log) earnings in the source country; and the random variable v_0 is i.i.d., measuring deviations from mean earnings and assumed to be normally distributed with mean zero and variance σ_0^2. For expositional convenience, equation (1.1) suppresses the subscript that indexes a particular individual.

If the *entire* population of the sending country were to emigrate, the earnings distribution that this population would face in the receiving country is:

$$\log w_1 = \mu_1 + v_1, \qquad (1.2)$$

where μ_1 gives the mean (log) earnings in the host country *for this particular population,* and the random variable v_1 is also i.i.d. and normally distributed with mean zero and variance σ_1^2. The parameter ρ_{01} gives the correlation coefficient between v_0 and v_1.

As defined, the population mean μ_1 need not equal the mean earnings of native workers in the receiving country. The average worker in the sending country may be more or less skilled than the average worker in the receiving country. It is convenient to initially assume that the average person in both countries is equally skilled (or, equivalently, that any differences in average skills have been controlled for), so that μ_1 also gives the mean earnings of natives in the receiving country. This assumption helps isolate the impact of the selection process on the skill composition of the immigrant population and provides a simple way to compare the skills of immigrants and natives in the receiving country.

Equations (1.1) and (1.2) describe the earnings opportunities available to persons residing in the source country. The insight that migration decisions are motivated mainly by wage differentials can be attributed to Sir John Hicks. In *The Theory of Wages,* Hicks (1932, p. 76) argued that "differences in net economic advantages, chiefly differences in wages, are the main causes of migration." Practically all studies of migration decisions use this conjecture as a point of departure. Suppose then that the migration decision is determined by a comparison of earnings opportunities across countries, net of migration costs.[1] Define the index function:

$$I = \log\left(\frac{w_1}{w_0 + C}\right) \approx (\mu_1 - \mu_0 - \pi) + (v_1 - v_0), \tag{1.3}$$

where C gives the level of migration costs, and π gives a "time-equivalent" measure of these costs ($\pi = C/w_0$). A person emigrates if $I > 0$, and remains in the source country otherwise.

Migration is costly, and these costs likely vary among persons. However, the nature of the correlation between costs (whether in absolute dollars or in time-equivalent terms) and skills is unclear. Migration costs involve direct expenditures (such as transportation costs), forgone earnings (such as the opportunity cost of a post-migration unemployment spell), and psychic costs (such as the disutility associated with leaving family and friends behind). Suppose that the distribution of the random variable π in the sending country's population is given by:

$$\pi = \mu_\pi + v_\pi, \tag{1.4}$$

where μ_π is the mean level of migration costs in the population, and the random variable v_π is i.i.d., and assumed to be normally distributed with mean zero and variance σ_π^2. The correlation coefficients between v_π and the random variables v_0 and v_1 are given by $\rho_{\pi 0}$ and $\rho_{\pi 1}$, respectively. Given the diverse components that enter the calculation of C, it is difficult to make any sensible *a priori* inferences about the relationship between time-equivalent migration costs and skills. The specification of migration costs in equation (1.4) implies that we can rewrite the index function in (1.3) as:

$$I = \log\left(\frac{w_1}{w_0 + C}\right) = (\mu_1 - \mu_0 - \mu_\pi) + (v_1 - v_0 - v_\pi). \tag{1.5}$$

The probability that a person migrates to the host country is given by:

$$P(z) = \Pr[I > 0] = \Pr[v > -(\mu_1 - \mu_0 - \mu_\pi)] = 1 - \Phi(z), \tag{1.6}$$

where $v = v_1 - v_0 - v_\pi$; $z = -(\mu_1 - \mu_0 - \mu_\pi)/\sigma_v$; and Φ is the standard normal distribution function. Equation (1.6) summarizes the economic content of the Hicksian theory of migration. In particular:

$$\frac{\partial P}{\partial \mu_0} < 0, \ \frac{\partial P}{\partial \mu_1} > 0, \text{ and } \frac{\partial P}{\partial \mu_\pi} < 0. \tag{1.7}$$

The migration rate falls when the mean income in the source country rises, when the mean income in the host country falls, and when (mean) time-equivalent migration costs rise. Most studies in the literature on the internal migration of persons within a particular country focus on testing these theoretical predictions. The evidence reported in the internal migration literature is generally supportive of the implications in equation (1.7).[2]

Why Are There So Few Immigrants?

There exist huge income differences across countries. The Penn World Table, for example, reports that the (PPP-adjusted) per capita GDP in 2010 ranged from $41,400 in the United States to $34,900 in Ireland, $10,400 in Turkey, and $1,100 in Uganda (Heston et al. 2012). These income gaps should generate very large flows of international migrants. In the absence of migration costs, these wage differences are sufficiently large that many countries should have "emptied out" by now if their populations were composed exclusively of rational, income-maximizing agents. Of course, most receiving countries enact restrictive immigration policies that prevent these flows from occurring, and the income differences persist.

It is easy to show, however, that the existence of restrictive immigration policies cannot be the sole factor explaining why many individuals do not move across countries in search of higher income opportunities. Even when there are no legal restrictions preventing entry into high-income regions, many people in low-income countries *choose* not to move. This type of behavior is consistent with the income-maximization model of migration only if migration costs C are very high. In fact, it is easy to apply the framework to get a back-of-the-envelope estimate of the magnitude of these costs.

Consider, for example, the existing wage differences between Puerto Rico and the United States. In 2012 the mean annual earnings of workers employed in production occupations was $22,600 in Puerto Rico and $34,500 in the United States (U.S. Bureau of Labor Statistics 2012).[3] Because Puerto Ricans are U.S. citizens by birth, there are no legal restrictions preventing their move to the United States. In fact, the large income gap has induced about a third of the Puerto Rican population to migrate to the United States since the end of World War II (Borjas 2008). But, just as important, two-thirds of Puerto Ricans chose not to move.

Let w_{PR} be the wage a production worker can earn in Puerto Rico, and w_{US} be the wage he can earn in the United States. For simplicity, assume these wages are constant over a worker's career and that workers live forever. The discounted present value in each location for the typical worker is then given by:

$$PV_{PR} = \frac{w_{PR}}{r} \quad \text{and} \quad PV_{US} = \frac{w_{US}}{r}, \tag{1.8}$$

where r is the rate of discount. The *marginal* Puerto Rican production worker is indifferent between moving and staying if the discounted gains from moving are exactly equal to migration costs:

$$\frac{(w_{US} - w_{PR})}{r} = C^* \tag{1.9}$$

where C^* gives the level of migration costs for the marginal worker. Let $\pi^* = C^*/w_{PR}$, so that π^* gives the costs of migration in time-equivalent terms. I can then rewrite equation (1.9) as:

$$\frac{1}{r}\frac{(w_{US} - w_{PR})}{w_{PR}} = \pi^* \tag{1.10}$$

The ratio $(w_{US} - w_{PR})/w_{PR}$ is around 0.5, indicating that a "typical" Puerto Rican production worker can increase his income by 50 percent by migrating to the United States. If the rate of discount is 5 percent, the left-hand side of equation (1.10) takes on the value of 10. In other words, migration costs for the marginal worker who is indifferent between migrating to the United States and staying in Puerto Rico are 10 times his salary. If this production worker earns the average salary in Puerto Rico, migration costs are around $226,000![4]

What exactly is the nature of these costs? They obviously do not represent the cost of transporting the family and household goods to a new location in the United States. Instead, the marginal Puerto Rican must attach a very high utility to the social and cultural amenities associated with remaining in his birthplace. Needless to say, migration costs could be even larger in other contexts—where there are much greater differences in language and culture between sending and receiving locations, and where the receiving country does not have a large and thriving network of compatriots to welcome and ease the entry of new migrants.[5] In short, the Puerto Rican example dramatically suggests that many people would choose not to migrate even if high-income receiving countries did not impose legal impediments.[6]

The Roy Model

Although it is important to determine the size and direction of migration flows, it is equally important to determine *which* persons find it most worthwhile to migrate to the receiving country. Even in the absence of legal restrictions impeding international migration, only a subset of persons in the host country chooses to move. The nature of the selection that generates a nonrandom sample of immigrants is closely related to the Roy model of occupational choice (Roy 1951). Roy's original setting examined a worker's choice between becoming a fisherman or a hunter, and provided an algorithm that described which types of people would go into each of the two occupations. The framework was first applied to answer the question "Should I stay or should I go?" in Borjas (1987b, 1991).[7]

Consider the conditional expectations $E(\log w_0 \,|\, I > 0)$ and $E(\log w_1 \,|\, I > 0)$. These expectations give the average earnings in both the source and the host country for the self-selected sample of migrants. It is important to emphasize that these expectations hold the parameters $(\mu_0, \mu_1, \sigma_0^2, \sigma_1^2, \rho_{01})$ of the income distributions constant. This is not a trivial assumption. For example, the model explicitly assumes that the migration flow is sufficiently small so that there are no feedback effects on the average income of immigrants (or natives) in the host country or on the average income of the "stayers" in the source country. A general equilibrium model would account for the fact that the parameters of the income distributions in both sending and receiving regions are endogenous, and likely depend on the size and skill composition of the immigrant flow.

Because the random variables v_0, v_1, and v_π are jointly normally distributed, it can be shown that these conditional means are given by:[8]

$$E(\log w_0 \,|\, I > 0) = \mu_0 + \frac{\sigma_0 \sigma_1}{\sigma_v} \left[\left(\rho_{01} - \frac{\sigma_0}{\sigma_1} \right) - \rho_{\pi 0} \frac{\sigma_\pi}{\sigma_1} \right] \lambda(z), \qquad (1.11)$$

$$E(\log w_1 \,|\, I > 0) = \mu_1 + \frac{\sigma_0 \sigma_1}{\sigma_v} \left[\left(\frac{\sigma_1}{\sigma_0} - \rho_{01} \right) - \rho_{\pi 1} \frac{\sigma_\pi}{\sigma_0} \right] \lambda(z), \qquad (1.12)$$

where $\lambda(z) = \phi(z)/(1 - \Phi(z)) \geq 0$, and ϕ is the density function of the standard normal distribution.

It is easier to grasp the economic intuition behind the implied selection mechanism by initially assuming that $\sigma_\pi = 0$, so that time-equivalent migration costs are constant in the population. To simplify the discussion, let $Q_0 = E(v_0 | I > 0)$ and $Q_1 = E(v_1 | I > 0)$. Manipulation of equations (1.11) and (1.12) shows that the Roy model demarcates three cases that summarize the pattern of skill differences between immigrants and natives:[9]

$$Q_0 > 0 \text{ and } Q_1 > 0, \quad \text{if} \quad \rho_{01} > \frac{\sigma_0}{\sigma_1} \text{ and } \frac{\sigma_0}{\sigma_1} < 1,$$

$$Q_0 < 0 \text{ and } Q_1 < 0, \quad \text{if} \quad \rho_{01} > \frac{\sigma_1}{\sigma_0} \text{ and } \frac{\sigma_0}{\sigma_1} > 1, \qquad (1.13)$$

$$Q_0 < 0 \text{ and } Q_1 > 0, \quad \text{if} \quad \rho_{01} < \min\left(\frac{\sigma_1}{\sigma_0}, \frac{\sigma_0}{\sigma_1} \right).$$

Define *positive selection* to occur when immigrants have above-average earnings in both the source and the host country ($Q_0 > 0$ and $Q_1 > 0$), and *negative selection* when immigrants have below-average earnings in both countries ($Q_0 < 0$ and $Q_1 < 0$). Equation (1.13) shows that either type of selection requires that skills be (sufficiently) positively correlated between the two countries. The variances σ_0^2 and σ_1^2 measure the "price" of skills: the greater the rewards to skills, the larger the inequality in wages.[10] Immigrants are then positively selected when the sending country—*relative to the receiving country*—offers a lower return to skills, "taxing" high-skill workers and "insuring" low-skill workers against poor labor market outcomes. In contrast, immigrants are negatively selected when the receiving country taxes high-skill workers and subsidizes low-skill workers.

The Roy model reveals that there exists a final selection possibility: the receiving country draws persons who have below-average earnings in the source country but do well in the host country ($Q_0 < 0$ and $Q_1 > 0$). This *inverse sorting* occurs when the correlation coefficient ρ_{01} is small or negative. The correlation could be negative when, for example, a source country experiences a political upheaval that results in the takeover of the government by a very redistributive regime, such as a communist revolution. In its initial stages, this political system often redistributes incomes by confiscating the assets of relatively successful persons. Immigrants from such systems will be in the lower tail of the post-revolution income distribution, but they will have the skills and wherewithal to perform quite well in the host country's market economy.

Equation (1.13) shows that neither differences in mean incomes across countries nor the mean level of migration costs determines the *type* of selection that characterizes the immigrant flow. Mean incomes and migration costs affect the size of the flow (and hence the extent to which the skills of the average immigrant differ from the mean skills of the base population) through the variable $\lambda(z)$, but they do not determine whether the immigrants are drawn mainly from the upper or lower tail of the skill distribution. Put differently, the gap in mean incomes and the level of migration costs influence the "intensity" of selection, but not the type.

It is important to examine what happens to the selection rules summarized in equation (1.13) if migration costs π are not constant across workers. It is easy to verify that variable migration costs do not alter any of the selection rules if (a) time-equivalent migration costs are uncorrelated with skills ($\rho_{\pi 0} = \rho_{\pi 1} = 0$), or (b) the ratio of variances σ_π / σ_j ($j = 0, 1$) is "small." In every other case, however, variable migration costs can change the nature of selection. Suppose, for example, that π is negatively correlated with skills, perhaps because high-skill workers are more proficient at collecting information about opportunities abroad or find it easier to adapt in a new environment. This negative correlation increases the likelihood that the bracketed term in equations (1.11) and (1.12) is positive, and the immigrant flow is more likely to be positively selected. Conversely, the likelihood of negative selection increases if time-equivalent migration costs and skills are positively correlated.

Inspection of equation (1.11) and (1.12) clarifies that it is not the heterogeneity in migration costs *per se* that can alter the nature of the selection, but the possibility that there exists a nonzero correlation between skills and migration costs. I would argue that the presence of such a correlation greatly reduces the empirical usefulness of the Roy model as a framework for thinking about the type of selection that characterizes the immigrant population. Put bluntly, *any* type of selection observed empirically can be explained by making the appropriate assumption about $\rho_{\pi 0}$ and $\rho_{\pi 1}$. This is particularly problematic because, as noted earlier, there is little reason to believe that we can figure out the nature of the distribution in migration costs by introspection.

For example, suppose that the pool of migrants from Mexico to the United States is composed of workers in the middle of the Mexican skill distribution (as reported in some of the empirical studies discussed below). The simplest version of the Roy model implies that Mexican migrants should be negatively selected because the rate of return to skills in Mexico is far higher than that found in the United States. Nevertheless, we can easily remedy the discrepancy between the data and the theory by assuming that migration costs are very high for the least-skilled Mexicans. These high migration costs remove the least-skilled workers from the sample of movers, leaving only workers in the middle of the skill distribution in the self-selected pool. The reverse-engineering of the "right" set of assumptions about the distribution of costs implies that the Roy model is no longer empirically falsifiable.

It is also of interest to generalize the selection rules summarized in (1.13) by examining the implications of the Roy model not only for the means of the income distributions among the relevant groups (movers and stayers), but also for the shape of the *entire* distributions. Consider the income distributions of two different populations, and let $F(x)$ and $G(x)$ represent the respective (cumulative) probability distributions, where x denotes the level of income for a particular person. By definition, $F(x)$ stochastically dominates $G(x)$ if:

$$F(x) < G(x), \forall\, x. \tag{1.14}$$

Stochastic dominance implies that a larger fraction of the workforce has incomes *above x* in the population represented by the dominating F distribution than by the G distribution. In other words, for any level of income, the population described by the probability distribution F is wealthier, because a larger fraction of the group exceeds that threshold. Note that stochastic dominance must imply a ranking of means where $\mu_F > \mu_G$, but the converse need not hold.

The selection that characterizes the sample of immigrants in the Roy model can be easily described in terms of the concept of stochastic dominance in the special case where $\sigma_\pi = 0$. In particular, let $F_M(v_0)$ be the distribution function of (pre-migration) earnings in the source country for the sample of movers, and let $F_S(v_0)$ be the respective distribution function for stayers. In short, $F_M(v_0)$ and $F_S(v_0)$ summarize the truncated earnings distributions—*prior to migration*—for the self-selected samples of movers and stayers, respectively. As shown in Appendix A, the Roy model predicts a unique stochastic ranking of these two truncated distributions. In particular:[11]

$$\mathbf{F_M}(v_0) < \mathbf{F_S}(v_0), \quad \text{if} \quad \frac{\sigma_0}{\sigma_1} < \rho_{01},$$

$$\mathbf{F_M}(v_0) > \mathbf{F_S}(v_0), \quad \text{if} \quad \frac{\sigma_0}{\sigma_1} > \rho_{01}.$$

(1.15)

Suppose that the rate of return to skills in the source country is sufficiently low, so that the ratio σ_0/σ_1 is below ρ_{01}. Equation (1.11) implies that the subsample of movers will necessarily have a higher mean income prior to moving than the stayers (so that the movers are positively selected in terms of mean incomes). Equation (1.15) further states that the distribution function of pre-migration incomes of movers stochastically dominates that of stayers, so that movers are "wealthier" than stayers at any point in the income distribution.

In contrast, suppose that the rate of return to skills is higher in the source country, implying that σ_0/σ_1 exceeds ρ_{01}. This situation might arise either because immigrants are negatively selected in the sense defined by equation (1.13), or because there is an inverse sorting of immigrants and the correlation coefficient ρ_{01} is small or negative. In either case, the pre-migration mean earnings of the migrants are lower than the pre-migration mean earnings of the stayers. Equation (1.15) shows that, for any level of income, a larger fraction of stayers is "wealthier."

Let me conclude by emphasizing that although this framework has become the canonical model of selection in the immigration literature, there is an important sense in which it is incomplete and could lead to misleading predictions about the skill composition of the immigrant population. As noted above, the Roy model provides a partial equilibrium framework for identifying the types of workers who find it most worthwhile to move. The immigrant flow is assumed to be "small," so that the impact of the labor supply shifts on the wage structures of both the source and the host country is negligible and can be ignored by the various agents in the model. In fact, the international movement of large numbers of workers will likely affect both wage structures, altering the optimal size and skill composition of the immigrant influx. However, the implications of a general equilibrium framework for the shape of the wage structures and for the selection predictions of the Roy model remain unexplored.[12]

A Special Case of the Roy Model and Extensions

There is a special case of the Roy model that can be illustrated graphically and that provides a simple point of departure for more complex situations. In particular, suppose that the correlation coefficient ρ_{01} is equal to one. This assumption effectively implies that earnings in both the source country and the United States depend on a single factor that is perfectly transferable across countries. In particular, let s denote the number of efficiency units embodied in the worker. The assumption that ρ_{01} is equal to one implies that we can write the income distributions in the two countries as:

$$\log w_0 = \alpha_0 + r_0\, s, \tag{1.16}$$

$$\log w_1 = \alpha_1 + r_1\, s, \tag{1.17}$$

where r_0 and r_1 are the rate of return to skills in the two countries, respectively.

The two panels of Figure 1.1 illustrate the linear relation between a worker's log wage and skills for each of the countries. In Figure 1.1A, the wage–skills profile is steeper in the host country, so the rate of return to skills is higher in the host country, while in Figure 1.1B, the rate of return to skills is higher in the source country. To easily illustrate the type of immigrant selection implied by this simplification, assume initially that workers do not incur any costs when they move. The decision rule determining im-

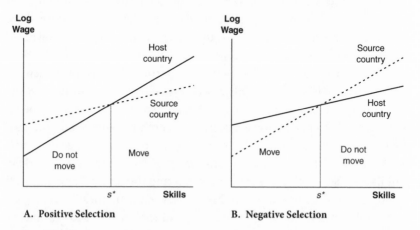

Figure 1.1. The Roy Model, Assuming Incomes Are Perfectly Correlated across Countries

migration is then quite simple: Workers originating in the source country emigrate whenever earnings are higher in the receiving country.[13]

Consider first the selection that occurs in Figure 1.1A. Workers with fewer than s^* efficiency units earn more if they stay in the source country than if they move. Workers with more than s^* efficiency units, however, earn more by moving. As long as the rate of return to skills is higher in the host than in the source country, therefore, the migration flow consists of workers in the upper tail of the skill distribution and immigrants are positively selected. Consider now Figure 1.1B. Workers with fewer than s^* efficiency units earn more in the host country and will want to move. When the returns to skills in the receiving country are relatively low, therefore, the immigrant flow is composed of the least-skilled workers in the source country and immigrants are negatively selected.

As Figure 1.1 shows, the assumption that ρ_{01} is equal to one leads to a simple separation of the pools of movers and stayers. Further, the graphical analysis can be easily extended to incorporate migration costs by simply shifting the respective wage profile accordingly. For example, the presence of constant time-equivalent migration costs would shift down the wage–skills profile in the host country (its intercept would now be given by $\alpha_1 - \pi$). As before, the introduction of constant migration costs does not change the nature of the selection (the movers would still be either positively or negatively selected), but would change its intensity because it would change the number of migrants.

The assumption that ρ_{01} is equal to one is useful because it permits several interesting and tractable generalizations. For example, consider the extension of the Roy model from a two-country to a multicountry framework, so that an individual residing in a particular source country must decide not only whether to leave that country, but also which potential destination to move to.

To simplify the exposition, assume that migration costs are equal to zero. A worker residing in a particular "base" country compares his earnings opportunities in all potential countries of residence and moves to the location that maximizes earnings. We can write the earnings distributions that workers in the base country would face if they all migrated to each of the n potential countries as:[14]

$$\log w_k = \alpha_k + r_k s, \qquad k = 1, \ldots, n. \tag{1.18}$$

An income-maximizing individual chooses to reside in country j whenever:

$$\log w_j > \max_{k \neq j} (\log w_k). \tag{1.19}$$

For convenience, rank countries such that $r_1 < r_2 < \ldots < r_n$. Figure 1.2 illustrates the nature of the sorting that takes place when $n = 3$. The least-skilled workers settle in the country with the lowest rate of return to skills, whereas the most-skilled workers settle in the country with the highest rate of return. In effect, income-maximizing behavior creates a positive correlation between the average skills of a country's inhabitants and the country's rate of return to skills:[15]

$$E(s \mid \text{choose } j) > E(s \mid \text{choose } k) \text{ if and only if } r_j > r_k. \tag{1.20}$$

The assumption that earnings are perfectly correlated across countries implies that individuals who rank highly in the income distribution in one country will also rank highly in the income distribution of any other country. Skilled workers, therefore, are attracted to countries that offer a relatively higher rate of return to skills. In contrast, low-skill workers choose countries that effectively "subsidize" their lack of human capital. As with the two-country Roy model, international differences in the returns to skills play an important allocative role in the sorting equilibrium.[16]

Another interesting extension, developed in Borjas and Bratsberg (1996), allows for the possibility of return migration. As in Rosen's (1972)

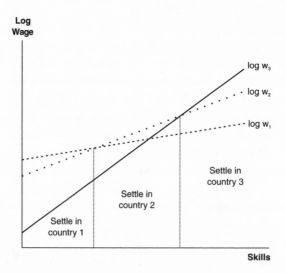

Figure 1.2. Selection in a Roy Model with Multiple Destinations

analysis of occupational mobility, return migration can occur as part of a "stepping stone" career path; it may be profitable to live abroad for a few years and acquire particular types of human capital that are valued in the source country's labor market. Return migration flows may also arise as workers correct mistakes in the initial migration decision (due perhaps to uncertainty in host country conditions). The Roy model helps to describe the type of selection that characterizes the return migrants.

To simplify the presentation, I illustrate the economic forces that determine return migration in the context of forward-looking workers who view temporary migration as a human capital investment. In a two-country framework, the log earnings distributions are given by equations (1.16) and (1.17). The worker also considers a third choice: migrating to country 1 for a fraction θ of his work life and returning home with an increased productivity. As a first-order approximation and ignoring discounting, the log wage associated with this choice is:

$$\log w_{10} = \theta \log w_1 + (1-\theta)(\log w_0 + \kappa), \qquad (1.21)$$

where $0 < \theta < 1$, and κ is the rate of return to temporary migration.

Suppose that the (time-equivalent) costs of migration and return migration equal π_{01} and π_{10}, respectively. These costs, as well as the parameters θ and κ, are assumed to be constant. A worker becomes an immigrant if:

$$\log w_1 - \pi_{01} > \log w_0 \quad or \quad \log w_{10} - \pi_{01} - \pi_{10} > \log w_0. \qquad (1.22)$$

In other words, a worker migrates if either the returns to permanently moving to the host country or the returns from a temporary sojourn surpass initial conditions (all net of migration costs). Similarly, a worker becomes a return migrant if:

$$\log w_{10} - \pi_{01} - \pi_{10} > \log w_0 \quad and \quad \log w_{10} - \pi_{01} - \pi_{10} > \log w_1 - \pi_{01}. \qquad (1.23)$$

The return migrants consist of the subsample of immigrants for whom the returns from temporary migration (net of migration costs) exceed the returns both of never moving and of moving permanently to the host country.

It is easy to characterize the various groups in terms of the distribution of efficiency units s in the population. In order for there to be *any* return migration, it must be the case that κ is sufficiently large. It is easy to show that the inequalities in equation (1.23) imply:

$$\kappa > \pi_{01} + \frac{\pi_{10}}{1-\theta}, \tag{1.24}$$

so that the rate of return to temporary migration must exceed the "expected" costs of migration. Assuming equation (1.24) holds, the subset of workers who become immigrants is given by:

$$(r_1 - r_0)s > (\alpha_0 - \alpha_1) + \kappa + \frac{\pi_{01} + \pi_{10} - \kappa}{\theta}, \tag{1.25}$$

and the subset of immigrants who become return migrants satisfies the inequality:

$$(\alpha_0 - \alpha_1) + \kappa + \frac{\pi_{01} + \pi_{10} - \kappa}{\theta} < (r_1 - r_0)s < (\alpha_0 - \alpha_1) + \kappa - \frac{\pi_{10}}{1-\theta}. \tag{1.26}$$

The two panels of Figure 1.3 illustrate the nature of selection in this model. The intuition for this sorting is obvious. Suppose, for example, that the immigrants were positively selected. The marginal immigrant in this self-selected sample is the least-skilled worker of a high-skill flow. The most-skilled workers in this sample have the most incentive to remain in the host country even if their economic opportunities improve in the source country. The marginal immigrant is most responsive to improving conditions in the

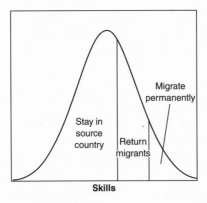

A. Positive Selection

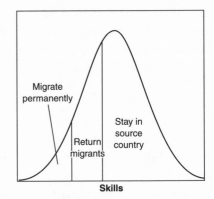

B. Negative Selection

Figure 1.3. Distribution of Skills and Selection in a Roy Model with Return Migration

source country and is most likely to become the return migrant. In contrast, if immigrants were negatively selected, the marginal immigrant is now the most-skilled person in a low-skill flow. Any improvements in source country conditions will particularly influence the return migration decision of the marginal immigrant, who happens to be the most-skilled worker.

In short, the return migration decision *reinforces* the original selection that characterized the immigrant population. Because it is the marginal immigrants who are most likely to become return migrants, the stayers are the "best of the best" if there is positive selection and the "worst of the worst" if there is negative selection.[17]

Linear Utility and "Generalized" Positive Selection

Although the Roy model has become a widely used framework for thinking about selection in the immigration context, its prediction that there exist plausible conditions under which the population of immigrants may be negatively selected has been disputed. In particular, it has been noted that many, if not most, immigrant flows are composed of workers who tend to have above-average education. For example, Docquier and Marfouk (2006) estimate the emigration rate from the less developed countries to be 1 percent for the general population, but over 13 percent for persons with tertiary education. These statistics suggest that the Roy model's predictive usefulness is limited, because most immigrant flows may be positively selected even though many of the source countries have very high rates of return to skills that should have generated negatively selected flows.

Grogger and Hanson (2011) propose an alternative model where positively selected flows naturally arise under most scenarios, particularly when examining migration flows from poor to rich countries. The nature of the prediction of "generalized" positive selection can be easily illustrated by examining a special case of this alternative framework. In particular, consider a situation where persons in a particular country, say 0, consider the possibility of settling in one of many potential destination countries, indexed by k. There are two skill groups in the population: high-skill (H) and low-skill (L). Finally, suppose that no other factors determine wages (so that the earnings distribution has zero variance for a particular skill group in a particular country). Let w_k^j give the wage that a worker in skill group j ($j = H, L$) would earn in country k. The log wage offers in country k for low- and high-skill workers are given by:

$$\log w_k^L = \mu_k, \tag{1.27a}$$

$$\log w_k^H = \mu_k + \delta_k, \tag{1.27b}$$

where δ_k gives the rate of return to skills in country k.[18] Suppose also that migration costs are composed simply of a fixed cost, C_{0k}, that is incurred by all workers—regardless of skill level—when migrating from country 0 to k.

The utility of worker i if he chooses to settle in country k is assumed to be linear in dollars and can be written as:

$$U_{i0k}^j = \alpha(w_k^j - C_{0k}) + \varepsilon_{i0k}^j, \tag{1.28}$$

where $\alpha > 0$, and ε is an unobserved random variable that summarizes the worker's preferences for particular places. Worker i calculates the utility associated from settling in each of the potential destinations, as well as the utility associated with not migrating at all (where $k = 0$ and $C_{00} = 0$).

Let P_{0k}^j be the fraction of the workforce in country 0 and in skill group j that chooses to move to country k. If ε_{i0k}^j has an i.i.d. extreme value distribution, it is well known (McFadden 1974) that the log odds of migrating from country 0 to country k are given by:

$$\log \frac{P_{0k}^j}{1 - P_{0k}^j} = \alpha(w_k^j - w_0^j) - \alpha C_{0k}, \tag{1.29}$$

where $w_k^L = e^{\mu_k}$ and $w_k^H = e^{\mu_k + \delta_k}$.

It is easy to see the type of selection implied by the linear utility framework by differencing the log odds ratio in equation (1.29) between the two skill groups. The differencing yields:

$$\log \frac{P_{0k}^H}{1 - P_{0k}^H} - \log \frac{P_{0k}^L}{1 - P_{0k}^L} = \alpha[(w_k^H - w_0^H) - (w_k^L - w_0^L)]. \tag{1.30}$$

Note that the differencing eliminates the fixed migration costs because they are independent of skill.

Equation (1.30) implies positive selection occurs as long as the differenced wage gap $\left[(w_k^H - w_0^H) - (w_k^L - w_0^L) \right]$ in the right-hand side of the equation is positive. Positive selection then requires that the *absolute* wage gap between the receiving and the source country be greater for high-skill than for low-skill workers. If migrants flow from poorer to richer countries (so that $\mu_k > \mu_0$), the differenced wage gap must necessarily be positive if $\delta_k > \delta_0$. The framework, therefore, replicates the Roy model prediction that countries offering a higher return to skills attract relatively more skilled immigrant flows.

The linear utility framework, however, also suggests that the migrant flow may be positively selected even if $\delta_k \leq \delta_0$. To see this, suppose that the rate of return to skills is the same in both countries ($\delta_k = \delta_0$). The larger absolute wage in the wealthier country ensures that $(w_k^H - w_k^L) > (w_0^H - w_0^L)$ even though the percent payoff to skills is the same in both countries.[19] In fact, if the absolute wage gap between poor and rich countries is sufficiently large, the rate of return to skills could be lower in the richer country and the immigrant flow would *still* be positively selected.

The linear utility framework has a dynamic implication that is interesting but may be troubling. Suppose that a worldwide skill-neutral technological shift continuously increases wages in all countries and for all skill groups. In the absence of migration costs, the Roy model would predict no change in the rate of international migration, because the *log* wage gap that summarizes migration incentives has not changed. The linear utility model, however, predicts either a substantial increase or a substantial decrease in the number of immigrants. This prediction follows directly from equation (1.29). Abstracting from migration costs, a steady rise in $(w_k^j - w_0^j)$ would continually increase the magnitude of the log odds ratio in the probability of moving for every skill group. If the log odds ratio were positive ($P_{0k}^j > 0.5$), the increase in world wealth would lead to exponential growth in the migration rate until it approaches 1. If the log odds ratio were negative ($P_{0k}^j < 0.5$), the migration rate would become vanishingly small. Because typically fewer than half of the people in most source countries emigrate, the linear utility model seems to suggest that the notion of international migration will become (or, perhaps, should have become) a distant memory as countries become wealthier, even though some countries will remain relatively poor.[20]

Regardless of whether this prediction of the model is empirically relevant or not, the wide array of results that can be derived from alternative selection models indicates that in the end, there will only be one way of determining which framework is most useful for understanding the nature of immigrant selection—by looking at the data.

Evidence on Selection

Cross-Country Regressions

It is well known that there is a large variance in skills and economic performance among immigrant groups residing in the United States but originating in different source countries. This dispersion across national origin groups inspired the methodology employed by the early empirical tests of the Roy model. Beginning with Borjas (1987b), a number of studies have estimated "cross-country regressions" to determine if post-migration earnings differences across national origin groups could be attributed to differences in the characteristics of the source countries. It is easy to illustrate (and update) this approach by using the Public Use Microdata Sample (PUMS) files from the 1980–2000 U.S. decennial censuses and the pooled 2009–2011 American Community Surveys (ACS). For expositional convenience, I refer to the pooled ACS data as the "2010 census." Appendix B contains a detailed description of the construction of the various data sets used throughout this book.

Each survey reports the earnings of workers belonging to specific national origin groups. To examine the differences in the skills that immigrants acquired prior to migration, I limit the analysis to those immigrants who entered the United States in the 5-year period just before the census cross-section. The sample consists of immigrant men aged 25–64, who worked at least one week in the year prior to the census, are not enrolled in school, and originated in one of the 80 largest sending countries.[21] An immigrant's weekly earnings is defined by the ratio of total earned income to annual weeks worked. The cross-country regression model is then given by:

$$\log \bar{w}_{kt} = \phi_t + Z_{kt}\alpha + \varepsilon, \tag{1.31}$$

where $\log \bar{w}_{kt}$ gives the mean log weekly wage of immigrants who originated in source country k and arrived just prior to the cross-section observed at time t; Z_{kt} is a vector of source-country characteristics; and ϕ_t is a vector of period fixed effects indicating the census of the observation.

Table 1.1 reports the coefficients from the cross-country regressions. The first regression specification uses the age-adjusted mean log weekly wage of the group as the dependent variable, while the second specification also adjusts for differences in educational attainment.[22] The model includes two variables summarizing the shape of the source country's income

Table 1.1 Cross-country determinants of entry earnings of immigrants

Variable	Specification	
	(1)	(2)
Log per capita GDP in source country	0.116	0.115
(PPP-adjusted)	(0.030)	(0.026)
Gini coefficient in source country	−0.013	−0.008
	(0.005)	(0.004)
Distance from United States (=1 if distance	0.400	0.252
exceeds 3,000 miles)	(0.094)	(0.074)
Repressive regime (=1 if curtailed civil liberties)	−0.313	−0.266
	(0.058)	(0.048)
R^2	0.756	0.716
Immigrant earnings are adjusted for		
Age	Yes	Yes
Educational attainment	No	Yes

Sources: U.S. Census PUMS, 1980–2010; the Penn World Table (Heston et al. 2012); the World Development Indicators (World Bank 2013); and the Freedom in the World index (Freedom House 2011). See Appendix B for details.

Notes: The sample consists of immigrant men, aged 25–64, who originated in one of the 80 largest source countries, and who migrated to the United States in the 5-year period prior to each census between 1980 and 2010. The unit of observation is a country-year cell. Standard errors are reported in parentheses and are clustered at the country level. The dependent variable gives the adjusted log weekly wage of workers in the cell. The regressions are weighted by the sample size in each country-year cell, and include fixed effects indicating the decade in which the cohort entered the United States. The regressions have 320 observations. The adjusted log weekly wage in the cell is given by the country-of-origin fixed effect from individual-level regressions estimated separately in each census that control for age (introduced as a third-order polynomial) and years of education [in specification (2)].

distribution: the log per capita GDP and the Gini coefficient.[23] Both of these variables strongly influence immigrant outcomes: earnings rise with per capita GDP and fall with the Gini coefficient. As illustrated in Figure 1.4, these correlations are an important feature of the raw cross-country data. A doubling of the source country's per capita GDP increases the earnings of newly arrived immigrants in the United States by 12 percent, whereas a rise in the Gini coefficient from 36 to 49 (or the difference between the United Kingdom and Mexico) lowers earnings by about 17 percent.

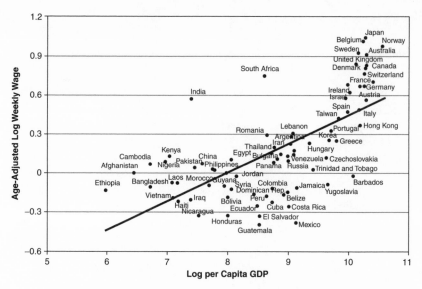

A. Immigrant Earnings and Per Capita GDP

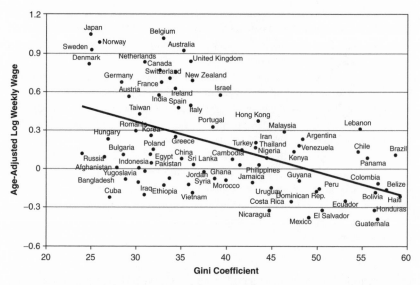

B. Immigrant Earnings and the Gini Coefficient

Figure 1.4. Source Country Determinants of Entry Earnings for 1995–1999 Immigrant Cohort

Source: U.S. Census PUMS, 2000; the Penn World Table (Heston et al. 2012), and the World Development Indicators (World Bank 2013). See Appendix B for details.

Notes: The construction of the age-adjusted log weekly wage for the national origin groups is described in the notes to Table 1.1. The *x*-axis gives either the (PPP-adjusted) log per capita GDP in the source country in 1995 (Panel A), or the average Gini coefficient in that country between 1978 and 2012 (Panel B).

The positive correlation between per capita income and immigrant earnings is sometimes interpreted as indicating that immigrants who originate in high-income countries find it easier to transfer their skills to other developed countries.[24] The negative correlation between immigrant earnings and the Gini coefficient is consistent with the Roy model prediction that immigrants who originate in countries with higher rates of return to skills should be, on average, relatively less skilled.[25]

The regression also includes a straightforward measure of "migration costs," defined by the distance between the United States and the source country. Immigrants originating in countries that are at least 3,000 miles away from the United States earn substantially more. Finally, the regression includes a civil liberties index constructed by Freedom House (2011).[26] Immigrants from countries with repressive regimes earn substantially less. Overall, the R^2 from these regressions is very high, so that a very small number of country-specific variables explain about 75 percent of the variation in mean entry earnings across national origin groups in the United States.

Grogger and Hanson (2011) use a variant of the cross-country empirical approach to estimate the (differenced) log odds ratio of migration implied by the linear utility model in equation (1.30). Specifically, they examine selection on educational attainment across a large number of sending and high-income receiving countries. The regression model compares the log odds ratio of migration for persons with a high level of education (13 or more years) with the log odds ratio for persons with a low-level of education (less than 9 years). As shown earlier, the linear utility model predicts a "generalized" form of positive selection. Skilled workers are more likely to migrate because the absolute wage gap between a poor and rich country widens at higher skill levels (even if the rate of return to skills were somewhat smaller in richer countries). The data confirm the positive correlation predicted by equation (1.30).

It is important to emphasize, however, that the empirical literature sometimes muddies the nature of the evidence by examining selection along different dimensions: selection in observables (such as educational attainment), selection in unobserved ability, and selection in the total value of the human capital stock. It is well known that education accounts for only a small portion of the variance in earnings across workers, suggesting that the nature of selection in educational attainment may not necessarily "transfer over" to a more comprehensive measure of a worker's human capital.[27] I will return to this point shortly in the context of a specific immigrant flow.

Finally, it is well known that correlations estimated in cross-country regressions are contaminated by many extraneous factors (Levine and Renelt 1992). It is also difficult to ascertain which underlying forces any specific regressor in the cross-country regression truly represents. As an example, a high level of per capita GDP in the source country may represent both a high average income as well as the ease of transferring skills to another industrialized economy. As a result, much of the empirical work in recent years has shifted away from estimating cross-country correlations and instead chosen to analyze specific case studies of migration flows to determine if the flows are consistent with a particular selection model.[28]

Mexico

In the past decade, several international data sets have become available that permit more direct tests of the implications of the Roy model. These data often allow a straightforward comparison of the skills of two distinct groups of persons in a particular source country: those who choose to move and those who choose to stay. The pioneering study by Chiquiar and Hanson (2005) represents the first use of this approach in a context that is of particular interest in the United States, the selection of Mexican migrants. The number of Mexican-born persons residing in the United States increased at an unprecedented rate in recent decades; they now account for about a third of the foreign-born population. In fact, the number of Mexican immigrants as a fraction of the Mexican population rose from 1.5 percent in 1960 to 10.5 percent by 2005 (Hanson and McIntosh 2010).

The Chiquiar-Hanson study introduced the methodological "trick" of comparing the skill distributions of Mexican stayers and Mexican movers by measuring the skills of Mexican stayers in the sample enumerated in the Mexican census, and measuring the skills of Mexican movers in the sample of Mexican-born persons enumerated in the U.S. census.[29] In terms of the Roy model, a comparison of the wage distributions of Mexico and the United States suggests that the migrant flow should be negatively selected, because the rate of return to skills is much larger in Mexico. In 2000 the wage gap between workers with a high school diploma and workers with 9 to 11 years of schooling was 24.7 percent in Mexico, as compared to only 7.9 percent among Mexican immigrants in the United States, and 10.2 percent among non-Mexican immigrants (Chiquiar and Hanson 2005, p. 256).

Table 1.2 summarizes the results of the Chiquiar-Hanson study by reporting the educational distribution in the samples of movers and stayers. There is no evidence that Mexican migrants to the United States are positively selected. In 2000, 11.3 percent of the Mexican "stayers" had at least 16 years of schooling as compared to only 5.0 percent of the immigrants. At the same time, however, the data indicate that Mexican migrants are not negatively selected: 69.4 percent of the Mexican stayers had less than 9 years of schooling, but only 60.1 percent of the Mexican immigrants did. Instead, the emigration rate is highest in the middle of the Mexican education distribution: 19.3 percent of the stayers have 10 to 15 years of schooling, as compared to 35.0 percent of the migrants.

Chiquiar and Hanson proposed a modified version of the Roy model that could fit the observed facts. In particular, it may be that the Roy model implication of negative selection is correct, but liquidity constraints and high mobility costs prevent the least-educated Mexicans from making the move. Even though the migrant sample is negatively selected, it is truncated from below because the high costs cut off the migration valve for the least skilled. The observed Mexican migrant sample would then be perceived as being characterized by "intermediate" selection.

An obvious problem with the Chiquiar-Hanson methodology is that the U.S. census does not provide a full count of the Mexican migrant population. A large fraction of the Mexican outflow is composed of

Table 1.2 Percent distribution of educational attainment for movers and stayers in Mexico, 2000

Educational attainment	Group			
	Mexican stayers	Mexican immigrants in the United States	Other immigrants in the United States	U.S. native born
0–9 years	69.4	60.1	14.4	4.5
10–15 years	19.3	35.0	46.2	68.9
16+ years	11.3	5.0	39.4	26.7

Source: Chiquiar and Hanson (2005, p. 248).

Notes: Columns may not add to 100 because of rounding error. All statistics refer to the distribution of educational attainment among men.

undocumented immigrants, and the U.S. census systematically under-counts both documented and undocumented immigrants, with the un-dercount rate being perhaps as high as 10 to 25 percent of Mexican mi-grants (Hanson 2006). It seems likely that the skill distribution of the "missing" Mexican immigrants differs systematically from that of the enumerated immigrants.

Fernández-Huertas (2011) revisited the issue by examining an alterna-tive data set that is not contaminated by the undercount problem. The En-cuesta Nacional de Empleo Trimestral (ENET) is a quarterly national labor force survey in Mexico that has a sampling structure similar to the Current Population Survey (CPS) in the United States. Specifically, the sample fol-lows a particular household for five consecutive quarters. This implies that the sample contains observations on workers who at some point during their participation in the survey choose to migrate to the United States (le-gally or otherwise). As a result, the survey allows the researcher to observe the skills of the migrants *prior* to the move.

The use of the ENET also addresses an additional limitation of the census-based approach. The ENET reports not only the educational at-tainment of the sample of (eventual) migrants, but also their pre-migration earnings. Hence, the analysis can determine the nature of selection on both observable and unobservable determinants of productivity.

The empirical results from the ENET seem more consistent with the im-plications of the Roy model. The ENET survey respondents who eventually left Mexico have less education and lower earnings than the Mexican work-ers who chose to stay. The average Mexican migrant has 7.2 years of school-ing, as compared to 8.5 years for the average stayer. Similarly, the average migrant earns about 29 percent less than the average stayer (Fernández-Huertas 2011, p. 76).

Figure 1.5 documents the negative selection in earnings by illustrating the probability distribution functions of the incomes of stayers and mov-ers in the ENET. Recall that the Roy model implies that the earnings dis-tribution of stayers will stochastically dominate that of movers if there is negative selection. Figure 1.5 confirms this implication of the theory, and a Kolmogorov-Smirnov test rejects the hypothesis that the two distribu-tions are the same. However, it is important to emphasize that the ENET evidence may itself be problematic, because the sample is not representa-tive of the Mexican population. By construction, the survey does not enu-merate anyone belonging to households where all the members left Mexico

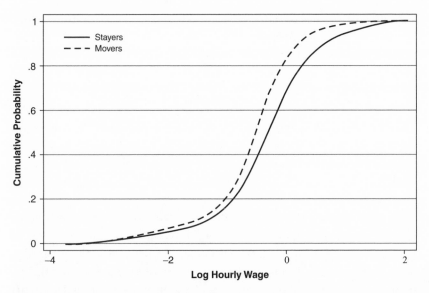

Figure 1.5. Negative Selection and Stochastic Dominance in Mexico

Source: Fernández-Huertas (2011, p. 79).

Note: The probability distribution functions are calculated using the sample of Mexican men working in the urban sector.

prior to the survey. Moreover, the ENET suffers from a high attrition rate: as many as 25 percent of the households do not survive the five quarters.

Kaestner and Malamud (2014) revisit the issue yet again using an alternative Mexico-based sample, the Mexican Family Life Survey (MxFLS), which is designed to be more representative than the ENET. Surprisingly, the MxFLS data suggest that Mexican migrants are intermediately selected in terms of educational attainment *and* negatively selected in terms of earnings. Specifically, Kaestner and Malamud document that the emigration rate for Mexican men with 7 to 9 years of education is higher than that of men with either more or less education. At the same time, however, the emigration rate is highest for workers in the lowest quintile of the income distribution and lowest for workers in the highest quintile.[30]

The Kaestner-Malamud study raises the interesting possibility that there could be different types of selection along different dimensions of skills. As noted earlier, evidence of positive or intermediate selection in terms of educational attainment may not accurately predict the selection that would be observed along other dimensions. We do not know, however, why the relative rates of return to skills between any two countries (which presumably drive the differential types of selection) should differ so dramatically between observed and unobserved skills.[31]

Puerto Rico

The Jones Act of 1917 granted U.S. citizenship to all Puerto Ricans, implying that Puerto Ricans can move freely to the United States. As a result, Puerto Rico provides an opportunity to test the implications of selection models in the absence of any distortions arising from immigration policy restrictions.[32]

By 2000, around a third of the Puerto Rican–born population lived in the United States. In addition to this outflow, there is an additional flow in the other direction that is less well known. In particular, there has also been a sizable in-migration *of persons not born in Puerto Rico,* and the in-migrants account for about 10 percent of the Puerto Rican population. Interestingly, nearly two-thirds of the in-migrants were born in the United States but had Puerto Rican ancestry. The Puerto Rican context, therefore, represents a unique opportunity: there are sizable inflows and outflows, and the Roy model has very different predictions for the skill composition of these two groups.

The rate of return to skills is higher in Puerto Rico than in the United States. The age-adjusted log wage gap between college graduates and high school graduates in 1990 was 0.623 in the United States and 0.811 in Puerto Rico. A straightforward application of the Roy model suggests a simple sorting: the least-skilled Puerto Rican–born workers have the greatest incentive to leave Puerto Rico, and Puerto Rico should attract high-skill workers from abroad.

It is easy to test these implications by manipulating the available U.S. and Puerto Rican census data to define the groups of movers and stayers (in the spirit of the Chiquiar-Hanson study). Consider first the migration flow from Puerto Rico to the United States. In this flow, the movers are persons born in Puerto Rico but living in the United States, whereas the stayers are persons born in Puerto Rico and still living in Puerto Rico. The data reported in Table 1.3 document the differences in the distribution of educational attainment between these two groups. It is evident that movers are more likely to be high school dropouts and less likely to be college graduates. In particular, 19.7 percent of the stayers are high school dropouts,

Table 1.3 Percent distribution of educational attainment for movers and stayers
in Puerto Rico, 2000

Educational attainment	1. Migration from Puerto Rico to the United States		2. Migration from the United States to Puerto Rico	
	Movers	Stayers	Movers	Stayers
0–11 years	26.2	19.7	10.8	18.0
12 years	35.7	33.6	29.9	38.6
13–15 years	23.8	26.1	34.9	30.6
16+ years	14.3	20.6	24.4	12.7

Source: Adapted from Borjas (2008, pp. 41–45).

Notes: Columns may not add to 100 because of rounding error. All statistics refer to the
distribution of educational attainment among men.

but this education group composes over a quarter of the movers. Similarly,
20.6 percent of the stayers are college graduates, but only 14.3 percent of
the movers are.

Consider instead the migration flow from the United States to Puerto
Rico. In this flow, the movers are persons born in the United States of
Puerto Rican ancestry, but living in Puerto Rico; while the stayers are persons born in the United States of Puerto Rican ancestry and still living in
the United States. Interestingly, the skill distributions of the movers and
stayers in this reverse flow are a mirror image of the Puerto Rico–to–U.S.
outflow. The movers are more likely to be college graduates and less likely
to be high school dropouts. In short, as implied by the Roy model, the evidence clearly indicates that the type of worker leaving Puerto Rico differs
dramatically from the type of worker moving in.

Norway, 1900

Although most of the existing studies use international migration flows in
the modern era to test the implications of selection models, the recent
availability of historical microdata sets has sparked interest in examining
the selection of immigrants during the Great Migration of 1880–1920. At
that time the United States imposed few restrictions limiting immigration
from many source countries, so the analysis, as in the Puerto Rican context, allows a "clean" test of the implications of income maximization. A

recent study by Abramitzky et al. (2012) shows the value and promise of analyzing these types of historical data sets.

During the (First) Great Migration, Norway had one of the highest out-migration rates in Europe; over a quarter of its population migrated to the United States. Abramitzky et al. exploited the fact that Norway has now digitized its two censuses from that period (1865 and 1890), and merged these data with newly available genealogical records in the United States (drawn from decennial censuses at the time) that contain information on all Norwegian-born men living in the United States.

Norway had a much more unequal income distribution than the United States at the beginning of the twentieth century: "United States workers below the fiftieth percentile of the earnings distribution out-earned similar Norwegians, while Norwegians above the ninetieth percentile commanded higher earnings than their U.S. counterparts" (Abramitzky et al. 2012, p. 1837). The Roy model would then imply that Norwegian immigrants to the United States should be negatively selected.

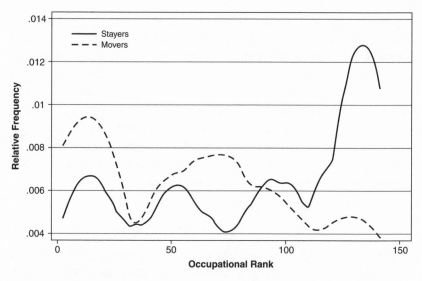

Figure 1.6. Selection of Migrants from Norway to the United States, circa 1900

Source: Abramitzky et al. (2012, p. 1843).

Note: Occupations are ranked from lowest to highest earnings. The figure gives the fraction of Norwegian men born in urban areas who are employed at each occupational rank.

The data in the various censuses report a worker's occupation in Norway (for the stayers) or in the United States (for the movers). The skills required by each occupation can be summarized by a measure of "occupational rank" (that is, the mean earnings that workers in a particular occupation earned in the United States in 1901). Figure 1.6 illustrates the nature of the selection by showing the fraction of either movers or stayers employed at a particular point in the occupational earnings distribution. Norwegian migrants in the United States are clearly more likely to be employed in low-paying occupations than the Norwegians who chose to remain in Norway, and less likely to be employed in high-paying occupations. The evidence, therefore, seems consistent with a simple version of the Roy model where high-skill Norwegians chose to remain in a country that, at the time, offered a relatively higher payoff for their abilities.

2

Economic Assimilation

———————————————◆———————————————

DECADES OF SOCIAL SCIENCE research establish an indisputable link between a worker's human capital stock and a wide array of social and economic outcomes. Chapter 1 examined the selection process that determines the preexisting skills of the subset of persons who become international migrants. The incentives to invest in human capital, however, do not end on the day the move takes place. In fact, because some of the preexisting skills may not be transferable across countries, and because the immigrant now has to compete in a labor market where he may lack even basic tools (such as fluency in the host country's language), an immigrant may face renewed incentives to continue the investment process and acquire new types of human capital that may be more marketable in the new environment.

This chapter examines the determinants of the rate of "economic assimilation" experienced by the immigrant population, which I define as the rate of convergence in economic outcomes between immigrants and natives in the post-migration period. The methodological issues surrounding the measurement of the assimilation rate form a classic question in labor economics, and, in fact, gave birth to the modern literature in immigration economics.

Cross-Section Evidence

The empirical analysis of the relative economic performance of immigrants in a host country was initially based on the cross-section regression model introduced by Chiswick (1978):

$$\log w_\ell = X_\ell \, \varphi + \varphi_A \, A_\ell + \varphi_F \, F_\ell + \varphi_Y \, y_\ell + \varepsilon_\ell, \qquad (2.1)$$

where w_ℓ is the wage rate of person ℓ in the host country; X_ℓ is a vector of socioeconomic characteristics, which often includes education; A_ℓ gives the worker's age (or labor market experience); F_ℓ is an indicator variable set to one if person ℓ is foreign-born; and y_ℓ gives the number of years that the immigrant has resided in the host country and is set to zero if ℓ is native-born. Although the model actually estimated in empirical studies typically includes higher-order polynomials in age and years-since-migration, I simplify the discussion by ignoring these nonlinearities. Note that the coefficient φ_Y measures the differential value that the host country's labor market attaches to time spent in the host country versus time spent in the source country.

The regression specification in equation (2.1) represents an important extension of the Mincer earnings function that forms the cornerstone of empirical analysis of the earnings distribution.[1] The Mincer framework presumes that the acquisition of general human capital is the key factor that explains how a worker's earnings evolve over time. Mincer showed that the optimal acquisition of skills over the life cycle generates an equation where the log earnings of a worker at a point in time depends linearly on the number of years of schooling that the worker has attained, and on the number of years of work experience (which enters as a quadratic). An important property of the Mincer model is that the regression coefficients of the schooling and experience variables can be interpreted in terms of the rates of return and volume of human capital investments.

Chiswick conjectured that even after controlling for educational attainment, the evolution of earnings in a host country's labor market may differ between comparably aged immigrants and natives, for two reasons: (1) the preexisting human capital of immigrants may be partly specific to the source country; and (2) immigrants may have different incentives to invest in the type of human capital valued by host country employers. As a result, the earnings function should include not only a measure of a person's total work experience, but also a measure of how long the person has resided in the host country.[2]

Table 2.1 reports estimates of the regression model using the 1970 U.S. census data that was also used in the original Chiswick study, and Figure 2.1 illustrates the implied path in the relative earnings of immigrants as they acquire labor market experience in the United States. The sample consists of men aged 25–64 (as of the time of the survey), who worked at some point in the calendar year prior to the census, and who were not enrolled in school. In addition, the sample of immigrants includes only those persons who were at least 18 years old at the time of their migration (ensuring that the observed assimilation is not contaminated by the labor market performance of "child immigrants"). The dependent variable is the log weekly wage of the worker.

As is well known, the coefficient φ_F is negative: for given levels of education, immigrants earn less than comparably aged natives at the time of arrival. In fact, the 1970 regression suggests that immigrants earned about 21 percent less than comparable natives at the time of entry, and their relative earnings grew rapidly thereafter. Befitting its human capital antecedents, Chiswick interpreted the steeper age-earnings profile of immigrants

Table 2.1 Cross-section earnings functions

Variable	Census				
	1970	1980	1990	2000	2010
Years of education	0.072	0.066	0.090	0.097	0.116
	(0.0002)	(0.0001)	(0.0002)	(0.0002)	(0.0002)
Immigrant indicator	−0.213	−0.241	−0.224	−0.164	−0.183
	(0.007)	(0.005)	(0.004)	(0.003)	(0.005)
Years residing in the	0.032	0.022	0.022	0.009	0.006
United States	(0.001)	(0.001)	(0.001)	(0.0005)	(0.001)
Years in the United	−0.068	−0.039	−0.029	0.0002	0.004
States squared (÷100)	(0.004)	(0.003)	(0.002)	(0.001)	(0.002)

Sources: U.S. Census PUMS, 1970–2010; see Appendix B for details.

Notes: The regressions are estimated in the sample of working men aged 25–64; the sample of immigrants is further restricted to those who entered the United States at age 18 or older. Standard errors are reported in parentheses. The dependent variable gives the worker's log weekly wage. The immigrant indicator variable is set to unity if the worker is foreign-born; zero otherwise. The variable giving the years of residence in the United States is set to zero for native-born workers. All regressions include the worker's age (introduced as a second-order polynomial). The number of observations in the regressions are: 1970: 945,579; 1980: 2,002,074; 1990: 2,373,285; 2000: 2,708,438; and 2010: 1,653,425.

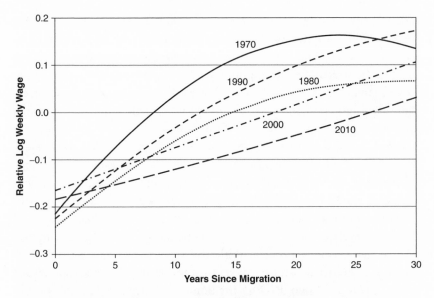

Figure 2.1. Cross-Section Assimilation Profiles, 1970–2010

Source: Regression coefficients reported in Table 2.1.

Notes: The relative earnings profiles in the figure give the log weekly wage gap between immigrants and natives, holding age and education constant.

through a Mincerian lens. When immigrants first arrive in the United States, they may lack the types of human capital valued by U.S. employers. As the "Americanization" process takes hold, immigrants acquire skills at a faster rate than natives, including English language fluency and learning the workings of the U.S. labor market, closing the wage gap between the two groups.

Define the rate of economic assimilation as the rate at which the wage gap between immigrants and natives narrows over time.[3] In the cross-section model given by equation (2.1), this rate is measured by the coefficient φ_Y. The 1970 cross-section, therefore, revealed that the estimated rate of assimilation was large, with the wage gap between immigrants and natives closing at the rate of more than 2 percent a year in the first decade.

However, as Figure 2.1 shows, the 1970 cross-section not only indicates that the foreign-born have a steeper age-earnings profile, but *also* that they overtake native earnings after about 8 years. Because there is little economic rationale for arguing that immigrants should continue to invest in U.S.-specific human capital long after they have caught up with comparable natives, the overtaking phenomenon was typically explained by resorting to a selection argument: immigrants are "more able and more highly motivated" than natives (Chiswick 1978, p. 900). As we have seen, however, these assumptions about selection are not necessarily implied by income-maximizing behavior on the part of immigrants.

Before proceeding to a detailed discussion of exactly what parameters the regression model in equation (2.1) identifies, it is important to note that there is a striking instability in the estimated coefficients if the *same* regression model were estimated in consecutive census cross-sections. The various columns of Table 2.1 report the coefficients when the model is estimated in every cross-section since 1970. Figure 2.1 illustrates the implied relative age-earnings profiles. Both the intercept of the relative age-earnings profile (that is, the coefficient φ_F) and its slope change from cross-section to cross-section. By 2010 the implied relative age-earnings profile was much flatter, with less than half the slope of the profile in the original 1970 cross-section, and the overtaking age had increased to over 25 years. In fact, Figure 2.1 illustrates what is surely a most peculiar finding in the human capital literature: the cross-section relative earnings profile of immigrants has gone from being quite concave to being slightly convex.

The obvious volatility in what seems to be a sensible empirical framework for examining the evolution of immigrant earnings raises suspicions about the interpretation of the evidence in terms of a straightforward Mincerian framework. This is the first time, but not the last, that we encounter evidence showing that correlations that seem superficially sensible change dramatically over time as the repercussions of continuing immigration in the host country ripple through the labor market. The volatility makes it very difficult, if not impossible, to draw inferences about "universal laws" that may summarize specific aspects of the economic impact of immigration.

The Identification of Aging and Cohort Effects

The instability in cross-section estimates of the parameters in equation (2.1) led Borjas (1985) to suggest an alternative interpretation of the evidence: The positive coefficient φ_Y might not be measuring the rate of economic assimilation, but might instead be revealing a decline in the relative "quality" of successive immigrant cohorts.[4] In the United States, for example, the postwar era witnessed major changes in immigration policy and in the size and national origin mix of the immigrant flow. If these changes generated a less-skilled flow, a positive φ_y may say little about the process of wage convergence, but may instead reflect the fact that more recent immigrant cohorts are inherently less able or less skilled.[5] More precisely, the cross-section correlation between earnings and years-since-migration captures both an aging effect (the presumed rate of economic assimilation), as well as a cohort effect (the change in the relative quality of successive immigrant cohorts).

The identification of aging and cohort effects raises difficult methodological problems in many demographic contexts.[6] Identification requires the availability of longitudinal data where a particular worker is observed over time, or, alternatively, the availability of a number of randomly drawn cross-sections so that the average worker in specific cohorts can be "tracked" across survey years. To simplify the presentation, suppose that two cross-section surveys are available, with cross-section τ ($\tau = 1, 2$) being observed in calendar year T_τ. Stack the data for immigrants and natives across the cross-sections, and consider the two-equation regression model:

$$\text{Immigrant earnings function: } \log w_{\ell\tau} = X_{\ell\tau}\,\varphi_i + \delta_i\,A_{\ell\tau} + \alpha\,y_{\ell\tau}$$
$$+ \beta C_\ell + \gamma_i\,\pi_{\ell 2} + \varepsilon_{\ell\tau}, \qquad (2.2a)$$

$$\text{Native earnings function: } \log w_{\ell\tau} = X_{\ell\tau}\,\varphi_n + \delta_n\,A_{\ell\tau} + \gamma_n\,\pi_{\ell 2} + \varepsilon'_{\ell\tau}, \qquad (2.2b)$$

where A gives the worker's age at the time of the cross-section survey; C gives the calendar year in which the immigrant arrived in the host country; y gives the number of years that the immigrant has resided in the host country ($y_{\ell\tau} = T_\tau - C_\ell$); and $\pi_{\ell 2}$ is an indicator variable set to unity if person ℓ was drawn from the second cross-section.

The parameter α in the immigrant earnings function measures the excess value of acquiring a year of experience in the host country's labor market, and represents an aging effect; the coefficient β indicates how the earnings of immigrants are changing across cohorts, and measures the cohort effect; and the coefficients γ_i and γ_n give the impact of changes in aggregate economic conditions on immigrant and native wages, respectively, and measure period effects. For expositional convenience, equation (2.2) uses a linear parameterization of the aging and cohort effects; it is trivial to incorporate a more general specification of these effects in empirical work. Finally, it is important to emphasize that the cohort effects captured by the specification in equation (2.2a) measure differences in the *level* of potential earnings across immigrant cohorts.

The instantaneous rate of economic assimilation implied by the framework is then given by:

$$\alpha^* = \frac{\partial \log w_\ell}{\partial t}\bigg|_{\text{Immigrant}} - \frac{\partial \log w_\ell}{\partial t}\bigg|_{\text{Native}} = (\delta_i + \alpha) - \delta_n, \qquad (2.3)$$

where the derivatives account for the fact that both age and the number of years-since-migration change over time.

The parameters measuring the aging, cohort, and period effects in equation (2.2a) are not separately identified. The identification problem arises from the identity:

$$y_{\ell\tau} \equiv T_1 + \pi_{\ell 2}(T_2 - T_1) - C_\ell. \qquad (2.4)$$

Equation (2.4) introduces perfect collinearity among the variables $y_{\ell\tau}$, C_ℓ, and $\pi_{\ell 2}$ in the immigrant earnings function. In fact, note that if only a single cross-section of data were available, the cross-section regression in the immigrant sample would collapse to:

$$\log w_{\ell\tau} = \gamma_\tau^* + X_{\ell\tau}\varphi_i + \delta_i A_{\ell\tau} + (\alpha - \beta)y_{\ell\tau} + \varepsilon_{\ell\tau}, \qquad (2.5)$$

so that the cross-section coefficient of the years-since-migration variable, which is a key ingredient in measuring the rate of economic assimilation, is contaminated by the potential presence of cohort effects.

To identify the parameters of interest, therefore, it is necessary to have not only a panel of data that tracks immigrant cohorts or specific workers over time, but also some type of restriction that breaks the perfect collinearity built in by equation (2.4).[7] Borjas (1985) proposed the restriction that the period effects were the same for immigrants and natives:

$$\gamma_i = \gamma_n. \qquad (2.6)$$

Put differently, trends in aggregate economic conditions change immigrant and native wages by the same percentage amount. A useful way of thinking about this restriction is that the value of the period effect for immigrants, γ_i, is determined *outside* the immigrant-specific labor market.[8]

Evidence on Aging and Cohort Effects

A voluminous literature examines the trends in the skills and wages of immigrants in the United States and other immigrant-receiving countries.[9] Most of these studies pool data from various census cross-sections to identify the relevant aging and cohort effects, although some of the studies also examine smaller-scale longitudinal data sets. This section summarizes and updates the evidence in the U.S. context.

It is instructive to begin by describing the basic patterns in the data. Specifically, I estimate the following regression model in each of the available census cross-sections:

$$\log w_{\ell\tau} = \phi_{c\tau} + X_{\ell\tau}\,\beta_{\tau} + \varepsilon_{\ell\tau}, \tag{2.7}$$

where $w_{\ell\tau}$ is the wage of person ℓ in cross-section τ; X is a vector of socioeconomic characteristics; and $\phi_{c\tau}$ is a vector of fixed effects indicating a specific immigrant cohort in the particular cross-section (with the native fixed effect being excluded from the regression). The regressions use the sample of men aged 25–64 introduced earlier in the chapter.

Table 2.2 reports the estimated cohort fixed effects when the vector X includes only the worker's age (introduced as a cubic polynomial). By construction, the cohort fixed effects give the age-adjusted wage gap between the typical worker in the immigrant cohort and natives at a point in time. Assuming that changes in aggregate economic conditions do not affect the *relative* wage of immigrants across cross-sections, the trends in cohort fixed effects across censuses can be used to measure the aging and cohort effects in the data. It is worth emphasizing, however, that the U.S. wage structure changed in dramatic ways in the past few decades, with a substantial decline in the relative wage of low-skill workers. A generalization of the framework that allows for the presence of skill-specific period effects is discussed later in this section.

An examination of the fixed effects $\phi_{c\tau}$ reported in Table 2.2 reveals two interesting findings. The first, which has received a great deal of attention in the literature, is the existence of sizable cohort differences in entry wages, with the more recent cohorts generally having lower earnings potential than earlier cohorts. In 1970, the most recent immigrant wave earned 23.5 percent less than comparable natives at the time of entry. By 1990 the entry wage disadvantage had grown to 33.1 percent, before contracting to 27.3 percent in 2000. By 2010, however, the long-term trend

Table 2.2 Age-adjusted relative log earnings of immigrant cohorts, by census

Cohort	1970	1980	1990	2000	2010
1960–1964 arrivals	−0.058	−0.041	0.046	0.074	—
	(0.001)	(0.001)	(0.004)	(0.004)	
1965–1969 arrivals	−0.235	−0.122	−0.020	−0.014	—
	(0.001)	(0.001)	(0.003)	(0.005)	
1970–1974 arrivals	—	−0.223	−0.124	−0.128	−0.053
		(0.001)	(0.002)	(0.006)	(0.004)
1975–1979 arrivals	—	−0.314	−0.185	−0.176	−0.134
		(0.001)	(0.001)	(0.005)	(0.004)
1980–1984 arrivals	—	—	−0.285	−0.236	−0.206
			(0.001)	(0.002)	(0.006)
1985–1989 arrivals	—	—	−0.331	−0.269	−0.259
			(0.001)	(0.002)	(0.005)
1990–1994 arrivals	—	—	—	−0.269	−0.271
				(0.003)	(0.003)
1995–1999 arrivals	—	—	—	−0.273	−0.278
				(0.004)	(0.001)
2000–2004 arrivals	—	—	—	—	−0.349
					(0.003)
2005–2009 arrivals	—	—	—	—	−0.326
					(0.004)

Sources: U.S. Census PUMS, 1970–2010; see Appendix B for details.

Notes: The samples are identical to those used in the cross-section regressions reported in Table 2.1. Standard errors are reported in parentheses and are clustered at the cohort level. The age-adjusted wage differentials between each cohort and natives are calculated from regressions estimated separately in each census, where the dependent variable gives the worker's log weekly wage and the regressors include year-of-entry fixed effects (if foreign-born) and the worker's age (introduced as a third-order polynomial). The regressions also include fixed effects for the cohort that entered the country in the 1950s and for the residual cohort that arrived before 1950.

seemed to have returned, and the latest wave of immigrants earned almost 33 percent less than comparable natives.

It is often argued that changes in U.S. immigration policy in the postwar period are likely responsible for the decline in the entry wage across immigrant cohorts. Prior to 1965, immigration policy favored the entry of persons originating in European countries. The "national origins quota system" was abolished in 1965 and replaced with a system that gave preferential treatment to visa applicants with relatives already residing in the

United States. There was a substantial increase in legal immigration from developing countries after the policy shift. In addition, the United States pursued a "policy" of permitting the entry of large numbers of low-skill undocumented immigrants (many of whom are enumerated in the census data). The evidence summarized in Chapter 1 suggests that these policy choices lowered the relative entry wage of immigrants.[10]

It is important to note, however, that little is actually known about the link between the pursuit of particular types of immigration policies and the resulting skill composition of immigrants.[11] The Canadian experience provides one glaring counterexample. Since 1967, Canadian immigration policy encourages the admission of high-skill workers through the use of a "point system" that awards points to particular types of socioeconomic characteristics (such as higher levels of education), and requires a minimum passing grade for a visa to be awarded. Despite the very different policies pursued by Canada and the United States, it turns out that Canada *too* experienced a decline in the relative entry wage of successive cohorts (Aydemir and Skuterud 2005, p. 649). It may well be that the differential policies pursued by host countries affect the skill composition of the immigrant influx at the margin, but the policy impacts could be swamped by changes in demographics or in worldwide economic conditions.

In addition to documenting the existence of sizable cohort differences in entry wages, the relative wage gaps reported in Table 2.2 suggest another interesting finding, one that is only beginning to receive systematic attention: there seems to have been a slowdown in the rate of economic assimilation (Borjas 2013a). Specifically, the immigrant cohorts that arrived prior to the early 1980s experienced much faster economic assimilation than the more recent cohorts. Put differently, there are cohort effects not only in the *level* of potential earnings, but in the *growth rate* of earnings as well.

The rate of economic assimilation can be measured by tracking a particular cohort across censuses, allowing us to observe changes in the relative wage as the cohort presumably assimilates into the U.S. labor market. Consider, for example, the cohort that entered the country between 1975 and 1979. The relative wage of this group improved from a disadvantage of 31.4 percent in 1980, to 18.5 percent in 1990, and to 17.6 percent by 2000—a growth of about 14 percentage points over two decades. In contrast, consider the cohort that migrated between 1985 and 1989. At the time of entry, they earned 33.1 percent less than natives. This wage disadvantage improved by only 6 percentage points between 1990 and 2000, and by another percentage point between 2000 and 2010.

The decline in the rate of economic assimilation implies that the regression model in equation (2.2a) needs to be generalized to allow for cohort differences in *both* the level and the growth rate of immigrant earnings. The cohort differences in the rate of assimilation can be characterized by a simple generalization of the model: the coefficient α varies across immigrant cohorts. One obvious solution is to interact the variable measuring the calendar year of arrival with the variable measuring the number of years since migration. The immigrant earnings function can then be rewritten as:

$$\log w_{\ell \tau} = X_{\ell \tau} \varphi_i + \delta_i A_{\ell \tau} + \alpha \, y_{\ell \tau} + \beta C_{\ell} + \theta (C_{\ell} \, y_{\ell \tau}) + \gamma_i \, \pi_{\ell 2} + \varepsilon_{\ell \tau}. \quad (2.2c)$$

The coefficient β would still measure the trend in the relative entry wage of immigrants, while the coefficient θ would be positive or negative depending on whether more recent cohorts have a larger or smaller rate of economic assimilation.[12] Note that no additional identification restrictions are required to estimate θ. The assumption that the period effects are the same for immigrants and natives, therefore, remains the only restriction that needs to be imposed to estimate both the level and the growth cohort effects in immigrant earnings.

The empirical analysis expands the specifications in equations (2.2b) and (2.2c) in three ways. First, I allow for third-order polynomials in the age and year-since-migration variables. Second, I define the variable C as a vector of year-of-entry fixed effects for each of the cohorts listed in Table 2.2 (that is, 1960–1964 arrivals, 1965–1969 arrivals, and so on). Third, I measure the cohort effects in the growth rate of earnings by interacting the linear term of the years-since-migration variable with each of the year-of-entry fixed effects. Put differently, the wage of each entry cohort is allowed to have its own growth path.[13]

The first specification in Table 2.3 reports selected coefficients from the regression estimated using the 1970–2010 pooled data. Although the regression model contains a full set of year-of-entry fixed effects, I report only selected coefficients in order to easily summarize the direction and magnitude of the level and growth cohort differences. The table also uses the coefficients of the cubic polynomials in age and years-since-migration to calculate the amount of wage convergence predicted to occur over the first 10 years in the United States.[14]

Table 2.3 Regression model allowing for cohort effects in wage levels and wage growth rates

Cohort	Specification		
	1. Basic model	2. Using age-education deflator	3. Using percentile deflator
Relative entry wage			
1965–1969 arrivals	−0.213	−0.206	−0.227
	(0.020)	(0.028)	(0.026)
1975–1979 arrivals	−0.301	−0.261	−0.279
	(0.020)	(0.029)	(0.027)
1985–1989 arrivals	−0.349	−0.303	−0.326
	(0.019)	(0.028)	(0.026)
1995–1999 arrivals	−0.270	−0.251	−0.259
	(0.016)	(0.021)	(0.021)
2005–2009 arrivals	−0.300	−0.212	−0.231
	(0.037)	(0.033)	(0.036)
Relative wage growth in first 10 years			
1965–1969 arrivals	0.132	0.112	0.132
	(0.024)	(0.038)	(0.036)
1975–1979 arrivals	0.111	0.086	0.088
	(0.025)	(0.039)	(0.037)
1985–1989 arrivals	0.090	0.063	0.064
	(0.024)	(0.038)	(0.035)
1995–1999 arrivals	0.025	0.039	0.019
	(0.020)	(0.025)	(0.026)

Sources: U.S. Census PUMS, 1970–2010; see Appendix B for details.

Notes: The regressions stack the cross-section samples used in Table 2.1. Standard errors are reported in parentheses and are clustered at the cohort level. The dependent variable gives the worker's log weekly wage. The regressors include a cubic in age (interacted with a variable indicating if the worker is an immigrant); a cubic in years-since-migration; a vector of year-of-entry fixed effects; and a vector of fixed effects giving the census year (in specification 1). The linear term in years-since-migration is interacted with the vector of year-of-entry fixed effects. The regression in specification 1 assumes that the coefficients of the census year fixed effects are the same for immigrants and natives. Specifications 2 and 3 "solve out" the period effects by using either a deflator giving the wage growth (among natives) between 2000 and the census year for a particular age-education group (specification 2) or a particular percentile of the weekly wage distribution (specification 3). The calculation of the relative wage growth in the first 10 years assumes that the immigrant arrives in the United States at age 25. The regressions have 9,682,801 observations.

The estimates of the *level* cohort effects are similar to those implied by the raw data summarized in Table 2.2. For example, the regression predicts an entry wage disadvantage of 21.3 percent for the cohort that entered the country in the late 1960s, while the raw data suggests a 23.5 percent wage disadvantage. The regression also reveals a steady decline in the rate of economic assimilation, with the decline accelerating in the 1990s. Immigrants who entered the country in the late 1960s could expect an increase in their relative earnings of about 13 percentage points during their first decade in the United States. However, the assimilation rate of the immigrants who entered in the late 1980s was about 9 percentage points, and the assimilation rate of the immigrants who entered in the late 1990s was near zero.

There are two competing explanations for the trends in entry wages and assimilation rates. The first is that they represent a failure of the regression model to properly account for various factors that may be leading to lower relative wages for immigrants in recent years and that have nothing to do with the underlying process of human capital accumulation. The second is that they reflect a tangible change in the relative skills of immigrants.

The most obvious "mechanical" explanation is that the period effects restriction in equation (2.6) is false. It is well known that the returns to skills increased dramatically during the past few decades (Katz and Murphy 1992; Lemieux 2006). Because the immigrant and native populations have a different skill mix, the assumption that the period effects are the same "on average" may not capture the impact of changing macroeconomic conditions on the two wage structures, biasing the other parameters of the model.

A simple way of addressing the problem is to assume that the period effects restriction in equation (2.6) operates at the level of a particular skill group at a particular point in time, rather than for the average immigrant and native at that point in time. For example, classify all workers into one of 40 narrowly defined skill groups (h) based on a worker's educational attainment and age.[15] I can then use the 1970–2010 cross-sections to calculate the nominal rate of wage growth experienced by *native* workers in each of these groups over the four-decade period. Let $\phi_{h\tau}$ be the implied "price index" that can be used to deflate the wages of a worker in skill group h and in cross section τ.[16] I then re-estimated the regression model after using the skill-specific deflator $\phi_{h\tau}$ to "solve out" the period effects from the earnings functions.

The second specification in Table 2.3 shows that controlling for skill-specific period effects dampens the rate of decline in the entry wage of immigrant cohorts. The entry wage of the 1985–1989 cohort is about 14 percentage points lower than that of the 1965–1969 cohort in the basic specification that uses the unadjusted wage, but only 10 percentage points lower after the model adjusts for skill-specific period effects. This finding replicates the evidence reported in Lubotsky (2011), who uses a structural framework to estimate the changing price of skills over the period and concludes that changes in the wage structure account for about a third of the observed decline in entry earnings typically associated with *level* cohort effects.[17] In addition, the adjustment for skill-specific period effects suggests a reversal in the direction of level cohort effects since 1990; the observed decline in cohort quality between 1970 and 1990 has been offset by an equivalent increase between 1990 and 2010. However, the regression also shows that the slowdown in the rate of economic assimilation seems impervious to the use of skill-specific price deflators.

An alternative way of adjusting the data for skill-specific period effects is to define the skill groups in terms of a worker's placement in the earnings distribution. In particular, I classify each worker into one of 100 skill groups depending on his percentile ranking in the *native* weekly earnings distribution.[18] I then use the 1970–2010 cross-sections to measure the nominal wage growth experienced by each percentile of the native distribution, and calculate the implied price index $\phi_{h\tau}$ that can be used to deflate the earnings of a worker in percentile ranking h and in cross-section τ. As the last column of Table 2.3 shows, defining the skill groups in terms of percentile ranking again reduces the difference in the relative entry wage between the late 1960s and the late 1980s cohorts by about one-third, and does not alter the conclusion that the most recent cohorts experience less economic assimilation than the earlier ones.[19]

Let me conclude by emphasizing two distinct conceptual problems that can easily contaminate any measurement of aging and cohort effects in the immigration context. First, the use of repeated cross-sections to measure economic assimilation introduces a potentially important flaw. Specifically, a fraction of the immigrants in a particular cohort are likely to return to their source countries (or migrate elsewhere), and the rate of economic assimilation is necessarily calculated from a sample that contains all immigrants at the beginning of the period and only the survivors at the end.[20] The measured rate of economic assimilation would be biased upward if the return migrants were those with the lowest wages in the United States, and downward if the return migrants had relatively high wages.

A few studies use longitudinal samples to examine how nonrandom return migration affects the rate of convergence implied by the census data. Hu (2000) and Lubotsky (2007) use data sets that match, at the individual level, the demographic records available in selected (and usually small) census-type samples with the complete earnings histories of workers maintained by the Social Security Administration. The administrative Social Security data, of course, are only available for immigrants who remain in the United States, making it possible to estimate the rate of economic assimilation among stayers, netting out the contaminating effect introduced by selective out-migration.

This type of longitudinal study, much of it using pre-1990 data, typically finds that the use of repeated cross-sections tends to *overestimate* the rate of economic assimilation. For example, Lubotsky (2007, p. 851) shows that applying a repeated-cross-section approach to the Social Security administrative data would imply a rate of economic assimilation of about 13.2 percentage points during the immigrant's first decade. The adjustment for selective out-migration, however, cuts the assimilation rate by half, to 6.0 percent. It seems, therefore, that the out-migrants tend to be the immigrants who have the lowest earnings in a particular cohort.[21]

Second, depending on the context, the nature of the evidence could hinge crucially on the identifying assumptions that are made about period effects and on the empirical methods that are used to adjust for differential period effects in the immigrant and native populations. An empirical analysis of the evolution of immigrant earnings, and particularly the interpretation of the earnings trends in terms of changes in underlying skills, can be credible only if it can document that the results are not driven by the imposed restrictions on period effects. To complicate matters, however, the period effects are endogenous in the sense that the laws of supply and demand imply that the immigrant influx *itself* differentially changes the relative wages of workers (both native- and foreign-born) in specific skill groups at different points in time. This conceptual issue has not been addressed in the literature, and would require a synthesis of the models and methods that are typically used to analyze the process of immigrant assimilation with those that are used to examine the labor market impact of immigration.

A Model of Economic Assimilation

The presence or absence of economic assimilation provides information about the rate at which immigrants accumulate human capital after arriving in a host country. In order to identify the factors that can either accelerate or impede the assimilation process, it is useful to derive the implications of a model of optimal human capital accumulation for the rate of economic assimilation.

A two-period model of the human capital accumulation process provides a valuable framework for thinking about these issues (Borjas 2000). Let K give the number of efficiency units an immigrant acquired in the source country. Because human capital may be partly specific to the country where it is acquired, a fraction δ of these efficiency units are not "marketable" in the host country's labor market. The worker's marketable human capital in the post-migration period is then given by $E = (1 - \delta) K$. The value of the depreciation rate δ provides a simple way to contrast the investment incentives faced by comparable immigrants and natives in the host country. The typical native can sell all of his K efficiency units in the labor market, so that $\delta = 0$ for natives and $0 < \delta < 1$ for immigrants.

An immigrant lives for two periods *after* migrating. During the investment period, the immigrant devotes a fraction π of his human capital to the production of additional human capital, and this investment increases the number of marketable efficiency units in the payoff period by $g \times 100$ percent. If the market-determined rental rate for an efficiency unit in the host country is one dollar, the present value of the post-migration income stream is:

$$V = (1 - \delta) K (1 - \pi) + \rho [(1 - \delta) K (1 + g)], \qquad (2.8)$$

where ρ is the discounting factor.

The human capital production function that generates the increase in the number of marketable efficiency units is given by:

$$gE = (\pi K)^\alpha K^\beta, \qquad (2.9)$$

where $\alpha < 1$. The production function in (2.9) is a simple adaptation of the one in the classic Ben-Porath (1967) model of human capital accumulation. In the Ben-Porath framework, a worker produces human capital by using part of his current human capital stock for the production of additional efficiency units. In equation (2.9), the worker uses a fraction of his *entire* human capital stock (or πK) as an input in production. Even though part of the preexisting human capital stock may not be marketable in the host country, it is still useful in the production of additional human capital. As an example, an immigrant with a specialized medical degree may not be able to market his skills in the host country's labor market due to licensing restrictions. Nevertheless, those skills do not entirely disappear; that knowledge is imbedded in the worker and would certainly be useful in the production of additional human capital. Note also that the production function in equation (2.9) allows for the possibility that the worker's preexisting human capital stock K is an independent input in the production process (as long as $\beta > 0$).

Workers choose the value of π that maximizes the present value of post-migration earnings. The implied optimal rate of accumulation of marketable efficiency units is:

$$g = (\alpha\rho)^{\frac{\alpha}{1-\alpha}} \left(\frac{1}{1-\delta} \right)^{\frac{1}{1-\alpha}} K^{\frac{\alpha+\beta-1}{1-\alpha}}. \tag{2.10}$$

Define "relative neutrality" as the case where the rate of human capital accumulation of marketable skills is independent of the initial level of human capital, so $\alpha + \beta = 1$. If $\alpha + \beta > 1$, the rate of human capital accumulation is positively related to initial skills, or "relative complementarity." If $\alpha + \beta < 1$, there is a negative relationship, or "relative substitutability."[22]

Equation (2.10) also implies a positive relation between the rate of human capital accumulation g and the depreciation rate δ. In fact, because $\delta = 0$ for native workers, the model predicts that immigrants accumulate human capital at a faster rate than comparable natives. The intuition is obvious: For comparable levels of "true" skills, immigrants face lower forgone earnings (a fraction δ of the preexisting human capital is not marketable in the host country), and hence have a greater incentive to acquire more skills. Finally, the model implies a positive relation between the rate of human capital accumulation and the discounting factor ρ: immigrants who discount their future earnings less heavily (that is, a higher ρ) acquire more post-migration human capital.

Let $\dot{w}$ be the rate of wage growth experienced by an immigrant in the host country. The rate of wage growth is given by:[23]

$$\dot{w} = \log \left(\frac{(1-\delta)K(1+g)}{(1-\delta)K(1-\pi)} \right) \approx g + \pi. \tag{2.11}$$

It is easy to show that:

$$\frac{\partial \dot{w}}{\partial \delta} > 0, \tag{2.12a}$$

$$sign\left(\frac{\partial \dot{w}}{\partial K}\bigg|_{\delta>0} - \frac{\partial \dot{w}}{\partial K}\bigg|_{\delta=0} \right) = sign(\alpha+\beta-1), \tag{2.12b}$$

$$\frac{\partial \dot{w}}{\partial \rho} > 0. \tag{2.12c}$$

Equation (2.12a) confirms that the rate of wage growth is larger for workers who have a larger depreciation rate δ. This result immediately implies that immigrants will experience faster wage growth than comparable natives, so that optimal investment behavior predicts a positive rate of economic assimilation. Interestingly, the model generates a positive rate of assimilation because, on average, immigrants are "different" from natives. Immigrants start their working life in the host country at a disadvantage (some of their skills have depreciated because $\delta > 0$) and have an incentive to catch up. Equation (2.12a) also implies that *within* the immigrant population, those immigrants originating in countries where the preexisting skills are least transferable to the host country will experience a *faster* rate of post-migration wage growth.

Equation (2.12b) shows that the sign of the correlation between the rate of economic assimilation and the preexisting human capital stock depends on whether there is relative substitution or relative complementarity in the production of skills. High-skill immigrants "assimilate faster" only if there is relative complementarity.

Finally, equation (2.12c) states that immigrants who are less likely to discount their future earnings in the host country's labor market (that is, have a higher ρ) will experience a higher rate of wage growth. This result suggests, for example, that immigrants who face higher return migration costs should assimilate faster.

Empirical Determinants of Assimilation:
A Cross-Country Analysis

Chapter 1 documented the sizable entry wage differences that exist across immigrants belonging to different national origin groups. Not surprisingly, there are equally large differences in the rate of economic assimilation. The model of human capital accumulation provides a useful framework for thinking about (and interpreting) these differences. The empirical analysis uses the 1980–2010 decennial census data. By definition, an immigrant cohort comprises a group of foreign-born persons who migrated to the United States at age i, from country k, at a particular calendar time t. Each (i, k, t) cohort is then tracked over the first 10 years after arrival by "jumping" to the next census and observing the now-older group at that point. The wage growth experienced by this cohort across censuses—relative to the wage growth experienced by a comparably aged group of native workers over the same period—measures the rate of economic assimilation.

The analysis is restricted to immigrant men originating in the largest 80 sending countries, and uses three age-at-migration "windows" to construct the cohorts: persons who were 25–34, 35–44, and 45–54 at the time of arrival. The analysis also uses three year-of-arrival groups: immigrants who arrived in 1975–1979, 1985–1989, and 1995–1999. The regression model is then given by:

$$\Delta \log w_{ik}(t) = \phi_i + \phi_t + Z_k(t)\,\beta + \varepsilon, \qquad (2.13)$$

where $\Delta \log w_{ik}(t)$ gives the (initial) 10-year change in the log weekly wage of a cohort of immigrants who arrived in the United States at age i, from country k, at time t relative to the wage growth experienced by comparably aged natives during the same decade; Z is a vector of country specific characteristics that may determine the rate of economic assimilation; and ϕ_i and ϕ_t are vectors of fixed effects that absorb any age- and year-of-entry-specific factors that determine the rate of assimilation.

The human capital accumulation model identifies three variables that play a central role in the investment decision: the initial human capital stock of the cohort (K); the depreciation rate of preexisting skills (δ); and the cohort's discounting factor (ρ). The empirical analysis uses the cohort's average years of educational attainment (measured at the time of arrival) to approximate for the preexisting human capital stock. The first regression specification in Table 2.4 shows that this variable has a positive impact on

Table 2.4 Cross-country determinants of economic assimilation
in first ten years

	Specification	
Variable	(1)	(2)
Educational attainment of cohort at time of entry	0.015	0.013
	(0.004)	(0.005)
Log per-capita GDP in source country (PPP-adjusted)	−0.026	−0.022
	(0.014)	(0.017)
Distance from the United States (=1 if distance exceeds 3,000 miles)	0.026	0.016
	(0.024)	(0.024)
Repressive regime (=1 if curtailed civil liberties)	0.050	0.063
	(0.021)	(0.030)
Preexisting size of national origin group (in millions)	—	−0.011
		(0.007)
R^2	0.253	0.261

Sources: U.S. Census PUMS, 1980–2010; the Penn World Table (Heston et al. 2012); the World Development Indicators (World Bank 2013); and the Freedom in the World index (Freedom House 2011). See Appendix B for details.

Notes: The analysis is restricted to cohorts of immigrant men aged 25–64 at the time of the census, who originated in the 80 largest source countries, and who migrated to the United States in the 5-year period prior to each census. The unit of observation is an immigrant cohort defined by age at arrival, source country, and calendar year of arrival. The age-at-arrival groups are: 25–34, 35–44, and 45–54. Standard errors are reported in parentheses and are clustered at the source country level. The dependent variable gives the change in the mean log weekly wage of the immigrant cohort (relative to that of comparably aged natives) during their first 10 years in the United States. The regressions include vectors of age-at-arrival and decade-of-arrival fixed effects, and are weighted by $n_0 n_1 / (n_0 + n_1)$, where n_0, is the sample size used to calculate the cohort's mean log wage at the beginning of the decade and n_1 is the respective sample size at the end of the decade. The regressions have 717 observations.

the rate of economic assimilation. Each additional year of education increases the (relative) rate of wage growth of immigrants by 1.5 percentage points. The evidence, therefore, suggests the presence of relative complementarity in the production of human capital.

The regression also includes a variable measuring the log per capita GDP in the country of origin at the time of migration. As shown in Chapter 1, there exists a strong positive correlation between immigrant earnings and per capita GDP in the source country. This correlation is sometimes explained by conjecturing that the skills of immigrants from high-income countries are more easily transferable to the U.S. labor market. Table 2.4 shows that the per capita GDP variable has a *negative* impact on economic assimilation. The negative effect is consistent with the theoretical prediction. Holding initial skills constant, the immigrants who can most easily transfer their skills from one industrialized economy to another are also the immigrants who find it most expensive to invest in the post-migration period.

The regression adds two variables that proxy for the discounting factor ρ. First, immigrants originating in countries that are geographically distant from the United States have a faster rate of assimilation (although the effect is not significant). One potential explanation is that these immigrants face a higher cost of return migration, so that they are less likely to discount their future earnings in the U.S. labor market. Similarly, the regression includes the civil liberties index constructed by Freedom House (2011). Immigrants from countries with repressive regimes have a larger rate of economic assimilation, presumably again because they are less likely to engage in return migration.

Finally, the payoff for immigrants to invest in U.S.-specific human capital (such as English-language fluency) depends on the frequency with which they will use those skills in their everyday interactions (Lazear 1999). Immigrants who find few of their compatriots living in the United States have a stronger incentive to make the investments that allow a wider range of social and economic exchanges.[24] Put differently, the depreciation rate δ is inversely correlated with the size of the potential audience that will value the immigrant's preexisting skills.

The second specification in Table 2.4 introduces a "group size" variable giving the number of immigrants from the same national origin group who resided in the United States at the time of the cohort's arrival. The preexisting group size has a (marginally significant) negative impact on economic assimilation: each million-person increase in the size of a national origin group reduces the rate of assimilation by about 1 percentage point.[25]

As with all cross-country regressions, it would be wise not to read too much into the evidence reported in Table 2.4. It is difficult to ascertain what the aggregate variables are "standing for," and the results are likely sensitive to the inclusion or exclusion of particular sets of variables. Nevertheless, the analysis suggests an important lesson: The process of economic assimilation is endogenous. Immigrants will make the necessary investments required for assimilation if and when it is profitable for them to do so.

Earnings Imputation: A Nontrivial Data Problem

Much of the empirical research summarized in this book uses U.S. census microdata. These data have many benefits. They are available over a long time span, consist of very large samples, and contain many of the variables that are crucial for a study of the economics of immigration, including birthplace, educational attainment, and earnings, at the individual level.

A critical feature of the public-use samples is that there typically is no missing information on *any* variable. Obviously, the completeness of the data is not because every single person bothered to take the time to answer every single question. The completeness is artificial and arises only because the U.S. Census Bureau systematically "fills in" the missing information whenever a survey respondent happened to skip a particular question.

The filling-in process, which is technically called a "hot deck imputation," is designed to provide a statistically valid way of approximating unobserved data (Andridge and Little, 2010). It works roughly as follows. Suppose a white man who is 40 years old, has a college degree, and lives in a neighborhood north of Chicago does not bother to report how much he earned. The Census Bureau will search for the "nearest neighbor" who is also a white 40-year-old male college graduate. If that matched neighbor, called the "donor," happened to earn $87,335 during the year, then the missing information for the original respondent, or the "recipient," will be imputed and take on a value of $87,335. The Census Bureau then adds a flag to the public microdata file indicating that the earnings for this particular respondent were imputed. The complete list of variables used to construct the sample of donors for earnings imputation is: geography, race, educational attainment, living arrangements, sex, occupation, class of worker, number of weeks worked, number of hours worked, and age. Notably, the hot deck algorithm does *not* use immigration status in order to identify the donors.

As long as the relative number of imputed observations is "small," the hot deck algorithm is not likely to create many problems for empirical work—although there are documented instances where problems arise

(Kaplan and Schulhofer 2012; Bollinger and Hirsch 2013). Unfortunately, the imputation rates have increased over time, and this increase is particularly dramatic in some segments of the foreign-born population. Table 2.5 reports that only 8.8 percent of native-born men in the 1980 census had imputed earnings. By 2010, however, their imputation rate had risen to 19.1 percent. The increase was even faster among immigrants, from 11 percent to 25 percent. In some important subsamples of the immigrant workforce, the imputation rate is even higher. For example, the imputation rate in the sample of newly arrived immigrants nearly doubled from 15 to 29 percent. And, perhaps most striking of all, the imputation rate for newly arrived Mexican immigrants increased from 17 to 38 percent.

To make matters worse, it is easy to show that the hot deck algorithm influences the measured immigrant–native wage differential. The immigrant–native wage gap should be the same regardless of whether the earnings information is "real" or imputed. Let F_ℓ be an indicator variable set to unity if person ℓ is foreign-born; and P_ℓ be an indicator variable set to unity if the earnings for that particular observation are imputed. Consider the regression model:

$$\log w_\ell = X_\ell \, \gamma_0 + \gamma_1 \, F_\ell + \gamma_2 \, P_\ell + \gamma_3 \, (F_\ell \times P_\ell) + \varepsilon. \qquad (2.14)$$

The coefficient of interest, γ_3, estimates the difference in the relative weekly wage of the foreign-born between the sample of workers with imputed earnings and the sample of workers with "real" earnings.

Table 2.6 reports estimates of the coefficient γ_3 when the model is estimated separately in each census cross-section. The simplest regression

Table 2.5 Percent of workers with imputed wage and salary income

Group	1980	1990	2000	2010
Natives	8.8	11.0	23.5	19.1
Immigrants	11.4	14.9	25.9	24.5
Immigrants, arrived in last 5 years	15.2	20.0	31.0	29.2
Mexican immigrants, arrived in last 5 years	16.7	19.8	40.2	38.2

Sources: U.S. Census PUMS, 1980–2010; see Appendix B for details.

Notes: The imputation rates are calculated in the sample of men who are 25–64 years old, do not live in group quarters, worked at least one week in the calendar year prior to the census cross-section, are not enrolled in school, and are employed in the wage-and-salary sector.

Table 2.6 Bias in imputed wages

Census cross-section	Specification		
	(1)	(2)	(3)
1980	.006	.034	.039
	(.007)	(.006)	(.006)
1990	.043	.072	.068
	(.005)	(.004)	(.004)
2000	.007	.049	.047
	(.003)	(.003)	(.003)
2010	.028	.075	.071
	(.004)	(.004)	(.003)
Variables included in regression			
Age-fixed effects	No	Yes	Yes
Education-fixed effects	No	Yes	Yes
Metropolitan area- and state-fixed effects	No	No	Yes

Sources: U.S. Census PUMS, 1980–2010; see Appendix B for details.

Notes: The regressions use the samples defined in the notes to Table 2.5 and are estimated separately in each census. The dependent variable gives the worker's log weekly wage. Standard errors are reported in parentheses. All regressions include a variable indicating if the worker is foreign-born and a variable indicating if his earnings were imputed. The table reports the coefficient of the interaction between those two variables. The number of observations in the regressions are: 1980: 1,769,419; 1990: 2,097,076; 2000: 2,425,339; and 2010: 1,491,684.

specification, which does not include any variables in the vector X, indicates that the coefficient γ_3 increased from essentially zero in 1980 to 2.8 percent by 2010. If the vector X includes educational attainment, age, and fixed effects indicating the worker's metropolitan area of residence, the coefficient γ_3 increased from 3.9 percent in 1980 to 7.1 percent in 2010. In other words, the set of donors generated by the hot deck algorithm systematically leads the census to impute relatively *higher* wages to immigrants than would otherwise be observed, and this bias has worsened over time.

In view of the rapid increase in the number of foreign-born workers with imputed earnings, the nonrandomness illustrated in Table 2.6 raises many concerns about the robustness of empirical findings in the immigration literature. Although it may seem sensible to test the robustness of the evidence by replicating the analysis in the subsample of workers where earnings are not imputed, it is unlikely that workers who *do* report their earnings compose a random sample in either the native or the immigrant population. In short, it may not be prudent to "bet the ranch" on the evidence when key subsamples of the immigrant workforce, such as recently arrived Mexicans, have nearly 40 percent imputation rates.

3

Immigration and the
Wage Structure: Theory

———————————◆———————————

THE SURGE IN INTERNATIONAL migration inspired a large literature examining what happens to labor markets in both receiving and sending countries as a result of immigration-induced supply shifts. The textbook model of a competitive labor market has clear implications about how wages should respond to immigration: Higher levels of immigration should lower the relative wage of competing workers and increase the relative wage of complementary workers. Despite the commonsense intuition behind these predictions, the empirical literature is full of contradictory results. Some studies claim that immigration has a substantial adverse impact on the wages of competing workers in receiving countries, while others claim the impact is negligible and perhaps even positive.

Before plunging into the empirical confusion, it is worth stepping back and asking a simpler question: What does factor demand theory have to say about the potential wage effects of immigration-induced supply shifts? Since Marshall's time, economists have had a good understanding of the factors that generate elastic or inelastic labor demand curves.[1] Unfortunately, much of the empirical literature on the wage impact of immigration (particularly in the 1990s) disregarded practically all of these theoretical insights, and instead took a data-mining approach: estimating regressions or difference-in-differences models to determine if the wage evolution in labor markets most affected by immigration differed from that observed in other markets. More recently, however, the literature has begun to pay much closer attention to the underlying economics of the problem.

Homogeneous Labor in a One-Good Closed Economy

It is instructive to begin with the simplest model of the labor market: a single good, Q, is produced using a production function that combines capital (K) and a single labor input (L).[2] The aggregate production function, $Q=f(K, L)$, is assumed to be linear homogeneous. The relevant derivatives of the production function exist, with f_K and $f_L > 0$, and f_{KK} and $f_{LL} < 0$. Linear homogeneity implies that $f_{KL} > 0$.

The elasticity of complementarity for input pair i and j is $c_{ij}=f_{ij}f/f_if_j$.[3] Linear homogeneity implies that a weighted average of these elasticities equals zero:

$$\sum_j s_j c_{ij} = 0, \tag{3.1}$$

where s_j is the income share accruing to input j.

The product price is fixed at p. In a competitive market, each input price is equal to its value of marginal product:

$$r=p f_K, \tag{3.2a}$$

$$w=p f_L, \tag{3.2b}$$

where r is the rental rate of capital and w is the wage rate.

It is instructive to consider two polar situations: the short run and the long run. By definition, the capital stock is fixed in the short run and the rental rate of capital is fixed in the long run. Suppose an immigrant influx increases the size of the workforce. By differentiating equation (3.2b), it is easy to show that the short-run factor price elasticity is given by:[4]

$$\left. \frac{d\log w}{d\log L} \right|_{dK=0} = s_L c_{LL} < 0. \tag{3.3}$$

For expositional convenience, the factor price elasticity will often be called the "wage elasticity" of immigration. The short-run wage elasticity must be negative, because $c_{LL} < 0$.

Although the wage falls in the short run, the return to capital must rise:

$$\frac{d\log r}{d\log L}\bigg|_{dK=0} = s_L c_{KL} > 0. \tag{3.4}$$

Linear homogeneity implies that capital and labor are complements, hence $c_{KL} > 0$. This complementarity ensures that capital becomes more valuable as immigration increases the number of workers. Immigration has a short-run distributional impact: wealth is shifted away from workers and toward those who own the productive resources in the immigrant-receiving country.

The distributional impact, however, disappears in the long run. The rise in the return to capital encourages capital inflows until the rental rate is again equalized across markets. Differentiating the marginal productivity condition in equation (3.2a) implies that the immigration-induced change in the capital stock is:

$$\frac{d\log K}{d\log L}\bigg|_{dr=0} = -\frac{s_L c_{KL}}{s_K c_{KK}} = 1, \tag{3.5}$$

where the last equality follows from equation (3.1). The capital stock will grow (in percentage terms) by exactly the same amount as the size of the workforce. The long-run wage elasticity is then given by:

$$\frac{d\log w}{d\log L}\bigg|_{dr=0} = s_K c_{LK} + s_L c_{LL} = 0, \tag{3.6}$$

where the last equality again follows from equation (3.1). In the long run, the host country's wage is independent of immigration. The intuition is clear: The linear homogeneity of the production function implies that input prices depend only on the capital/labor ratio. The assumption that the price of capital is constant builds in the restriction that the capital/labor ratio is also constant. If immigrants increase the size of the workforce by 10 percent, the capital stock must eventually also increase by 10 percent. In the long run, the labor market returns to its pre-immigration equilibrium and immigration does not alter input prices.

It is possible to obtain some sense of the *magnitude* of the short-run wage elasticity by specifying a functional form for the production function. Suppose, in particular, that the aggregate production function has a constant elasticity of substitution (CES), so that $Q=[\alpha K^{\delta}+(1-\alpha)L^{\delta}]^{1/\delta}$, where $\delta \leq 1$, and the elasticity of substitution between labor and capital is $\sigma_{KL}=1/(1-\delta)$. The short-run wage elasticity is then given by:

$$\frac{d\log w}{d\log L}\bigg|_{dK=0} = -(1-\delta)s_{K}. \tag{3.7}$$

If the production function were Cobb-Douglas (so that $\delta=0$, or equivalently, $\sigma_{KL}=1$), the theory has very specific implications about the numerical size of the short-run wage effect. In particular, labor's share of income in the United States has hovered around 0.7 for many decades. Equation (3.7) then implies that the short-run wage elasticity is -0.3. One would then expect the wage elasticity to lie between 0.0 and -0.3, depending on the extent to which capital has adjusted to the presence of the immigrant influx.

Heterogeneous Labor in a One-Good Closed Economy

The linear-homogeneous production function for the single aggregate good is now given by $Q=f(K, L_1, \ldots, L_Z)$, and the price of the output, p, is again assumed to be constant. The existence of Z labor inputs makes it important to specify precisely what is meant by an immigration-induced supply shift. After all, immigration may increase the supply of each of the inputs, but the quantity of some of these inputs may increase (proportionately) more than the others. Define the percent increase in supply experienced by group i as:[5]

$$m_i = \frac{dL_i}{L_i}. \tag{3.8}$$

The vector $\mathbf{m}=[m_1, \ldots, m_Z]$ represents the generalized supply shift in the host country's labor market.

Consider initially the situation in the short run, with a fixed capital stock. By differentiating the marginal productivity condition for capital, it follows that the change in the rental price of capital is:

$$d\log r\big|_{dK=0} = \sum_{\ell} s_{\ell} c_{K\ell} m_{\ell}, \tag{3.9}$$

where $c_{K\ell}$ gives the elasticity of complementarity between capital and labor input ℓ. The impact of the generalized supply shift on the rental price of capital cannot be signed unambiguously. Instead, it roughly depends on the sign of the "average" elasticity of complementarity between capital and labor. Equation (3.1) states that the weighted average of the elasticities of complementarity between capital and all inputs is zero. Hence, the "average" labor input must be complementary with capital. It seems reasonable to suspect, therefore, that immigration will increase the returns to capital.

Differentiating the marginal productivity condition for labor input i yields:

$$d\log w_i\big|_{dK=0} = \sum_{\ell} s_{\ell} c_{i\ell} m_{\ell}. \tag{3.10}$$

Equation (3.10) shows the difficulty of determining how immigration alters the wage structure in the presence of heterogeneous labor: the wage impact on a particular group depends not only on the size of the "own" supply shift, but also on the size of the supply shift in every other group. An interesting special case occurs when immigration only increases the supply of input i, so that $\mathbf{m} = [0, \ldots 0, m_i, 0, \ldots 0]$. In that case:

$$d\log w_i\big|_{dK=0} = s_i c_{ii} m_i < 0, \tag{3.11}$$

and the wage of input i must fall.

Define the *average* wage change as $d\log \bar{w} = \sum_{\ell} s_{\ell} d\log w_{\ell} / s_L$, where s_L is the share of income accruing to labor ($s_L = s_1 + \ldots + s_Z$). By substituting equation (3.10) into the definition of the average wage change, it is easy to show that:

$$d\log \bar{w}\big|_{dK=0} = -\frac{s_K}{s_L}\left[d\log r\big|_{dK=0}\right]. \tag{3.12}$$

The average wage impact of immigration must be opposite in sign to the impact of immigration on the rental price of capital. If immigration raises the return to capital, it must lower the average wage. Immigration redistributes wealth between labor and capital in the short run.

It is also possible to sign the average short-run wage effect when the generalized supply shift is "balanced," so that $m_i = \bar{m}$ for all groups. Equation (3.12) then reduces to:

$$d\log\bar{w}\Big|_{dK=0} = \frac{s_K^2 c_{KK}\bar{m}}{s_L} < 0. \tag{3.13}$$

In other words, if immigration increases the supply of every type of labor by x percent, the short-run impact is to lower the average wage by an amount proportional to x.

Let us now examine the implications of factor demand theory for the long-run wage effects when there is heterogeneous labor. The impact of the generalized supply shift **m** on the wage of group i is:

$$d\log w_i\Big|_{dr=0} = \sum_{\ell} s_\ell c_{i\ell} m_\ell + s_K c_{Ki}\Big[d\log K\Big|_{dr=0}\Big]. \tag{3.14}$$

Note that the short- and long-run effects given by equations (3.10) and (3.14) differ only by the presence of the last term in (3.14). Differentiating the marginal productivity condition for capital yields:

$$d\log K\Big|_{dr=0} = \frac{-\displaystyle\sum_{\ell} s_\ell c_{K\ell} m_\ell}{s_K c_{KK}}. \tag{3.15}$$

The percent change in the capital stock is a weighted average of the group-specific supply shifts.[6] By substituting equation (3.15) into (3.14), the long-run wage change experienced by group i can be rewritten as:

$$d\log w_i\Big|_{dr=0} = \frac{\displaystyle\sum_{\ell} s_i s_K (c_{i\ell} c_{KK} - c_{Ki} c_{K\ell}) m_\ell}{s_K c_{KK}}. \tag{3.16}$$

Equation (3.16) can be signed in a very special case. Suppose, in particular, that immigration increases only the supply of group i. Equation (3.16) then reduces to:

$$d\log w_i\big|_{dr=0} = \frac{s_i s_K (c_{ii} c_{KK} - c_{Ki}^2) m_i}{s_K c_{KK}} < 0. \tag{3.17}$$

The isoquant between capital and labor input i (holding constant the quantities of all other inputs) will have the usual convex shape if $c_{ii} c_{KK} - c_{Ki}^2 > 0$. The wage elasticity in (3.17) will then be negative.

There is one other long-run wage effect that is of interest. In particular, consider what happens to the average wage. After some algebra, it can be shown that:

$$d\log \bar{w}\big|_{dr=0} = 0. \tag{3.18}$$

It is worth emphasizing that the theoretical prediction in (3.18) makes no assumption whatsoever about the nature of the generalized supply shift **m,** so that immigration leaves the *average* wage unaffected regardless of how it changed supply. In the long run, neither the rental rate of capital r nor the average wage $\bar{w}$ changes as a result of an immigration-induced supply shift. The long-run effects are restricted to the labor market and must be distributional—changing the relative wage of the various labor groups. Generally, those groups that experience the largest supply shifts lose relative to the ones that experience the smallest supply shifts. It follows trivially that if the supply shift is balanced (that is, $m_i = \bar{m}$), then $d\log w_i = 0 \; \forall \; i$. Put differently, a balanced supply shift represents the only situation where immigration (in the heterogeneous labor context) does not have any long-run economic consequence.

The Nested CES

The presence of heterogeneous labor implies that the impact of immigration on the wage of any single group of workers depends on how immigration affects the supply of *every* group. In both theoretical and empirical work, therefore, the need arises to reduce the dimensionality of the problem, typically by limiting the types of permissible cross-effects among inputs.

The nested CES framework is relatively tractable, easy to implement empirically, and has become popular in the immigration literature since its introduction into that context by Borjas (2003).[7] The generic two-level nested CES system can be written as:

$$Q = [\alpha K^{\delta} + (1-\alpha)L^{\delta}]^{1/\delta}, \tag{3.19a}$$

$$L = [\theta_1 L_1^{\beta} + \theta_2 L_2^{\beta}]^{1/\beta}. \tag{3.19b}$$

Equation (3.19a) gives the aggregate production function. The labor input L should now be interpreted as the number of efficiency units available in the labor market, an agglomeration of workers belonging to different skill groups. The elasticity of substitution between capital and the labor aggregate is defined by $\sigma_{KL} = 1/(1-\delta)$. Equation (3.19b) gives the Armington aggregator that homogenizes different types of workers into standardized efficiency units, with L_i giving the number of workers in group i. The elasticity of substitution between groups 1 and 2 is defined by $\sigma_{12} = 1/(1-\beta)$, with $\beta \leq 1$; and $\theta_1 + \theta_2 = 1$. Although the exposition uses only two labor inputs, it will be evident that all of the results extend easily to any finite number.

Immigrants can shift the supply of either of the two groups. As before, $m_i = dL_i/L_i$ gives the immigration-induced percent supply shift for group i. Appendix A shows that the percent shift in the number of standardized efficiency units is given by:

$$d\log L = \frac{s_1 m_1 + s_2 m_2}{s_L} = \overline{m}. \tag{3.20}$$

Equation (3.20) reveals an interesting technical feature of the nested CES framework: It is not necessary to know the value of the elasticities of substitution σ_{12} and σ_{KL} to calculate the size of the percent shift in the labor aggregate L. All of the pertinent information is contained in the income shares accruing to the various skill groups. As will be seen in what follows, this "averaging" mathematical property has important empirical implications.

The condition that the wage of input i equals its value of marginal product is:

$$w_i = \left[(1-\alpha)Q^{1-\delta} L^{\delta-1} \right] \theta_i L^{1-\beta} L_i^{\beta-1}. \tag{3.21}$$

The bracketed term in (3.21) represents the marginal productivity condition in the homogeneous labor case. The fact that there are now two different skill groups simply adds the multiplicative term that appears to the right of the bracket. Let w be equal to the bracketed term in (3.21). By differentiating equation (3.21) and using the averaging property in (3.20), it is easy to show that the effect of immigration on the wage of group i is given by:

$$d\log w_i = d\log w + (1-\beta)d\log L + (\beta-1)d\log L_i,$$
$$= d\log w + (1-\beta)(\bar{m} - m_i).$$

(3.22)

Equation (3.22) has a number of interesting implications. Consider, for example, the impact of immigration on the relative wage of the two skill groups. This distributional effect is given by:

$$d\log w_1 - d\log w_2 = -\frac{1}{\sigma_{12}}(m_1 - m_2).$$

(3.23)

The impact of immigration on relative wages depends only on the elasticity of substitution between the two groups and is proportional to the relative supply shift. If the two groups are perfect substitutes ($\sigma_{12} = \infty$), immigration has no relative wage effect. If the two groups are imperfect substitutes, the group that experiences the larger supply shock will *always* experience a decline in its relative wage.

In addition to its distributional effects, immigration also changes the average wage in the labor market. Define the average wage effect as $d\log\bar{w} = (s_1 d\log w_1 + s_2 d\log w_2)/s_L$. It is easy to manipulate equation (3.22) to show that:

$$d\log\bar{w} = d\log w.$$

(3.24)

The nested CES framework implies that the impact of immigration on the average wage in a model with heterogeneous labor is identical to its impact in a model with homogeneous labor.[8]

Consider the implications of this prediction if the aggregate production function in equation (3.19a) were Cobb-Douglas. Regardless of the value of the elasticity of substitution σ_{12}, it must still be the case that the wage elasticity of immigration is −0.3 in the short run and 0.0 in the long run. In other words, the effect of immigration on the economy-wide average wage *level* has been "predetermined" by the Cobb-Douglas assumption and is independent of whatever complementarities may or may not exist among labor inputs in the production process.

The presence of imperfect substitution across skill groups simply "places" the wage effect for each of the groups around this predetermined mean wage effect. Suppose that an immigrant influx increases the size of the (efficiency-units adjusted) workforce by 10 percent. In a short-run Cobb-Douglas world, the wage effect on one group must be greater than

−3 percent (or -0.3×10), while the wage impact on the other group must be below −3 percent. The deviations from −3 percent will depend on (a) the disparity in the size of the supply shocks experienced by the two groups, and (b) the value of σ_{12}. A weighted average of the two wage effects, however, must be identically equal to −3 percent. In short, *the constraints imposed by factor demand theory and the nested CES framework greatly limit the structure of immigration wage effects that can possibly be estimated by any data.*

It is worth reemphasizing the same point in a different way. As I will show in Chapter 5, the literature now contains a number of empirical exercises claiming that the *estimation* of general equilibrium structural models indicates that the impact of immigration on the average wage is x percent, or that the impact of immigration on the average wage of workers in a particular skill group is y percent. These simulations often use a Cobb-Douglas aggregate production function. However, the Cobb-Douglas functional form builds in *numerically* what the mean wage effect of immigration must be in both the short run and the long run. In other words, the wage level effects reported by these studies have nothing to do with the underlying data; they are often simply regurgitating the constraints imposed by factor demand theory.

Imperfect Substitution between Immigrants and Natives

Some recent studies conjecture that immigrants and natives belonging to the same skill group may be imperfect substitutes—and that the resulting complementarities can greatly attenuate the adverse wage impact of immigration on the native workforce (Ottaviano and Peri 2012; Manacorda et al. 2012). These models typically expand the nested CES framework by adding yet another level that homogenizes the contribution of immigrants and natives into the efficiency units provided by skill group i:

$$L_i = [\rho_N N_i^\gamma + \rho_F M_i^\gamma]^{1/\gamma}, \tag{3.25}$$

where N_i and M_i give the number of native and foreign-born workers in group i, respectively; and the elasticity of substitution between native and immigrant workers is $\sigma_{MN} = 1/(1-\gamma)$, with $\gamma \leq 1$; and $\rho_N + \rho_F = 1$.

There now exist separate marginal productivity conditions for native and immigrant workers in each skill group. These conditions are:

$$w_i^N = [(1-\alpha)Q^{1-\delta}L^{\delta-1}](\theta_i L^{1-\beta}L_i^{\beta-1})(\rho_N L_i^{1-\gamma}N_i^{\gamma-1}), \quad (3.26a)$$

$$w_i^M = [(1-\alpha)Q^{1-\delta}L^{\delta-1}](\theta_i L^{1-\beta}L_i^{\beta-1})(\rho_F L_i^{1-\gamma}M_i^{\gamma-1}), \quad (3.26b)$$

where w_i^N and w_i^M give the wage of native- and foreign-born workers in skill group i, respectively.

By comparing equations (3.26a) and (3.26b) with equation (3.21), it is obvious that the presence of within-group complementarities simply adds yet another multiplicative term to the marginal productivity conditions. The bracketed term still represents the "average" wage in the economy, aggregated across all skill groups. The product of this bracketed term and $\theta_i L^{1-\beta}L_i^{\beta-1}$ gives equation (3.21), the wage for group i.

The multiplicatively separable property of the marginal productivity conditions makes it easy to evaluate the potential importance of immigrant-native complementarities as the host country's wage structure digests the impact of a supply shock. Differentiating equations (3.26a) and (3.26b) gives the impact of a generalized supply shift on the wage of native and immigrant workers in group i:

$$d\log w_i^N = d\log w + (1-\beta)[d\log L - d\log L_i]$$
$$+ (1-\gamma)[d\log L_i - d\log N_i], \quad (3.27a)$$

$$d\log w_i^M = d\log w + (1-\beta)[d\log L - d\log L_i]$$
$$+ (1-\gamma)[d\log L_i - d\log M_i]. \quad (3.27b)$$

Consider a supply shock that changes the number of immigrants in each of the skill groups but leaves the number of native workers unchanged. Let $\bar{m}$ be the immigration-induced percent change in L, the efficiency units-adjusted size of the workforce, and m_i be the percent change in L_i, the efficiency units-adjusted size of skill group i. The averaging mathematical property of the nested CES framework implies that these supply shifts can be written as:

$$d\log L_i = m_i = \frac{s_i^M}{s_i} d\log M_i, \quad (3.28a)$$

$$d\log L = \bar{m} = \frac{s_1 m_1 + s_2 m_2}{s_L}, \quad (3.28b)$$

where s_i^M is the share of income accruing to immigrants in group i, and $s_i = s_i^M + s_i^N$.

The presence of within-group complementarities can have important implications for within-group inequality. After all, the relative wage effect within group i is:

$$d\log w_i^M - d\log w_i^N = -\frac{1}{\sigma_{MN}} d\log M_i. \tag{3.29}$$

The distributional effect in (3.29) depends *only* on the value of the elasticity of substitution between immigrants and natives and on the size of the increase in the group's foreign-born workforce. The wage of natives in skill group i (relative to that of immigrants in that skill group) could increase substantially if immigrants and natives in that group were not perfect substitutes. However, the value of the elasticity σ_{MN} does not have *any* implications for the impact of immigration on either the average wage level in the labor market or the average wage level of any skill group. For instance, consider the impact of immigration on the average wage of group i, where $d\log \bar{w}_i = (s_i^N d\log w_i^N + s_i^M d\log w_i^M)/s_i$. It is easy to show that:

$$d\log \bar{w}_i = d\log w + (1-\beta)(\bar{m} - m_i), \tag{3.30}$$

which is identical to equation (3.22), the implied wage effect in the simpler model that assumed that immigrants and natives in a skill group were perfect substitutes.[9] Put differently, the value of σ_{MN} does not influence how immigration changes the average wage of preexisting workers in a particular skill group.[10] It is trivial to move up yet another level in the CES nesting and calculate the average wage effect across all skill groups. This exercise would again yield equation (3.24), so that the average wage effect does not depend on the value of either σ_{12} or σ_{MN}.

Although empirically tractable, the nested CES framework imposes an important restriction on any study of the wage effects of immigration: The impact of immigration on the average wage at a particular level of the nesting depends only on the elasticities of substitution that enter the model at or above that level. Hence, the impact of immigration on the average economy-wide wage does not depend on the value of the elasticity of substitution across skill groups or on the presence or absence of within-group complementarities; it depends only on the value of the elasticity of substitution between labor and capital. Similarly, the impact of immigration on the average wage of a particular skill group is unaffected by within-group complementarities between immigrants and natives.

A Two-Good Open Economy with Homogeneous Labor

Up to this point I have simplified the analysis by focusing on a stylized economy that produces a single good. The introduction of a second good is crucial if one wishes to examine how immigration affects aggregate product demand and prices. After all, if there were only one good in the economy, all units of that good must be sold regardless of the price. Borjas (2013b) expands the framework by assuming that there are two goods in a large, open economy; one good is produced domestically and the other is imported.[11] This generalization allows for changes in product demand both because immigration may change the price of the domestically produced product (encouraging preexisting consumers to change their quantity demanded) and because immigrants themselves consume the product.

Suppose good q is produced domestically and good y is imported. Suppose further that the imported good y is produced at constant marginal cost (or, alternatively, that its price is set in the global marketplace). In this context, the price of y is the numeraire and set to unity.[12] Each consumer j has the quasilinear utility function:

$$U(y,q) = y + g_j^* q^\varepsilon, \tag{3.31}$$

where the weight g_j^* reflects the consumer's relative preference for the domestic good and may differ across consumers. The utility function is quasiconcave for $0 < \varepsilon < 1$, a restriction that is assumed to hold. Let W be the consumer's income. The budget constraint is given by:

$$W = y + pq. \tag{3.32}$$

Utility maximization implies that the product demand function for the domestic good is:

$$q_j = g_j \, p^{-1/(1-\varepsilon)}, \tag{3.33}$$

where q_j is the quantity demanded by consumer j; and g_j is a rescaled person-specific weight. The quasilinear utility function implies that the consumer's demand for the domestic product does not depend on his income.

Three types of persons consume q: domestic workers, domestic capitalists, and consumers in other countries. Let C_L be the number of domestic workers, C_K be the number of domestic capitalists, and C_X be the number of consumers in the "rest of the world." I assume that all groups have the same quasilinear utility function in (3.31), but that the weighting factor g may differ among the groups. The total quantity demanded by domestic consumers (Q_D) and foreign consumers (Q_X) is then given by:

$$Q_D = (g_L C_L + g_K C_K) p^{-1/(1-\varepsilon)}, \tag{3.34a}$$

$$Q_X = g_X C_X p^{-1/(1-\varepsilon)}. \tag{3.34b}$$

Balanced trade requires that expenditures on the imported good y equal the value of the exports of good q:

$$wL + rK - (g_L C_L + g_K C_K) p^{-\varepsilon/(1-\varepsilon)} = g_X C_X p^{-\varepsilon/(1-\varepsilon)}, \tag{3.35}$$

where ($wL + rK$) gives the total payment to domestic factors of production L and K. In a competitive market, the payment to each factor of production equals its value of marginal product. If the production function is linear homogeneous, Euler's theorem implies that the expression in (3.35) can be rewritten as:

$$wL + rK = p(f_L L + f_K K) = pQ = [g_L C_L + g_K C_K + g_X C_X] p^{-\varepsilon/(1-\varepsilon)}. \tag{3.36}$$

where f_i is the marginal product of factor i. It follows that aggregate market demand for the domestic good is given by:

$$Q = C p^{-1/(1-\varepsilon)}, \tag{3.37}$$

where $C = g_L C_L + g_K C_K + g_x C_X$, the (weighted) number of consumers.

A crucial question immediately arises: How does an immigration-induced increase in the size of the workforce affect the size of the consumer base C for the domestic product? Let $C(L)$ be the function that relates the number of consumers to the number of workers, and let $\phi = d \log C / d \log L$. An important special case occurs when the elasticity $\phi = 1$, so that the immigrant influx leads to a proportionately equal increase in the (weighted) number of consumers and the number of workers. I will refer to the assumption that $\phi = 1$ as the case of *product market neutrality*. The "neutrality," of course, refers to the fact that the immigration-induced supply shift has the same relative impact on the size of the consumer base and the size of the workforce.

Equation (3.37) suggests that an immigration-induced supply shift has two distinct effects in the domestic labor market through product demand: First, the price of the domestic good might change, moving current consumers along the existing product demand curve; second, because immigrants are themselves "new" consumers, the market product demand curve will shift out and the magnitude of this shift will depend on ϕ.[13]

It is analytically convenient to solve the model by using the inverse product demand function:

$$p = C^{\eta} Q^{-\eta}, \tag{3.38}$$

where η is the inverse price elasticity of demand, with $\eta = 1 - \varepsilon$. Note that the assumption of a quasiconcave utility function imposes the restriction that $0 < \eta < 1$.

To easily grasp the implications of the framework, suppose that the production technology for the domestic product is given by a Cobb-Douglas production function, $Q = K^{\alpha} L^{1-\alpha}$. In a competitive market, input prices equal the value of marginal product:[14]

$$r = p(\alpha Q K^{-1}) = \alpha C^{\eta} Q^{1-\eta} K^{-1}. \tag{3.39a}$$

$$w = p((1-\alpha)Q L^{-1}) = (1-\alpha) C^{\eta} Q^{1-\eta} L^{-1}. \tag{3.39b}$$

Appendix A shows that the short- and long-run wage elasticities associated with an immigration-induced increase in supply are given by:[15]

$$\left. \frac{d\log w}{d\log L} \right|_{dK=0} = -(1-\eta)s_K - \eta(1-\phi), \tag{3.40}$$

$$\left. \frac{d\log w}{d\log L} \right|_{dr=0} = \frac{-\eta(1-\phi)}{1-(1-\eta)s_K}. \tag{3.41}$$

Consider initially the case of product market neutrality ($\phi = 1$). Equation (3.41) shows that the long-run wage effect disappears, as in the one-good, closed economy model. In the short run, however, immigration will continue to have a negative effect on wages, despite the impact that immigrants have on product demand. In particular, the short-run wage elasticity in (3.40) is given by $-(1-\eta)s_K$. By contrasting this elasticity with the analogous effect in the one-good, closed-economy model, it is easy to see that the short-run scale effect equals ηs_K. Note that this positive scale effect cannot reverse the sign of the short-run wage elasticity, because the quasiconcave utility function implies that $0 < \eta < 1$. In other words, the scale effect resulting from immigration cannot be sufficiently strong to generate a wage increase in the short run.[16]

The situation becomes far more interesting if the product market neutrality assumption fails to hold. Specifically, immigration now has a long-run wage effect. Consider, for example, the case where immigration does not expand the size of the consumer base as rapidly as it expands the size of the workforce ($\phi < 1$). Equation (3.41) shows that the long-run wage elasticity will be negative. There is a permanent wage reduction because there are "too many" workers and "too few" consumers. Moreover, this effect will augment the already-negative short-run wage effect. Note, however, that it is also possible for immigration to generate permanent wage *gains* for native workers if $\phi > 1$ and immigrants are "conspicuous consumers" of the domestic product.[17]

The possibility that ϕ might be less than one has interesting implications for a host country when immigrants remit a large fraction of their earnings to the source country. In this case, immigrants increase the size of the workforce without having a commensurate impact on the size of the host country's consumer base. There is a lot of evidence indicating that remittances are very valuable for the receiving countries (Yang, 2011). Remittances, however, can also have a mirror-image negative wage effect on the host country's labor market that has been overlooked.[18]

In sum, accounting for the feedback effects of immigration through changes in product demand does not alter the insight that the short-run wage elasticity is likely to be negative in a wide array of possible scenarios. Moreover, even the long-run wage effect may be negative if immigration increases the size of the consumer base by less than it increases the size of the workforce. In fact, generalizing the model to allow for these types of feedback effects raises an important question: By how much does immigration expand the consumer base of the host country? It turns out that the answer to this question, which has not yet received any empirical examination, plays a crucial role in determining the wage impact of immigration, in both the short and the long run.

4

The Wage Effects of Immigration: Descriptive Evidence

———————————◆———————————

How DOES INTERNATIONAL migration affect the labor market opportunities of workers in receiving and sending countries? Remarkably, there was no empirical study of this central question in immigration economics prior to the 1980s. Greenwood and McDowell's (1986) survey of the literature concludes that "substantive empirical evidence regarding the effects of immigration is generally scarce.... Little direct evidence is available on immigration's impact on the employment opportunities and wages of domestic workers" (p. 1750). The situation has changed dramatically since, as the conceptual and methodological issues involved in measuring the labor market impact of immigration became a central question in labor economics.

As we saw in Chapter 3, economic theory suggests that immigrants will lower the wage of competing workers, at least in the short run. The empirical literature of the past three decades can be viewed as a continuing search for this presumed effect. The early studies were structural in the sense that they assumed a particular functional form for the production technology, such as the translog, and attempted to estimate the technological parameters. Equally important, these early studies introduced the working assumption that the labor market could be defined in terms of a particular geographic area, most often a metropolitan area. Subsequent work typically discarded the structural aspect of the early research but maintained the operational assumption that a geographic region delineates the boundaries of the labor market. It was argued that the resulting coefficient, which I call a *spatial correlation,* measured the impact of immigration on the native wage structure.

This chapter summarizes the evidence that typically results from using this type of "descriptive" framework. It is easy to summarize the most striking lesson of the exercise: the inferred impact of immigration on the native wage structure depends almost entirely on how the analyst chooses to define the labor market.

Spatial Correlations

Grossman's (1982) pioneering study conjectured that it should be possible to measure the wage impact of immigration by comparing the evolution of wages in labor markets that are affected differentially by these labor flows. The wages of substitutable workers, for instance, should decline more in those markets that had a larger immigrant influx. Grossman operationalized this insight by introducing a modeling assumption that greatly influenced subsequent work. She defined the labor market in terms of a specific geographic region. Specifically, she assumed that a labor market is delineated by the boundaries of a metropolitan area. Her empirical analysis, therefore, consisted of comparing wage outcomes in local labor markets that received many immigrants to the outcomes in localities that received few.

Grossman's regression specification used an additional modeling assumption: the production technology in each local labor market can be characterized by a translog production function.[1] This technical assumption leads to a system of regression equations where the income share accruing to the various labor inputs in a particular labor market is related to the (log) quantity of the various types of workers in that market. Grossman's evidence, based on data drawn from the 1970 census cross-section, indicated that there was only a weak correlation between the income share accruing to native workers in a particular metropolitan area and the size of the immigrant workforce in that area. Immigration, she inferred, had little impact on the native wage structure.

Although Grossman's structural approach was discarded by the atheoretical research style that became increasingly influential in mainstream labor economics in the 1990s, her seemingly innocuous choice of metropolitan areas as the unit of analysis played a fundamental role in the subsequent development of the academic literature.[2] The typical post-Grossman empirical study dispensed with the structural details and simply regressed native wages in a locality (or the change in the wage) on the relative quantity of immigrants in that locality (or the change in the relative number). The resulting spatial correlation was then interpreted as giving the impact of immigration on the native wage.[3]

This section summarizes the nature of the empirical evidence implied by the spatial correlation approach in the U.S. context. I use decennial data that summarize conditions in the U.S. labor market between 1960 and 2010. Specifically, I use data drawn from the 1960–2000 Public Use Microdata Samples (PUMS) of the decennial censuses, and the pooled 2007–2011 American Community Surveys (ACS). For expositional convenience, I refer to the pooled ACS samples as the "2010 census." Appendix B provides a detailed description of the construction of the data extracts and of the variables used in the analysis.

Within a labor market, I classify workers into skill groups defined by education and work experience. In particular, workers are classified into five distinct education groups: persons who are high school dropouts (they completed less than 12 years of schooling), high school graduates (exactly 12 years of schooling), persons who have some college (13 to 15 years of schooling), college graduates (exactly 16 years of schooling), and persons who have post-college education (more than 16 years of schooling). Further, I define work experience as the number of years that have elapsed since the person completed school. I capture the similarity across workers with roughly similar years of experience by aggregating the data into 5-year experience intervals, indicating if the worker has 1 to 5 years of experience, 6 to 10 years, and so on. The sample consists of workers with 40 or fewer years of experience, so that there are a total of 40 skill groups in the analysis (five education groups and eight experience groups).

Let $M_{exr}(t)$ give the total number of hours worked by immigrants in education group e, experience group x, living in region r, in calendar year t; and $N_{exr}(t)$ give the corresponding labor supply of natives. The immigrant share in the workforce in cell (e, x, r, t) is:

$$p_{exr}(t) = \frac{M_{exr}(t)}{M_{exr}(t) + N_{exr}(t)}. \tag{4.1}$$

The immigrant share $p_{exr}(t)$ gives the fraction of total work hours supplied by foreign-born workers in the relevant labor market.[4]

The dispersion in the immigrant share across metropolitan statistical areas (MSAs) is striking. In 2010 the immigrant share for high school dropouts was around 80 percent in New York and Los Angeles, but only 38 percent in Philadelphia and 26 percent in Detroit. There is also a large variance in the growth rate within metropolitan areas. The immigrant share in Dallas rose from a negligible 1.9 percent in 1970 to 23.0 percent in 2010, while in San Francisco it "only" tripled from 11.8 to 35.6 percent. The geographic dispersion, of course, reflects the substantial clustering of immigrants in a relatively small number of places. In 2010, for instance, 36.5 percent of all hours worked by immigrants were supplied in just five metropolitan areas (the comparable statistic for natives was only 13.9 percent).[5] It is this clustering that initially motivated Grossman (1982) to exploit geographic differences in immigrant penetration to identify the wage impact of immigration.

I begin by estimating the spatial correlation in each cross-section. Consider the following regression model:

$$\log w_{exr}(t) = \phi_H + \phi_R + \alpha_t \, p_{exr}(t) + \varepsilon, \qquad (4.2)$$

where $\log w_{exr}(t)$ gives the mean log weekly wage of *natives* in cell (e, x, r, t); ϕ_H is a vector of skill fixed effects indicating all possible education-experience permutations; and ϕ_R is a vector of metropolitan area fixed effects.[6] The coefficient α_t measures the spatial correlation between wages and immigration in cross-section t. I calculate the mean log weekly wage separately in samples of only men and of both men and women. The wage is obviously a more precise measure of the price of a skill unit in the male sample; the inclusion of working women in the analysis introduces selection issues that are difficult to address and resolve.

Table 4.1 shows the problem with using the estimated α_t to infer the wage impact of immigration: The estimate of the spatial correlation changes drastically over time. At the beginning of the sample period (using the same 1970 census data as in the initial Grossman study), the correlation was positive and weak, but it turned negative after the 1990s. In particular, the spatial correlation is $+0.028$ (with a standard error of 0.127) in the male regression in 1970, but becomes -0.159 (0.046) by 2000. Put differently, the near-zero spatial correlations that were initially reported in the literature seem to be an artifact of the choice of sample period. Those

Table 4.1 Cross-section spatial correlations across metropolitan areas (MSAs)

Sample	1970	1980	1990	2000	2010
1. Men	0.028	−0.037	−0.063	−0.159	−0.145
	(0.127)	(0.079)	(0.044)	(0.046)	(0.042)
2. Men and women	0.102	−0.025	−0.069	−0.158	−0.113
	(0.099)	(0.053)	(0.033)	(0.045)	(0.040)

Sources: U.S. Census PUMS 1970–2010; see Appendix B for details.

Notes: The sample consists of workers aged 18–64, who are classified into five education groups and eight experience groups. The unit of observation is a skill-MSA cell, where a skill group represents an education-experience pairing. Standard errors are reported in parentheses, and are clustered at the skill-MSA level. The dependent variable is the mean log weekly wage of natives in a skill-MSA cell, while the independent variable is the respective immigrant share. The log weekly wage is calculated in the sample of natives (men in row 1; men and women in row 2) employed in the wage-and-salary sector who are not enrolled in school; the immigrant share is defined as the fraction of work hours supplied by all foreign-born workers (including men and women). Each cross-section regression includes vectors of skill fixed effects and MSA fixed effects. The regressions are weighted by the number of observations used to calculate the dependent variable. The male regressions have 4,684 observations in 1970; 10,191 observations in 1980; 9,954 observations in 1990; 11,315 observations in 2000; and 11,310 observations in 2010.

same studies would have necessarily reached the opposite conclusion (that is, the presence of a strong negative correlation between wages and immigration) if they had been written two or three decades later, using either the 2000 or 2010 census data.

The dramatic sign switching in the cross-section spatial correlation illustrates a fundamental flaw of the approach. The geographic sorting of immigrants (and natives) across metropolitan areas or regions is not random. The settlement patterns of immigrants changed drastically over the past few decades; relatively fewer immigrants now settle in the traditional high-wage gateways (such as New York and California), and more settle in areas that have had little historic experience with immigration and offer lower wages (such as Arkansas and Georgia). Even though the regression model in (4.2) includes a vector of region fixed effects, these fixed effects cannot entirely control for the spurious correlation created by the possibility that the regional distribution of wages is not the same for all skill groups.

One way of controlling for the potential presence of skill-region fixed effects is to difference the data, so as to examine how the wage of a skill group in a particular area changes as competing immigrants enter that area. Stacking all of the data across the various cross-sections yields the longitudinal regression model:

$$\log w_{exr}(t) = \phi_H + \phi_R + \phi_T + \phi_{HT} + \phi_{RT} + \phi_{HR} + \theta\, p_{exr}(t) + \varepsilon', \qquad (4.3)$$

where ϕ_T is a vector of fixed effects indicating the census year; ϕ_{HT} and ϕ_{RT} are vectors that interact the period fixed effects with the skill group or region fixed effects, respectively; and ϕ_{HR} is a vector that interacts the skill group fixed effects with the region fixed effects. The interacted fixed effects ϕ_{HT} and ϕ_{RT} control for secular changes in the returns to skills and in the regional wage structure during the sample period. The inclusion of the vector ϕ_{HR} implies that the longitudinal spatial correlation θ is being identified from changes in wages and immigration that occur *within* skill-region cells. Equation (4.3) can be roughly interpreted as a "reduced-form" regression that relates the change in the wage in a particular skill cell to a (presumably exogenous) supply shift.

The various columns of Table 4.2 report the estimated θ's from various specifications of the stacked regression model.[7] The regression is estimated separately using metropolitan areas, states or regions as the geographic definition of the labor market. Consider initially the traditional regression estimated at the level of metropolitan areas. The coefficient θ is −0.058 (0.018) in the male sample, so that there seems to be a modest negative correlation between wage growth and the immigrant influx into a metropolitan area.

There is a great deal of confusion in the literature as to how to quantify the wage impact of immigration. Many studies measure the impact in terms of the wage change resulting from an x-percent change in the number of immigrants. This metric, however, is useless unless one knows something about the size of the base workforce. A 10-percent change in the number of immigrants, for instance, implies very different things for labor markets that have a few immigrants in a relatively large population than for labor markets that have the same number of immigrants but a far smaller population. A parameterization that is more informative and better aligned with factor demand theory would ask: What is the implied wage impact of an immigration-induced supply shift that increases the *total* number of workers in the labor market by x percent?

Table 4.2 Ordinary least-squares estimates of longitudinal spatial correlation

	Definition of regional labor market		
	Metropolitan area	State	Census division
1. Men	−0.058	−0.186	−0.237
	(0.018)	(0.029)	(0.048)
2. Men and women	−0.074	−0.227	−0.309
	(0.017)	(0.031)	(0.054)

Sources: U.S. Census PUMS 1960–2010; see Appendix B for details.

Notes: The MSA-level regressions stack the cross-section data sets used in Table 4.1; the stacked samples for the state and census division regressions were constructed analogously. The regressions use all available data between 1960 and 2010 at the state and census division levels, and between 1980 and 2010 at the MSA level. The unit of observation is a skill-region-year cell (where the definition of the region varies across the columns). Standard errors are reported in parentheses and are clustered at the skill-region level. The dependent variable is the mean log weekly wage of natives in the skill-region-year cell, and the independent variable is the respective immigrant share. All regressions include skill-year, region-year, and skill-region fixed effects. The regressions are weighted by the scaled number of observations used to calculate the dependent variable, where the scaling ensures that each cross-section has the same weight. The male MSA-level regressions have 42,770 observations, the state-level regressions have 12,215 observations, and the census-division-level regressions have 2,160 observations.

It is easy to rescale the reduced form coefficient θ in terms of this metric. Let $m_{exr} = M_{exr}/N_{exr}$, or the immigration-induced percent increase in the labor supply of group (e, x, r). The relevant wage elasticity is given by:

$$\frac{\partial \log w_{exr}}{\partial m_{exr}} = \theta(1 - p_{exr})^2. \tag{4.4}$$

By 2010 the immigrant share in the total number of hours supplied to the U.S. labor market was 16.7 percent. Equation (4.4) implies that the wage elasticity—evaluated at the marginal value of the immigrant share—can be obtained by multiplying θ by approximately 0.7. Hence, the wage elasticity implied by the longitudinal regression at the metropolitan-area level is −0.04.[8]

Interestingly, as first noted by Borjas, Freeman, and Katz (1996), Table 4.2 shows that the magnitude of the wage effect depends on the geographic definition of the labor market. In particular, the observed spatial correlation is more negative the larger the market. The estimate of the coefficient θ triples in size, to -0.186 (0.029), when using state-level data, implying a wage elasticity of -0.13. Moreover, the coefficient gets even larger when the regression defines the labor market in terms of a census division. This instability is troubling, suggesting that other factors are perhaps diffusing the impact of immigration across local labor markets or that there may be measurement error in the observed immigrant share for smaller geographic units. Both of these issues will be addressed in greater detail in what follows.

It is recognized that the sorting of immigrants across local labor markets is not random, and income-maximizing immigrants would settle in those areas that offer the best economic opportunities. Altonji and Card (1991, p. 222) proposed using the lagged measure of the immigrant share in the labor market as an instrument. The justification is that new immigrants tend to settle in the same places where earlier waves settled, perhaps because of lower information costs associated with ethnic networks. Although this instrument (or some variation thereof) is commonly used in the literature, it may not be conceptually valid. After all, the settlement decision of the earlier immigrant waves may be endogenous. Perhaps those "pioneering" waves settled in high-wage places. Any serial correlation in wages at the skill-region level would invalidate the instrument.

To illustrate the sensitivity of the estimated longitudinal spatial correlation to the correction for endogeneity, I reestimated the model in equation (4.3) using two alternative instruments. The first instrument is simply the lagged foreign-born share in the local labor market, where the lag refers to the value observed in the previous census. More precisely, the instrument for the immigrant workforce share $p_{exr}(t)$ is given by $p_{exr}(t-1)$.

The second instrument is a more sophisticated version that explicitly incorporates the "ethnic network" justification (Lewis 2011; Peri 2012). In particular, let $M_{exr}^k(t_0)$ be the labor supply of immigrants in baseline year t_0 who belong to skill group (e, x), live in region r, and were born in country k. The share of immigrants in this particular skill-origin group who lived in a particular geographic region is then defined by:

$$g_{exr}^k(t_0) = \frac{M_{exr}^k(t_0)}{\sum_r M_{exr}^k(t_0)}, \tag{4.5}$$

Suppose that the geographic sorting of type-k immigrants in the baseline year (assumed to be 1980 in the empirical analysis) can be treated as exogenous. We can then predict the number of immigrants in a particular skill group who would live in region r in any subsequent period. The predicted number is defined by $\hat{M}_{exr}(t) = \sum_{k} g^k_{exr}(t_0) M^k_{ex}(t)$, where $M^k_{ex}(t)$ is the nationwide number of immigrants originating in country k in skill cell (e, x) at time t. The instrument for the immigrant share at time t is then given by:[9]

$$\hat{p}_{exr}(t) = \frac{\hat{M}_{exr}(t)}{\hat{M}_{exr}(t) + N_{exr}(t)}. \qquad (4.6)$$

Equation (4.6) gives the predicted immigrant share after the immigrant population present in the United States at time t is allocated to the various regions based on the baseline geographic sorting of each national origin group.

Table 4.3 reports the instrumental variables (IV) estimates of the spatial correlation θ using the MSA-level data. The table also reports the key coefficient from the first-stage regression (that is, the coefficient of the immigrant share on the instrument). Perhaps the most striking finding is the variance in the estimated coefficients. In fact, depending on the instrument and the time period, the first-stage coefficient is sometimes negative. The estimate of θ (in the male sample) ranges from -1.1 to $+4.4$ when using the lagged share instrument, but is much less volatile when using the more sophisticated predicted share instrument. Note also that the wage elasticities implied by the predicted share instrument are more negative than the ones implied by the ordinary least squares (OLS) regressions. The OLS elasticity in Table 4.2 is -0.04, while the corresponding IV elasticity is -0.17. Although the predicted share instrument seems to "work," there are good reasons to question its validity, because (a) the baseline geographic sorting of immigrants originating in country k was partly determined by preexisting regional differences in wage and employment opportunities; (b) there is serial correlation in wage and employment opportunities within metropolitan areas; and (c) the corresponding endogeneity that determines the geographic sorting of natives is ignored.

Although the vast majority of studies in the spatial correlation literature estimate cross-city regressions similar to those reported above, the most influential study in this genre attempts to measure the impact of an immigrant influx that affected only a single locality. On April 20, 1980, Fidel Castro declared that Cuban nationals wishing to move to the United States could

Table 4.3 Instrumental-variables estimates of longitudinal spatial correlation at the
MSA level

| | Instrument | | | |
| | Lagged immigrant share | | Predicted share | |
	First-stage coefficient	Spatial correlation	First-stage coefficient	Spatial correlation
1. Men, 1990–2010	0.150	−1.087	0.564	−0.239
	(0.017)	(0.225)	(0.023)	(0.051)
2. Men, 1990–2000	−0.053	4.357	0.567	−0.496
	(0.028)	(2.165)	(0.026)	(0.084)
3. Men, 2000–2010	−0.087	1.003	0.637	−0.122
	(0.024)	(0.441)	(0.026)	(0.065)
4. Men and women, 1990–2010	0.144	−1.267	0.559	−0.208
	(0.017)	(0.235)	(0.022)	(0.046)

Sources: U.S. Census PUMS 1980–2010; see Appendix B for details.

Notes: The regressions stack the cross-section data sets used in Table 4.1, as indicated in each row.
The unit of observation is a skill-MSA-year cell. Standard errors are reported in parentheses and are
clustered at the skill-MSA level. The dependent variable is the mean log weekly wage of natives in the
cell, and the independent variable is the respective immigrant share. All regressions include skill-year,
region-year, and skill-region fixed effects. The regressions are weighted by the scaled number of
observations used to calculate the dependent variable, where the scaling ensures that each cross-section
has the same weight. The "lagged share" instrument gives the value of the immigrant share in the previous
census; the "predicted share" instrument treats the 1980 geographic sorting of immigrants from specific
national origin groups as a baseline, and uses this sorting to allocate the immigrants in subsequent
censuses across metropolitan areas. The male regressions have 27,847 observations in the first row.

leave freely from the port of Mariel. By September 1980, about 125,000
Cubans, mostly low-skill workers, accepted Castro's offer and Miami's labor force grew by 7 percent.

Card's (1990) ingenious study used a straightforward difference-in-
differences methodology to determine if this "natural experiment" affected
labor market opportunities for Miami's preexisting workforce. Table 4.4
summarizes some of the evidence. In 1979, prior to the Mariel flow, the
black unemployment rate in Miami was 8.3 percent. This unemployment
rate rose to 9.6 percent by 1981, after the Mariel flow. However, black unemployment was rising even faster in the other cities that form the "control group" (as the aggregate economy was entering a recession), from 10.3
to 12.6 percent. If anything, therefore, it seems that the Mariel flow actually attenuated the rise in black unemployment in Miami.[10]

Table 4.4 The Mariel boatlift

	The Mariel flow		The Mariel flow that did not happen	
Unemployment rate of blacks in	1979	1981	1993	1995
Miami	8.3	9.6	10.1	13.7
Comparison cities	10.3	12.6	11.5	8.8
Difference-in-differences estimate	−1.0		+6.3	

Sources: Card (1990, p. 251) for the Mariel flow; Angrist and Krueger (1999, p. 1329) for the Mariel flow that did not happen.

Despite its natural experiment underpinnings, the Mariel study exemplifies the spatial correlation approach. It essentially correlates changes in economic outcomes and immigrant flows in a small subset of metropolitan areas, and the labor market impact of immigration is again inferred from the sign and magnitude of the spatial correlation.

Given the short-run nature of the empirical exercise—the changes in Miami's labor market over a 2-year period—it would be difficult to argue that the study identifies the perfectly elastic long-run labor demand curve that the theory predicts might prevail after the market adjusts fully to the immigrant supply shock. The Mariel study, therefore, presents a puzzling set of results, contradicting basic notions of how economists think about labor market equilibrium.

Subsequent research, however, raises reservations about the inferences that can be drawn from the Mariel data. In 1994, economic and political conditions in Cuba were ripe for the onset of a new refugee influx into the Miami area, and thousands of Cubans began the hazardous journey. To prevent the refugees from reaching the Florida shore, the Clinton administration ordered that all refugees be redirected toward the American military base at Guantanamo. As a result, few of the potential migrants reached Miami.

Angrist and Krueger (1999) replicated the methodological design of Card's Mariel study by comparing Miami's labor market conditions—relative to those in the same control group—before and after "the Mariel boatlift that didn't happen." This non-event had a remarkable *adverse* impact on the unemployment rate of Miami's black workforce. Table 4.4 shows that the black unemployment rate in Miami rose from 10.1 to 13.7 percent between 1993 and 1995, as compared to a drop from 11.5 to 8.8 percent in the control group.

Interpreted in the usual way, the evidence suggests that a phantom immigrant flow harmed the economic opportunities of black workers. This nonsensical inference obviously raises suspicions about whether one should interpret the evidence for the Mariel boatlift that *did* happen as indicating that immigration had little impact on Miami's labor market.

As with the regression-based spatial correlation evidence, the conflicting results reported in Table 4.4 most likely indicate that local labor markets are continually affected by many shocks. It seems impossible to draw specific conclusions about the wage impact of immigration unless we have a much better understanding of the many other factors that are shifting supply and demand curves in these labor markets at different points in time.

So what do we learn from spatial correlations? An objective reading of the evidence suggests that they do not contain as much information as we would like. The estimated spatial correlation—in terms of sign and magnitude—does not seem robust to specification changes. Why did the cross-section correlation change drastically over the past half century, and what does this change imply for estimates of the wage impact of immigration? Why is there an intimate link between the size of the spatial correlation and the size of the geographic area covered by the labor market? And why should an instrument based on a lagged measure of immigration be presumed to be valid when labor economists apply far more stringent requirements to the construction of instruments outside the immigration context? Put simply, spatial correlations are unlikely to identify the structural parameter that measures the wage effect of an immigration-induced supply shift.

The National Labor Market

Although estimates of the spatial correlation are sensitive to specification changes, a consensus quickly developed: the labor market impact of immigration is negligible. A well-cited survey by Friedberg and Hunt (1995, p. 42) concluded: "The effect of immigration on the labor market outcomes of natives is small." Similarly, the 1997 National Academy of Sciences report on the economic impact of immigration argued: "The weight of the empirical evidence suggests that the impact of immigration on the wages of competing native workers is small" (Smith and Edmonston 1997, p. 220).

These conclusions are potentially inconsistent with factor demand theory, because the post-1970 immigration-induced supply shock in the United States was very large, and most studies of labor demand (outside

the immigration context) report that the labor demand curve is not perfectly elastic (Hamermesh 1993).[11] The incongruity between the data and
the theory inspired the growth of a large literature that attempts to explain
these differences.[12]

There are two widely recognized problems with the spatial correlation
approach. First, immigrants might not be randomly distributed across labor markets. If the areas where immigrants cluster have done well over
some time periods, this would produce a spurious correlation between immigration and area outcomes both in the cross-section and in the time-
series.[13] A positive or near-zero spatial correlation would simply indicate
that immigrants choose to reside in areas that are doing relatively well,
and this spurious correlation could swamp the presumed negative effect of
immigration on the wage of competing workers. Ideally, this issue would
be handled by using an appropriate instrument for the geographic settlement of immigrants *and* natives. As noted above, however, the instrument
of choice in the literature—some transformation of the lagged immigrant
share in the relevant labor market—is problematic.

A second difficulty is that natives may respond to the entry of immigrants in a locality by moving their labor or capital to other places until
native wages and returns to capital are again equalized across regions. A
comparison of the wage of native workers across cities or states might
show little or no difference because the internal flows have diffused the effects of immigration throughout the national economy. Chapter 6 will discuss in detail the behavioral response of native agents to the supply shock.

To avoid some of these pitfalls, Borjas (2003) introduced an alternative
approach that dispenses with the comparison of geographically distinct
labor markets altogether. Instead, the impact of immigration is identified
by examining how the evolution of the average wage across skill groups
has been affected by differences in the size of the supply shocks.

The examination of wage trends across skill groups in the national labor
market has much in common with the literature that identifies the factors
responsible for the increase in U.S. wage inequality. The wage structure
literature demonstrates that shifts in both the relative demand and the
relative supply curves for skills help explain the trend in the wage gap between high- and low-skill workers. For example, Murphy and Welch
(1992), Katz and Murphy (1992), and Card and Lemieux (2001) document
that shifts in the relative supply of workers in a particular skill group help
determine their relative wage.

In contrast to the immigration literature discussed in the previous section, none of these landmark studies exploit geographic variations in the skill composition of the workforce to identify the impact of supply shifts on the wage structure. Instead, these studies aggregated the available data to the level of the national labor market and examined whether the evolution of the national wage structure was related to the supply (and/or demand) shifts. In an important sense, the Borjas (2003) study placed the question of how to estimate the labor market impact of immigration squarely in the context of the wage structure literature that was a central focus of labor economics throughout the 1990s.

It is easy to carry out the national-level analysis of the wage impact of immigration by aggregating—within each census—the skill-group specific data introduced earlier. This aggregation produces a data set giving the mean log weekly wage and the immigrant share for each skill group in each census cross-section.

It turns out that immigration to the United States—even within a particular education group—is not balanced evenly across all age groups, and the nature of the supply imbalance changes over time. This fact generates a great deal of variation—across schooling and experience groups, and over time—that helps to identify the impact of immigration on the labor market. Equally important, the composition of the native workforce in each of the skill groups is somewhat fixed, so that there is less potential for native flows to contaminate the comparison of outcomes across skill groups.[14]

Figure 4.1 illustrates the supply shock experienced by selected skill groups between 1960 and 2010. It is well known that immigration greatly increased the supply of high school dropouts in recent decades. What is less well known is that this supply shift did not affect all age groups within the population of high school dropouts equally. Moreover, the nature of the imbalance changed over time. As Panel A of the figure shows, immigrants made up 60 percent of all high school dropouts with 15 to 20 years of experience in 2010, but only 30 percent of those with less than 5 years. In 1960, however, the immigration of high school dropouts most increased the supply of the oldest workers. Similarly, Panel B shows that in 1990 the immigrant supply shock for workers with more than a college education was reasonably balanced across all experience groups, generally increasing supply by around 10 percent. By 2010, however, the supply shock for these highly educated workers was far larger for those with 5 to 10 years of experience.

As noted earlier, changes in U.S. immigration policy may be partly responsible for both the increase in the number of immigrants and the changing

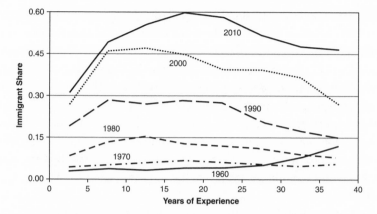

A. High School Dropouts (Less than 12 Years of Schooling)

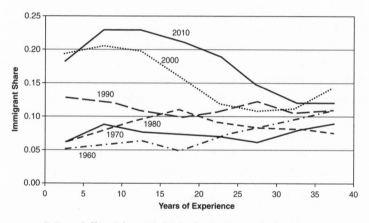

B. Post-College Education (More than 16 Years of Schooling)

Figure 4.1. Immigrant Shares by Skill Group, 1960–2010

Sources: U.S. Census PUMS 1960–2010; see Appendix B for details.

Notes: The sample consists of workers aged 18–64, who are classified into five education groups and eight experience groups. The immigrant share is given by the fraction of work hours supplied by all foreign-born workers (including men and women) in each education-experience cell.

skill composition. Prior to 1965, immigration policy favored the entry of persons originating in some European countries. Since 1965, immigration policy gives preferential treatment to visa applicants with relatives in the United States. In addition, there has been a sizable increase in the number of undocumented immigrants. The national-level approach exploits the resulting variation in the size of the supply shock across skill groups and over time to identify the wage impact of immigration. Crucially, the analysis treats these supply shifts as exogenous. In fact, immigration policy is likely to respond to political and economic forces so that many of the supply shifts illustrated in Figure 4.1 happened for a reason: some group of persons benefited sufficiently to influence policy in a particular direction. In the absence of a more general framework that ties together the changes in the policy with the underlying economic forces and an understanding of how the policy shifts actually affect the skill composition of immigrants, it is difficult to ascertain how the endogeneity of immigration policy affects the measured labor market impact of immigration.

Abstracting from the potential endogeneity of the supply shifts, the aggregated data reveal a strong link between trends in the log weekly wage and the immigrant share *within* schooling-experience cells. In particular, Figure 4.2 presents the scatter diagram relating the within-group change in the log weekly wage to the within-group change in the immigrant share, after removing decade effects from the data.[15] The figure clearly suggests a negative relation between wage growth and immigrant penetration across skill groups. Put simply, the raw data at the national level show that weekly wages grew fastest for workers in those education-experience groups that were least affected by immigration.

By stacking the data for the 40 education-experience groups across the various cross-sections, it is possible to estimate the model:

$$\log w_{ex}(t) = \phi_E + \phi_X + \phi_T + \phi_{ET} + \phi_{XT} + \phi_{EX} + \beta\, p_{ex}(t) + \varepsilon, \qquad (4.7)$$

where ϕ_E and ϕ_X are vectors of fixed effects indicating the group's education and experience, and the interactions ϕ_{ET} and ϕ_{XT} allow for the impact of these fixed effects to vary over time. The inclusion of the education-experience interactions ϕ_{XE} implies that the impact of immigration on labor market outcomes is identified from changes that occur *within* an education-experience cell over time.

Table 4.5 reports the estimates of the coefficient β. In the male sample, the coefficient is -0.529 (0.102). The implied wage elasticity is -0.37 (or -0.529×0.7). Put differently, an immigrant flow that increases the number of workers in the skill group by 10 percent reduces weekly earnings by about 4 percent.[16]

It is instructive to compare the results from the national-level regressions to those obtained at the metropolitan area or state levels. It is evident

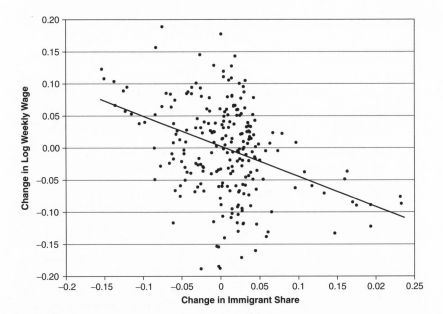

Figure 4.2. Relation between Wages and Immigration across Skill Groups and over Time, 1960–2010

Sources: U.S. Census PUMS 1960–2010; see Appendix B for details.

Notes: The sample consists of workers aged 18–64, who are classified into five education groups and eight experience groups. Each point in the scatter represents an education-experience-year cell, stacked across the 1960–2010 censuses. The notes to Table 4.1 describe the construction of the mean log weekly wage and immigrant share for each cell. The "change in log weekly wage" and "change in immigrant share" variables are residuals from regressions of the log weekly wage or the immigrant share on vectors of education-experience fixed effects and census year fixed effects. These residuals give the log wage or the immigrant share in the specific education-experience-year cell relative to that skill group's mean over the sample period, after removing decade effects.

that the larger the geographic area, the larger the estimated wage impact of immigration. The wage elasticity is −0.04 in the MSA data, −0.13 in the state data, −0.17 in the Census division data, and −0.37 in the national data. Note that (roughly) the same underlying data are being used in all four sets of regressions.[17] It is only the geographic definition of the labor market that differs.

The remaining rows of Table 4.5 report a number of sensitivity tests.[18] First, the magnitude of the coefficient β, like the spatial correlation estimated

Table 4.5 Estimates of wage effects at the national level

Sample	Men	Men and women
1. All workers	−0.529	−0.355
	(0.102)	(0.134)
2. 1960–1990 censuses	−0.660	−0.473
	(0.209)	(0.187)
3. 1990–2010 censuses	−0.287	−0.271
	(0.122)	(0.130)
4. At least twelve years of schooling	−0.590	−0.218
	(0.392)	(0.466)
5. At most sixteen years of schooling	−0.601	−0.534
	(0.118)	(0.127)

Sources: U.S. Census PUMS 1960–2010; see Appendix B for details.

Notes: The sample consists of workers aged 18–64, who are classified into five education groups and eight experience groups. The unit of observation is an education-experience-year cell. Standard errors are reported in parentheses and are clustered at the education-experience level. The dependent variable is the mean log weekly wage of natives in the cell, and the independent variable is the respective immigrant share; the notes to Table 4.1 describe the construction of these variables. All regressions include education-year, experience-year, and education-experience fixed effects. The regressions are weighted by the scaled number of observations used to calculate the dependent variable, where the scaling ensures that each cross-section has the same weight. The regressions have 240 observations in row 1; 160 in row 2; 120 in row 3; and 192 in rows 4 and 5.

earlier, is sensitive to the choice of time period. Nevertheless, the national-level wage elasticity is negative and significant (in the male sample) regardless of whether it is estimated using data from the 1960–1990 or the 1990–2010 periods.[19] Similarly, the table shows that if the skill cells involving high school dropouts (the cells that received the largest supply shifts) are excluded from the analysis, the measured wage effect is much less precisely estimated, but remains marginally significant in the sample of men. Some of the instability in the national-level results (and the larger standard errors) is inherent in the framework: there is much less skill-time variation that can be exploited to estimate the wage elasticity.[20]

It is interesting that the wage elasticity estimated at the national level resembles the one implied by the spatial correlation approach when both regressions are estimated over the same sample period *and* the MSA-level regression uses the predicted immigrant share instrument.[21] Specifically, the national-level elasticity estimated over the 1990–2010 period is −0.20 while the corresponding MSA-level IV elasticity in Table 4.3 is −0.17.[22] It is difficult to determine if this striking resemblance indicates that the instrument "solved" the endogeneity problem, or if it represents a statistical fluke. It is probably wise to remain skeptical about the validity of the instrument, because the geographic sorting of national origin groups in 1980 (used as the baseline in the construction of the predicted immigrant share) is itself not independent from persistent wage differences across local labor markets.

There also exists a conceptual problem that can easily contaminate the estimates of the longitudinal correlation between immigration and wages (regardless of the level of geographic aggregation), as well as the parameters estimated by structural methods in Chapter 5. The correlation may arise spuriously, a numerical artifact resulting from the changing composition of native workers in a particular skill cell over time. For example, the fraction of native-born high school dropouts declined dramatically in the past few decades, and it is unlikely that the ability of the average native worker in that group today is the same as that of his counterpart 30 years ago. Similarly, the fraction of natives who have a college degree increased during the period, and again it is unlikely that the typical native-born worker in that group has the same ability as the typical college graduate a few decades ago.

In both cases, in fact, it seems reasonable to suspect that the average native worker in the specific skill group today is less able than his counterpart in the past. As a result, the changing composition of native-born workers in narrowly defined groups could generate a spurious correlation between wages in those cells and any variable that is trending over time, such as the fraction of foreign-born workers. The sign of the spurious correlation would depend on whether immigration is increasing at a faster or slower rate in those skill groups that experienced the largest compositional change.[23] Despite the potential importance of this problem, however, there have not been any empirical studies that evaluate the sensitivity of the evidence to the changing composition of the native workforce.

The simple methodology underlying the national-level approach summarized in Table 4.5 has inspired a number of replications in other settings. One particularly interesting context is given by the Canadian experience. As noted earlier, since the 1960s Canada has used a point system designed specifically to select high-skill immigrants. The first row of Table 4.6 reports the estimates of the coefficient β when equation (4.7) is estimated using data from the 1971–2001 Canadian censuses. The coefficient is −0.507 (0.202). Evaluated at a 15 percent immigrant share, the implied wage elasticity is −0.35.

In contrast, Mexico is a major source country for international migrants, with almost all of the emigrants moving to the United States. Mishra (2007) used data from the 1970–2000 Mexican and U.S. censuses to calculate an out-migration rate for each education-experience group and estimated equation (4.7) using the mean earnings of workers *in Mexico* as the dependent variable. As shown in Table 4.6, there is a strong positive correlation between the log earnings of Mexican stayers in a particular skill group and the out-migration rate of that group. The estimated coefficient is +0.44 (0.11), implying a wage elasticity of −0.31.

Puerto Rico provides a unique case study because, as noted in Chapter 1, it exhibits large in-migrant and out-migrant flows simultaneously. Borjas (2008) pooled the data from the 1970–2000 U.S. and Puerto Rican decen-

Table 4.6 Relation between wages and supply shocks in other countries

	Measure of supply shock	
Country	Immigrant share	Out-migrant share
1. Canada (Aydemir and Borjas 2007, p. 682)	−0.507 (0.202)	—
2. Mexico (Mishra 2007, p. 187)	—	0.440 (0.110)
3. Puerto Rico (Borjas 2008, p. 57)	−0.543 (0.269)	0.537 (0.185)
4. Germany (Bonin 2005, p. 25)	−0.105 (0.036)	—
5. Germany (Steinhardt 2011, p. 19)	−0.163 (0.035)	—
6. Norway (Bratsberg et al. 2013, p. 17)	−0.380 (0.183)	—

Notes: Standard errors are reported in parentheses. All coefficients are obtained from national-level regressions using the regression model specified in equation (4.7). Steinhardt (2011) uses occupation-experience cells rather than education-experience cells to define the skill groups.

nial censuses to calculate both the immigrant share and the out-migrant share. Table 4.6 reports the coefficients obtained from a regression of the mean log earnings of Puerto Rican workers on both the immigrant and out-migrant shares. The data confirm the mirror-image prediction of economic theory: A larger out-migration flow increases the wage of those who remain in the island, while a larger immigrant influx decreases their wage. The wage elasticity implied by the coefficients of both shares is −0.38.

Finally, a number of studies have replicated the analysis in the European context. In Germany, for example, the immigrant share increased from 9 to 11 percent in the 1990s. Some of the studies report a statistically significant, though numerically weaker, negative correlation between immigration and wage growth in the German labor market, even though wages are thought to be relatively rigid in Germany (Franz and Pfeiffer 2006). The wage elasticity implied by the studies summarized in Table 4.6 is around −0.1.[24] Similarly, Bratsberg et al. (2013) estimate the model using Norwegian data. The immigrant share in Norway increased from 2 to 10 percent in the past three decades. Using administrative data that cover all workers in Norway from 1993 through 2006, the study estimates a significant negative relation between immigration and wage growth. The implied wage elasticity is −0.27.[25]

Sampling Error and Attenuation Bias

The generic regression model used in the literature, whether estimated at the level of the metropolitan area or the national labor market, introduces a specific type of measurement error into the estimation. The analyst typically does not have an independent measure of the size of the immigration-induced supply shock in the relevant labor market. Instead, both the market's average log wage and the fraction of the workforce that is foreign-born are estimated from the sample of workers observed in that particular labor market and are subject to sampling error.

As shown by Aydemir and Borjas (2011), the sampling error in the immigrant share can lead to substantial attenuation bias in the estimated wage elasticity because of the longitudinal nature of the empirical exercise. The typical study examines the relation between the wage and the immigrant share across labor markets and over time. To net out market-specific factors, the regression usually includes various vectors of fixed effects (such as region fixed effects and/or skill fixed effects). The inclusion of these fixed effects implies that there may be little identifying variation remaining in the immigrant share variable, permitting any sampling error in the immigrant share to play a disproportionately large role. Even very small amounts of sampling error get magnified and can easily bias the results.

To illustrate, consider the generic regression model:

$$\log w_k = \beta \pi_k + Z_k \alpha + \varepsilon_k, \tag{4.8}$$

where w_k gives the wage in labor market k ($k = 1, \ldots, K$); π_k gives the immigrant share; the vector Z contains control variables that may include period fixed effects, region fixed effects, skill fixed effects, and any other variables that generate wage differences across markets; and ε is an i.i.d. error term, with mean 0 and variance σ_ε^2.

A crucial feature of this empirical exercise is that the analyst calculates the immigrant share from the microdata available for market k. To fix ideas, suppose that all other variables in the regression model are measured correctly.[26] Suppose further that the only type of measurement error in the observed immigrant share p_k is the one that arises due to sampling error and not to any possible misclassification of workers by immigration status. The relation between the observed immigrant share and the true immigrant share is:

$$p_k = \pi_k + u_k. \tag{4.9}$$

When a sample of size n_k is obtained by sampling with replacement from a population of size N_k, the observed immigrant share is calculated from a sample of independent Bernoulli draws, so that $E(u_k) = 0$ and $\mathrm{Var}(u_k) = \pi_k(1 - \pi_k)/n_k$. However, census sampling is without replacement. The error term in (4.9) then has a hypergeometric distribution with moments:

$$E(u_k) = 0, \; \mathrm{Var}(u_k) = \frac{N_k - n_k}{N_k - 1} \times \frac{\pi_k(1 - \pi_k)}{n_k}. \tag{4.10}$$

The expected value of the ratio n_k/N_k equals the sampling rate τ that generates the census sample (such as a $1/100$ sample). It is convenient to approximate the variance of the error term by $\mathrm{Var}(u_k) \approx (1 - \tau) \pi_k (1 - \pi_k)/n_k$.

It is well known that the probability limit of $\hat{\beta}$ in a multivariate regression model when only the regressor p_k is measured with error is:[27]

$$\text{plim}\,\hat{\beta}=\beta\left(1-\frac{\text{plim}\dfrac{1}{K}\displaystyle\sum_{k}u_{k}^{2}}{(1-R^{2})\sigma_{p}^{2}}\right),\tag{4.11}$$

where σ_{p}^{2} is the variance of the observed immigrant share across the K labor markets, and R^2 is the multiple correlation of an auxiliary regression that relates the observed immigrant share to all other right-hand-side variables in the model.

The typical study in the literature stacks data on particular labor markets over time and adds fixed effects that net out persistent wage variation across markets. This type of regression model, of course, effectively differences the data so that the wage impact of immigration is identified from within-market changes in the immigrant share. The multiple correlation of the auxiliary regression in this type of longitudinal study is usually well above 0.9. Much of the systematic variation in the immigrant share is "explained away" and measurement error will inevitably play a crucial role.

Aydemir and Borjas (2011, p. 75) show that the probability limit of $\hat{\beta}$ as the number of labor markets $K \to \infty$ can be approximated by:

$$\text{plim}\,\hat{\beta}\approx\beta\left(1-(1-\tau)\frac{\bar{p}(1-\bar{p})/\bar{n}}{(1-R^{2})\sigma_{p}^{2}}\right),\tag{4.12}$$

where $\bar{p}$ is the average observed immigrant share across the K labor markets, and $\bar{n}$ is the average number of observations used to calculate the immigrant share in each cell. The percent bias generated by sampling error is:

$$\frac{\text{plim}\,\hat{\beta}-\beta}{\beta}=(1-\tau)\frac{\bar{p}(1-\bar{p})/\bar{n}}{(1-R^{2})\sigma_{p}^{2}}.\tag{4.13}$$

To grasp the quantitative importance of attenuation bias, consider the following exercise. The average immigrant share in the United States in the 1960–2010 national-level data used in the previous section is 0.11, and the variance across labor markets defined on the basis of education and experience is 0.007. The explanatory power of the auxiliary regression of the immigrant share on all the other variables in the model (such as fixed effects for education and experience) is very high, around 0.95. Suppose that the sampling rate τ is small ($\tau \to 0$). Equation (4.13) then implies that the percent bias is 28 percent when the average cell has 1,000 observations and 47 percent when there are 600 observations.

Aydemir and Borjas (2011) had access to the *entire* (and confidential) Canadian census data maintained at Statistics Canada for the 1971–2001 period.[28] Statistics Canada releases a subset of these data as Public Use Microdata Files (PUMFs). As a result, Aydemir and Borjas could examine the consequences of estimating the *same* regression model using both "population" data and the much smaller samples that are made available to the research community.

Table 4.7 reports that the estimate of β is −0.507 (0.202) when the generic national-level regression given by equation (4.7) is estimated using the population files maintained by Statistics Canada. The average cell has 30,416 observations in this large sample. The remaining columns in Panel A of the table illustrate the behavior of $\hat{\beta}$ as one considers progressively smaller samples of the Canadian workforce. In particular, the table reports the sensitivity of the estimated coefficient when using a data set that comprises a 5/100 random sample of the Canadian population, a 1/100 random sample, and so on. For each of these sampling rates, Aydemir and Borjas drew 500 random samples from the population files, and the statistics reported in the table are the averages of the 500 replications.

The coefficient is −0.468 when the sampling rate is 5/100, so that the estimated wage impact of immigration falls by 7.7 percent even when the average cell size contains 7,001 workers. The attenuation becomes more pronounced as one moves to smaller samples. Consider, in particular, the results from the replications that use the PUMF sampling rate. The estimated coefficient drops to −0.403 (a 20.5 percent drop from the estimate in the population files). The typical researcher using the publicly available random sample of Canadian workers would inevitably conclude that immigration had a smaller numerical impact on wages.

Equation (4.12) provides a simple method for correcting these estimated coefficients. The R^2 of the auxiliary regression in the population file maintained by Statistics Canada was 0.967, suggesting that attenuation bias could easily play an important role even for relatively large samples. The back-of-the-envelope correction generates adjusted coefficients that typically approximate the coefficient estimated in the population files as long as the mean cell size is relatively large. The adjustment, however, breaks down at the 1/100 sampling rate.[29]

Of course, sampling error will also affect the estimated wage impact of immigration when the labor market is defined at a narrower geographic

Table 4.7 Sampling error and the wage impact of immigration in Canada

	Sampling rate					
	Statistics Canada	5/100	PUMF	1/100	1/1,000	1/10,000
A. National level						
1. $\hat{\beta}$	−0.507	−0.468	−0.403	−0.342	−0.076	−0.011
2. Standard error of $\hat{\beta}$	0.202	0.196	0.189	0.180	0.191	0.200
3. Auxiliary R^2	0.967	0.965	0.960	0.953	0.845	0.590
4. Corrected coefficient	−0.520	−0.531	−0.524	−0.638	1.174	0.044
5. $\bar{n}$	30416.3	7000.7	3426.9	1399.8	139.9	14.4
B. Metropolitan-area level						
1. $\hat{\beta}$	−0.053	−0.022	−0.012	−0.004	—	—
2. Standard error of $\hat{\beta}$	0.037	0.039	0.040	0.042	—	—
3. Auxiliary R^2	0.982	0.959	0.929	0.864	—	—
4. Corrected coefficient	−0.112	0.328	0.065	0.009	—	—
5. $\bar{n}$	659.5	165.1	83.9	34.1	—	—

Source: Aydemir and Borjas (2011, pp. 81, 84).

Notes: The coefficient $\hat{\beta}$ gives the estimated wage impact of immigration, estimated from a regression of the mean log wage in an education-experience-year cell (or education-experience-MSA-year cell in Panel B) on the respective immigrant share, holding constant the relevant vectors of fixed effects (listed in Table 4.5 for the national-level regressions, and Table 4.2 for the metropolitan-area-level regressions); the R^2 of the auxiliary regression gives the multiple correlation of the regression of the immigrant share on all other explanatory variables; the "corrected coefficient" uses the correction formula in equation (4.12); and $\bar{n}$ gives the average number of observations used to calculate the cell's immigrant share. All statistics reported in the table, except those referring to the Statistics Canada file, are averages across 500 replications of random samples at the given sampling rate. The PUMF sampling rate is the one used by Statistics Canada to create the Public Use Microdata File.

level, such as metropolitan areas. The bottom panel of Table 4.7 reports the results when the longitudinal spatial correlation model in equation (4.3) is estimated at the MSA-level. In Canada, the coefficient $\hat{\beta}$ is substantially smaller than that found in the national-level analysis, even when one uses the population sample; the estimated coefficient using the Statistics Canada file is −0.053 (0.037).

Because the sample size used to calculate the immigrant share variable is relatively small even when using the population files available at Statistics

Canada, the estimated wage effect of approximately −0.05 may have already been attenuated by sampling error. The corrected coefficient confirms this suspicion. The simplest back-of-the-envelope correction more than doubles the estimated wage impact to −0.112, so that the bias in the spatial correlation using the large Statistics Canada file is around 53 percent.[30]

Much of the empirical research in immigration economics has been conducted under the false sense of security provided by the fact that the analysis is often carried out using very large samples (such as the 5 percent random samples from the U.S. census). The use of these large microdata sets would seem to suggest that measurement error washes out as we aggregate across individuals in these samples. It turns out, however, that even a 5/100 sampling rate can easily generate substantial sampling error in the immigrant share—and that this sampling error will almost certainly play a crucial role in longitudinal-type studies that attempt to measure the wage impact of immigration. In short, measurement error has probably led to an attenuation of the measured wage effect.

5

The Wage Effects of Immigration: Structural Estimates

———————————◆———————————

THE STRUCTURAL APPROACH to estimating the labor market impact of immigration has an interesting intellectual history. As noted earlier, the initial empirical studies actually imposed a structure on the technology of the local labor market, such as the translog production function, and used the resulting estimates to predict the various wage effects. The obvious problem was one of dimensionality: for a reasonably detailed specification of the skill groups that populate the labor market, the methodology quickly strained the available data. Even if there were only 10 skill groups in the workforce, for example, the researcher needed to estimate over 50 parameters to describe how a particular supply shock affected the wage of all directly competing and potentially complementary workers.

Although this approach fell out of favor in the 1990s, the past decade has witnessed renewed and increasing interest in structural methods. Keeping in mind the lesson from the early structural estimates, however, the new studies emphasize the construction of models that both reduce the dimensionality of the parameter space and build a closer link between the key theoretical concepts and the variables that are actually used in the empirical research.

A Nested CES Model

A structural approach is required if the purpose of the analysis is not simply to estimate the "own" effect of a particular immigrant influx on the wage of directly competing native workers, but also the "cross" effects on the wage of other native workers.[1] The assumption of a specific functional form for the aggregate production function allows for the estimation of the complete set of factor price elasticities that determine how immigration affects the entire wage structure. One particularly tractable approach, introduced into the immigration literature in Borjas (2003), assumes that the aggregate technology of the labor market can be represented in terms of a three-level nested CES production function where the "primitive" labor inputs are the skill groups defined by education and experience. This section presents and estimates the nested CES framework before proceeding to discuss extensions that have been proposed in the subsequent literature.

Suppose the aggregate production function for the national labor market at time t can be written as:

$$Q_t = [\lambda_{Kt} K_t^\delta + \lambda_{Lt} L_t^\delta]^{1/\delta}, \tag{5.1}$$

where Q_t is output, K_t is capital, L_t denotes the aggregate labor input measured in efficiency units; and $\delta = 1 - 1/\sigma_{KL}$, with σ_{KL} being the elasticity of substitution between capital and labor ($-\infty < \delta \leq 1$). The vector λ gives (potentially) time-varying technology parameters that shift the production frontier, with $\lambda_{Kt} + \lambda_{Lt} = 1$. The total number of efficiency units L_t incorporates the contributions of workers who differ in both education and experience.

The Armington aggregator giving the total number of efficiency units in the workforce is:

$$L_t = \left[\sum_e \theta_{et} L_{et}^\beta \right]^{1/\beta}, \tag{5.2}$$

where L_{et} gives the effective supply of workers with education e at time t, and $\beta = 1 - 1/\sigma_E$, with σ_E being the elasticity of substitution across these education aggregates ($-\infty < \beta \leq 1$). The θ_{et} give (potentially) time-varying technology parameters that shift the relative productivity of education groups, with $\sum_e \theta_{et} = 1$.

Finally, the effective supply of workers in each education group is itself given by an Armington aggregation of the contribution of similarly educated workers with different levels of work experience. In particular:

$$L_{et} = \left[\sum_x \alpha_{ex} L_{ext}^{\eta} \right]^{1/\eta}, \tag{5.3}$$

where L_{ext} gives the number of work hours provided by workers in education group e and experience group x at time t; and $\eta = 1 - 1/\sigma_X$, with σ_X being the elasticity of substitution across experience classes within an education group $(-\infty < \eta \le 1)$. Equation (5.3) incorporates an important identifying assumption: the coefficients α_{ex} are time-invariant, with $\sum_x \alpha_{ex} = 1$.

The nested CES framework has two features that make it extremely useful for empirical analysis. First, it greatly reduces the dimensionality of the problem. The descriptive analysis presented in Chapter 4 classified workers into 40 different education-experience groups, so that there are 41 factors of production (including capital). Even after imposing the symmetry restrictions implied by factor demand theory, a general specification of the technology, such as the translog, would require the estimation of 861 different parameters (or $n(n+1)/2$). The nested CES drastically reduces the size of the parameter space; the technology can be summarized in terms of *three* elasticities of substitution.[2] Obviously, this simplification comes at a cost: the CES specification restricts the types of substitution that can exist among the various factors. The elasticity of substitution across experience groups takes on the same value for workers in adjacent experience categories as for workers who differ greatly in their experience; the elasticity of substitution between high school dropouts and high school graduates is the same as that between high school dropouts and college graduates; and the elasticity of substitution between capital and labor is the same for all the different types of workers as long as the labor input is measured in efficiency units.

Second, the nested CES framework is easily estimable using the national-level census data by education and experience introduced in Chapter 4. In particular, note that the marginal productivity condition implies that the wage for cell (e, x, t) is:

$$\log w_{ext} = \log \lambda_{Lt} + (1-\delta) \log Q_t + (\delta - \beta) \log L_t + \log \theta_{et}$$
$$+ (\beta - \eta) \log L_{et} + \log \alpha_{ex} + (\eta - 1) \log L_{ext}. \tag{5.4}$$

This marginal productivity condition can be rewritten as:

$$\log w_{ext} = \phi_t + \phi_{et} + \phi_{ex} - \frac{1}{\sigma_X} \log L_{ext}, \tag{5.5}$$

where $\phi_t = \log \lambda_{Lt} + (1-\delta) \log Q_t + (\delta - \beta) \log L_t$, and is absorbed by period fixed effects; $\phi_{et} = \log \theta_{et} + (\beta - \eta) \log L_{et}$, and is absorbed by interactions between education and period fixed effects; and $\phi_{ex} = \log \alpha_{ex}$, and is absorbed by interactions between education and experience fixed effects. In short, a regression of the log wage for a particular skill group on the log quantity of that skill group, holding constant the relevant vectors of fixed effects, identifies the elasticity of substitution across experience groups.

Because the coefficients of the education-experience fixed effects in (5.5) identify the parameters $\log \alpha_{ex}$, it is trivial to estimate the actual weights α_{ex} by imposing the restriction that $\Sigma_x \, \alpha_{ex} = 1$.[3] As implied by the Armington aggregator in equation (5.3), the estimates of α_{ex} and σ_X then permit the calculation of L_{et}, the total number of efficiency units supplied by education group e at time t. One can then move up one level in the CES technology, and recover an additional unknown parameter. Let $\log w_{et}$ be the mean log wage paid to workers in education group e at time t. The marginal productivity condition determining the wage for this group implies that:

$$\log w_{et} = \phi_t + \log \theta_{et} - \frac{1}{\sigma_E} \log L_{et}. \tag{5.6}$$

Equation (5.6) is closely related to the Katz-Murphy (1992) relative demand function that examines how the wage differential between college and high school graduates is affected by changes in relative supplies. As in the Katz-Murphy framework, equation (5.6) introduces a technical issue with important empirical ramifications. Note that the presence of $\log \theta_{et}$ suggests that the model must include a full set of education-time fixed effects to adjust for unobservable shifts in the productivity of different education groups. However, it is impossible to include all of these interactions, because they would be perfectly collinear with L_{et}, the effective supply of education group e at time t. Katz and Murphy (1992) circumvented the problem by assuming that the technology shifters $\log \theta_{et}$ can be approximated by a *linear* trend that varies across education groups. Given this operational assumption, the regression model in (5.6) then yields an estimate of the elasticity of substitution σ_E. It turns out, however, that this assumption "may not be innocuous" (Card and Lemieux 2001, p. 713).

The nested CES framework raises a number of methodological issues. First, note that OLS regressions of equations (5.5) and (5.6) yield biased estimates of σ_X and σ_E because the supply of workers to the various skill groups is likely to be endogenous over the 50-year period spanned by the data used below. The economic question at the core of the analysis, however, suggests an instrument for the (effective) size of the workforce in each skill group: the size of the population of foreign-born workers in that group. In other words, the immigrant influx into particular skill groups provides the supply shifter required to identify the labor demand curve. This instrument would be valid if the immigrant influx into particular skill groups were independent of the relative wages offered to the various skill categories. The number of immigrants in a skill group, however, likely responds to shifts in the wage structure. Income-maximizing behavior on the part of potential immigrants would generate larger flows into those skill cells that offered relatively higher wages. This behavioral response would tend to build in a *positive* correlation between the size of the immigrant influx and wages in a skill group. The estimated regression coefficients would then understate the negative wage impact of a relative supply increase.[4]

Second, the regressions of mean log wages on log quantities in equations (5.5) and (5.6) yield only two of the three elasticities of substitution (σ_X and σ_E) that summarize the nested CES technology. The estimation of the elasticity of substitution between capital and labor σ_{KL} requires additional data on the aggregate capital stock or the rate of return to capital.[5] The literature typically evades this problem by assuming that the aggregate production function in equation (5.1), the top level of the nested CES system, is Cobb-Douglas (or, more generally, linear homogeneous). *This assumption is definitely not innocuous.* As I showed in Chapter 3, the Cobb-Douglas assumption predetermines the numerical value of the average wage effect of immigration. Specifically, a 10 percent immigration-induced increase in supply *must* lower the average wage by 3.0 percent in the short run and by 0.0 percent in the long run. Similarly, the more general assumption of a linear, homogeneous production function at the top level of the nesting builds in the restriction that immigration *cannot* change the average wage in the long run.

The data used to estimate the structural CES model were introduced in Chapter 4 and give the mean log weekly wage and the total hours supplied for each of the 40 education-experience groups in the national labor market between 1960 and 2010. Table 5.1 summarizes the estimated coefficients.

Table 5.1 Estimates of (inverse) elasticities of substitution in nested CES framework

	Men	Men and women
1. Estimate of $-1/\sigma_X$	−0.153	−0.112
	(0.060)	(0.051)
2. Estimate of $-1/\sigma_E$		
a. Linear trend for demand shocks, efficiency unit counts	−0.257	−0.252
	(0.137)	(0.111)
b. Linear trend for demand shocks, actual hours counts	−0.234	−0.233
	(0.115)	(0.095)
c. Linear trend and post-1990 spline, efficiency unit counts	−0.215	−0.222
	(0.097)	(0.072)
d. Linear trend and post-1990 spline, actual hours counts	−0.200	−0.208
	(0.084)	(0.063)
e. Quadratic trend, efficiency unit counts	−0.297	−0.223
	(0.353)	(0.274)
f. Cubic trend, efficiency unit counts	−0.234	−0.218
	(0.245)	(0.244)
g. Log trend, efficiency unit counts	0.099	0.061
	(0.067)	(0.060)

Sources: U.S. Census PUMS, 1960–2010; see Appendix B for details.

Notes: The analysis is restricted to workers aged 18–64, who are classified into five education groups and eight experience groups. Robust standard errors are reported in parentheses and are clustered at the education-experience level in row 1. The dependent variable is the mean log weekly wage of natives in an education-experience-year cell in row 1 (men in the first data column; men and women in the second); and the mean log weekly wage of natives in an education-year cell in rows 2a–2g. The independent variable is the log size of the workforce in that cell, either in "efficiency units" or "actual hours" counts, The mean log weekly wage is calculated in the sample of natives employed in the wage-and-salary sector who are not enrolled in school; the size of the workforce is calculated over all workers (including men and women). All regressions are estimated using instrumental variables, where the instrument is the log of the number of foreign-born persons (both men and women) in the cell. The regressions in row 1 include vectors of year, education-year, and education-experience fixed effects. The regressions in rows 2a–2g include education-specific trends; the trend variable is initialized at 1 in 1960. The "post-1990" spline regressions add interactions between the education fixed effects and an indicator variable set to one in the 1990–2010 censuses. The regressions are weighted by the number of observations used to calculate the dependent variable. The regressions reported in row 1 have 240 observations; the regressions in rows 2a–2g have 30 observations.

The first row of the table reports that the IV estimation of equation (5.5) yields an estimate of $-1/\sigma_X$ equal to -0.153 (0.060). The implied estimate of the elasticity of substitution across experience groups is 6.7.

Given the estimate of σ_X and of the weights α_{ex}, it is then possible to use the aggregator in equation (5.3) to calculate L_{et}. This calculation, in turn, allows the estimation of equation (5.6), which yields an estimate of σ_E, the elasticity of substitution across education groups. As noted above, the estimation of this equation requires that some assumption be made about the differential *and unobserved* trends in productivity across education groups (that is, the time variation in θ_{et}). Row 2a of Table 5.1 shows that the estimate of $-1/\sigma_E$ is -0.257 (0.137) if we maintain the original Katz-Murphy assumption of a linear trend that differs across education groups. The implied elasticity of substitution across education groups is 3.9. Row 2b reestimates the regression by using the total number of hours worked by workers in each education group, rather than the Armington aggregation that relies on σ_X and the estimated α_{ex}. The implied elasticity of substitution across education groups is robust to this specification change.

Autor et al. (2008) argue that the original Katz-Murphy linear trend assumption fails to capture some of what happened to the U.S. wage structure in the 1990s. Specifically, they document that the growth in the relative demand for skilled workers slowed in the 1990s. To capture this break in the linear trend, I included additional interactions in equation (5.6) that allow for differential shifts in the education-specific trends since 1990. Specifically, row 2c estimates a regression that allows for a "spline" by including not only interactions between the education fixed effects and a linear trend, but also interactions between the education fixed effects and an indicator that "turns on" in 1990.[6] Row 2c shows that the estimate of $-1/\sigma_E$ with this expanded spline specification is -0.215 (0.097), implying that the elasticity of substitution across education groups is around 5.0. I will use this implied value of the elasticity of substitution across education groups in the simulations reported in the next section.

It is important to emphasize, however, that the estimate of the inverse elasticity becomes much more imprecise (and can even change sign) under alternative trend assumptions. Row 2e, for example, assumes that the unobserved demand shifts across education groups follow a quadratic trend, while row 2f assumes a cubic trend. Both of these alternative assumptions lead to a dramatic increase in the standard error so that the elasticity of substitution σ_E is no longer statistically significant. Finally, the assumption of a log trend in row 2g leads to a breakdown of the empirical approach: the implied elasticity of substitution has the wrong sign.

Simulating the Wage Effects of Immigration

The nested CES model provides a simple method for calculating the predicted wage effects of immigration. Consider, in particular, the impact of a "generalized" supply shift on the wage of a skill group with education e and labor market experience x. By differentiating the marginal productivity condition for this group, it is easy to show that:

$$d\log w_{ex} = \frac{s_K}{\sigma_{KL}} d\log K + \left(\frac{1}{\sigma_E} - \frac{s_K}{\sigma_{KL}}\right)\bar{m}$$
$$+ \left(\frac{1}{\sigma_X} - \frac{1}{\sigma_E}\right)m_e - \frac{1}{\sigma_X}m_{ex}, \tag{5.7}$$

where $m_{ex} = d\log L_{ex}$, the percent shift in the supply of skill group (e, x); $m_e = d\log L_e$; and $\bar{m} = d\log L$.

Equation (5.7) has a number of interesting properties. First, as emphasized in Chapter 3, it is not necessary to estimate any regressions to calculate the magnitudes of the immigration-induced supply shifts m_e and $\bar{m}$. Specifically, $m_e = \sum_x s_{ex} m_{ex} / s_e$, and $\bar{m} = \sum_e s_e m_e / s_L$. In other words, the supply shift occurring at any level of the nested CES framework is simply a weighted average of the supply shifts observed at a lower level of aggregation—where the weights are given by income shares.[7]

Second, one important "deliverable" from this type of empirical exercise is the prediction of the wage impact of immigration across the various education groups. It is easy to calculate the mean wage effect for the various education groups by taking a weighted average of the wage effects in equation (5.7) across the experience groups for a particular education group e. The weight implied by factor demand theory would be the relative income share accruing to each of the experience groups in education group e, or (s_{ex}/s_e). This weighted average yields:[8]

$$d\log w_e = \frac{s_K}{\sigma_{KL}} d\log K + \left(\frac{1}{\sigma_E} - \frac{s_K}{\sigma_{KL}}\right)\bar{m} - \frac{1}{\sigma_E}m_e, \tag{5.8}$$

Equation (5.8) again illustrates a remarkable property of the nested CES: the impact of an immigration-induced supply shift on the average wage of education group e is independent of any elasticities of substitution that enter the model *below* the education level in the CES nesting (in the current context, it is independent of σ_X). The predicted wage effect on education group e depends only on the elasticity of substitution between labor and capital, and on the elasticity of substitution across education groups.[9]

Finally, recall that the generic model in the literature does not attempt to estimate the elasticity of substitution between labor and capital, σ_{KL}. Instead, the numerical value of this elasticity is built in by the assumption that the aggregate production function in the nested CES framework is Cobb-Douglas, or $\sigma_{KL} = 1$. The impact of an immigration-induced supply shift on the mean wage in the labor market can again be obtained by taking a weighted average of the mean wage effect across education groups using relative income shares (or s_e/s_L) as the weights. The average wage effect is:

$$d\log \bar{w} = \frac{s_K}{\sigma_{KL}}(d\log K - \bar{m}) = s_K(d\log K - \bar{m}). \qquad (5.9)$$

As expected, equation (5.9) implies that the mean wage effect is zero in the long run (when $d\log K = \bar{m}$) and would simply equal $-s_K$ times $\bar{m}$ in the short run, when $d\log K = 0$. Again, note the property that the aggregate wage effect does not depend directly on any of the elasticities of substitution that enter the nested CES framework below the level of the aggregate labor input (specifically, it does not depend on σ_E and σ_X). Put bluntly, the voluminous amount of empirical work that relates mean wages in specific skill groups to group-specific quantities *provides no information whatsoever* to help calculate the mean wage effect of immigration on the host country's labor market. The mean wage effect reported in these types of simulations is the mechanical result of the assumption that the aggregate production function is Cobb-Douglas (or linear homogeneous) and has nothing to do with the underlying data.

Table 5.2 summarizes the results of the simulation. Specifically, the table uses the estimated elasticities of substitution reported in rows 1 and 2c of Table 5.1 (that is, $\sigma_X = 6.7$ and $\sigma_E = 5.0$) to calculate the percent wage impact resulting from the generalized supply shift induced by immigration between 1990 and 2010. The first row of Table 5.2 shows that the supply shift was particularly large for workers at the bottom and top of the

Table 5.2 Simulated wage impact of 1990–2010 immigrant influx on the
preexisting workforce

	High school dropouts	High school graduates	Some college	College graduates	Post-college	All workers
Percent supply shift	25.9	8.4	6.1	10.9	15.0	10.6
Percent wage effects						
Short run	−6.2	−2.7	−2.3	−3.2	−4.1	−3.2
Long run	−3.1	0.4	0.9	−0.1	−0.9	0.0

Source: Elasticities estimated in Table 5.1, male sample, rows 1 and 2c.

Notes: The simulations use the nested CES framework, set $\sigma_X = 6.7$, $\sigma_E = 5.0$, and assume that the aggregate production function is Cobb-Douglas, implying $\sigma_{KL} = 1.0$. The preexisting workforce includes both natives and immigrants residing in the United States in 1990. The short-run simulation assumes that the capital stock is constant; the long-run simulation assumes that the rate of return to capital is constant. Relative wage effects may differ between the short and long runs due to rounding error.

education distribution.[10] Immigration increased the effective number of work hours of high school dropouts by 25.9, and those of workers with more than a college degree by 15.0 percent. In contrast, immigration increased the number of hours supplied by workers with 12 to 15 years of school by 6 to 8 percent. Overall, immigration increased effective supply by 10.6 percent during the two-decade period.

Because of the U-shaped nature of the supply shift, the simulation necessarily shows that immigration most affected the wage of workers at the two ends of the education distribution. The estimated elasticity of substitution across education groups implies that the large immigration-induced supply shift experienced by high school dropouts reduced the wage of this group by 6.2 percent in the short run and 3.1 percent in the long run. Similarly, the wage effect for the most highly skilled workers (those with more than a college degree) were −4.1 percent in the short run and −0.9 percent in the long run.[11]

If we take the weighted average of the wage effects across education groups, we find that the average wage of a preexisting worker fell by 3.2 percent in the short run and 0.0 percent in the long run. It is important to reemphasize, however, that these aggregate effects have nothing to do with the underlying data. They are the mechanical predictions of the assumption that the aggregate production function is Cobb-Douglas (so, for example, the short-run average wage effect of 3.2 percent is simply the product of capital's share of income, 0.3, times the aggregate supply shift, 10.6 percent).

The mechanical nature of these aggregate wage effects suggests that we should view the absolute numerical values provided by a simulation that relies on a nested CES/Cobb-Douglas framework with *more* than the usual skepticism. The Cobb-Douglas assumption implies that the average wage effect in the short run *must be* −3.2 percent. Therefore, some education groups must have experienced a wage loss that is somewhat larger than 3.2 percent, while other education groups must have experienced a somewhat smaller wage loss. Despite its simplicity and elegance, the nested CES framework carries a great deal of baggage as well, and this baggage suggests that the only valuable results that come out of the simulation deal with the impact of immigration on *relative* wages. Although obvious, this fact has not been sufficiently emphasized or appreciated in the existing literature.

In addition, it is worth stressing that the distinction between the short run and the long run used in the simulations is a purely theoretical construct. As will be noted in Chapter 6, remarkably little is known about how labor markets actually adjust to immigration and about the speed of that adjustment. The available evidence simply does not provide a useful guide to help us discern which of the two sets of simulation results seems more representative of what happens in real-world labor markets. Moreover, the only results that are data-driven in these simulations measure the impact of immigration on relative wages. However, as equation (5.8) shows, the algebra of the nested CES *forces* these relative wage effects to be the same in both the short and the long run. In the end, therefore, the distinction between short run and long run is a red herring. The simulated wage effects can be made to look "small" or "large" by choosing a particular time horizon, but this choice does not offer any real-world informational content.

Within-Group Complementarity between Immigrants and Natives

Both the descriptive empirical analysis reported in Chapter 4 and the structural analysis presented in the previous section assumed that immigrant and native workers belonging to a particular skill group (e, x) are perfect substitutes.[12] The question of whether there is *within-group* imperfect substitution—giving rise to potential complementarities between similarly skilled immigrants and natives—was first examined in the context of a structural framework by Jaeger (1996), who concluded that the two groups were indeed perfect substitutes. More recently, however, Ottaviano and Peri (2006, 2012) revisited this question and report some evidence for within-group complementaries. In fact, in the original version of their work, they concluded that the complementarities were sufficiently strong that an immigration-induced supply shock would increase the wage of almost all native workers.

The extent of within-group complementarities can be easily determined in the nested CES framework by adding a fourth level to the production technology. In particular, let N_{ext} and M_{ext} be the total number of work hours supplied by natives and immigrants, respectively, with education e, experience x, at time t. The Armington aggregator describing the interactions between these two groups is given by:

$$L_{ext} = [\varphi_{ext} N_{ext}^{\gamma} + (1 - \varphi_{ext}) M_{ext}^{\gamma}]^{1/\gamma}, \tag{5.10}$$

where $\gamma = 1 - 1/\sigma_{MN}$, with σ_{MN} being the elasticity of substitution between equally skilled foreign- and native-born workers (and $-\infty < \gamma \le 1$).

Note that the type of complementarity measured by σ_{MN} is quite specific and narrow. It does not describe how low-skill immigrants and high-skill natives may interact in the production process—which is the type of complementarity that could easily be presumed to be empirically relevant in the context of immigration to many developed countries. Instead, it describes the complementarities that arise when a 30-year-old foreign-born high school dropout interacts with a 30-year-old native-born high school dropout.[13]

Equating wages to the value of marginal product of labor yields the estimable relative labor demand function:

$$\log \frac{w_{ext}^{M}}{w_{ext}^{N}} = \varphi_{ext}^{*} - \frac{1}{\sigma_{MN}} \log\left(\frac{M_{ext}}{N_{ext}}\right), \tag{5.11}$$

where w_{ext}^{M} and w_{ext}^{N} give the wage of immigrant and native workers in cell (e, x, t), respectively; and $\varphi_{ext}^{*} = \log[(1 - \varphi_{ext}) / \varphi_{ext}]$, a (potentially) time- and skill-varying relative demand shifter that will presumably need to be approximated by a vector of observed variables.

The first row of Table 5.3 reports the inverse elasticity of substitution estimated in the Ottaviano and Peri (2012) study. The inverse elasticity of substitution estimated using the simplest specification is -0.053 (0.008), implying that σ_{MN} is around 20.[14] It is important to emphasize that this

Table 5.3 Estimates of inverse elasticity of substitution between equally skilled immigrants and natives $(-1/\sigma_{MN})$

	Specification			
	(1)	(2)	(3)	(4)
A. Log of the mean wage (Ottaviano-Peri, 2012)				
Men	−0.053	—	−0.033	—
	(0.008)		(0.013)	
Men and women	−0.032	—	−0.024	—
	(0.008)		(0.015)	
B. Mean of the log wage (Borjas et al. 2012)				
Men	−0.008	0.008	0.008	0.009
	(0.017)	(0.021)	(0.013)	(0.034)
Men and women	−0.002	0.004	0.001	−0.034
	(0.015)	(0.018)	(0.012)	(0.036)
C. Mean of the log wage, updated to 2010				
Men	−0.018	0.005	−0.003	0.029
	(0.007)	(0.009)	(0.009)	(0.019)
Men and women	−0.036	−0.011	−0.017	0.016
	(0.006)	(0.006)	(0.015)	(0.017)
Fixed effects included				
Year	No	Yes	Yes	Yes
Education × experience	No	No	Yes	Yes
Education × year	No	No	No	Yes
Experience × year	No	No	No	Yes

Sources: Adapted from Borjas et al. (2012, p. 202). The inverse elasticities reported in Panel A are drawn from Ottaviano and Peri (2012, p. 171, columns 1 and 2).

Notes: Robust standard errors reported in parentheses. The unit of observation is an education-experience-year cell. The dependent variable is the difference in the log weekly wage between immigrants and natives in the cell, and the independent variable is the corresponding difference in the log total hours supplied. Panel A defines the log wage of a group as the log of the mean wage across workers in that group; Panels B and C define it as the mean of the log wage across workers. The regressions reported in Panel A use total employment in the skill group as the weight; in all other panels, the weight is the inverse of the sampling variance of the dependent variable. The regressions in Panel C use the same data employed in the regressions reported in row 1 of Table 5.1 (with the mean log wage for an education-experience group being calculated separately for natives and immigrants).

"preferred" estimate is based on a regression model that treats φ_{ext}^{*} in equation (5.11) as a constant and simply regresses the log of relative wages on the log of relative quantities.

It turns out, however, that an estimated elasticity of 20 exaggerates the within-group complementarities that are actually revealed by the census data. Borjas et al. (2012) replicated the Ottaviano-Peri study and found that the estimate of σ_{MN} would have been much larger had the regression analysis used modeling assumptions that are widely accepted in the labor economics literature. Specifically, Ottaviano and Peri define the value of marginal product for a skill group as the *log of the mean wage* for a particular cell. The standard approach in the literature is to use the *mean of the log wage*.[15] By Jensen's inequality, the log mean wage and the mean log wage are not the same. The mean log wage corresponds to the geometric mean wage, which has the interpretation of a marginal product index in which weights are each worker's share of total hours worked. The log mean wage does not have such an economic interpretation. It turns out that this seemingly trivial definitional change has a major impact on the estimates.

Panel B of Table 5.3 reports the estimated inverse elasticity resulting from a regression that uses the mean log wage. The regression coefficient is now −0.008 (0.017). The coefficient is no longer statistically significant and has an implied substitution elasticity of 125. Finally, Panel C reports the coefficients from regressions that use the updated 1960–2010 census data. The estimate of the inverse elasticity of substitution is −0.018, implying an elasticity of over 50.

Further, note that the coefficients reported using the simplest regression specification ignore the possibility of time-skill variation in the intercept φ_{ext}^{*} in equation (5.11). Because the dependent variable in this regression is the difference in immigrant-native log wages, factors that affect immigrant and native labor demand equally are automatically removed from the equation. Remaining factors that affect immigrant-native relative wages include differences in the composition of immigrants and natives within skill groups and differential shifts in demand.[16] One solution is to control for skill-group and period fixed effects. The inclusion of these fixed effects consistently produces estimated inverse elasticities that are both numerically and statistically equal to zero. Put simply, the available evidence suggests that within-group complementarities between foreign- and native-born workers are not an important factor in an assessment of the labor market impact of immigration in the United States.[17]

It is instructive to illustrate the role played by potential within-group complementarities in simulations of the labor market impact of immigration. By differentiating the marginal productivity conditions giving the wage of foreign- and native-born workers in a particular skill group, it is easy to show that the wage impact of an immigration-induced supply shift is given by:

$$d\log w_{ex}^M = \frac{s_K}{\sigma_{KL}}d\log K + \left(\frac{1}{\sigma_E} - \frac{s_K}{\sigma_{KL}}\right)\bar{m} + \left(\frac{1}{\sigma_X} - \frac{1}{\sigma_E}\right)m_e$$
$$+ \left(\frac{1}{\sigma_{MN}} - \frac{1}{\sigma_X}\right)m_{ex} - \frac{1}{\sigma_{MN}}d\log M_{ex},$$

$$(5.12)$$

$$d\log w_{ex}^N = \frac{s_K}{\sigma_{KL}}d\log K + \left(\frac{1}{\sigma_E} - \frac{s_K}{\sigma_{KL}}\right)\bar{m} + \left(\frac{1}{\sigma_X} - \frac{1}{\sigma_E}\right)m_e$$
$$+ \left(\frac{1}{\sigma_{MN}} - \frac{1}{\sigma_X}\right)m_{ex}.$$

$$(5.13)$$

Equations (5.12) and (5.13) imply that the impact of immigration on the wage differential between equally skilled foreign- and native-born workers, or $d\log(w_{ex}^M / w_{ex}^N)$, depends on the product of the inverse elasticity σ_{MN} and $d\log M_{ex}$, the percent change in the number of work hours supplied by foreign-born workers. If the elasticity of substitution σ_{MN} were small, the within-group complementarities would inevitably have a substantial impact on the wage gap between comparably skilled foreign- and native-born workers.

However, the nested CES framework also implies that the value of σ_{MN} plays no role in determining the impact of immigration on the average wage of the preexisting workforce for any particular skill group—where the preexisting workforce includes both the native-born and the preexisting foreign-born workers. In other words, the average wage effect on all preexisting workers in a particular education group *must be identical* to that estimated in the previous section, regardless of the value of σ_{MN}.

Table 5.4 summarizes the results of the simulation, using two alternative values for the elasticity: 20 and infinity. The elasticity of 20 is the Ottaviano-Peri preferred estimate; and an elasticity of infinity is the estimate that, in fact, seems most consistent with the 1960–2010 census data. To simplify the exposition, the table reports only the long-run wage impacts. It

Table 5.4 Simulated long-run wage impact of 1990–2010 immigrant influx, allowing for within-group complementarities

	High school dropouts	High school graduates	Some college	College graduates	Post-college	All workers
Percent wage effects, $\sigma_{MN} = 20.0$						
Native-born	−1.7	0.9	1.2	0.5	−0.1	0.6
Foreign-born	−5.3	−3.4	−2.7	−4.9	−5.3	−4.4
All workers	−3.1	0.4	0.9	−0.1	−0.9	0.0
Percent wage effects, $\sigma_{MN} = \infty$						
All workers	−3.1	0.4	0.9	−0.1	−0.9	0.0

Source: Elasticities estimated in the male sample of Table 5.1, rows 1 and 2c; Table 5.3, Panel A, data column 1.

Notes: The simulations use the nested CES framework, set $\sigma_X = 6.7$, $\sigma_E = 5.0$, and assume that the aggregate production function is Cobb-Douglas, implying $\sigma_{KL} = 1.0$. The long-run simulation assumes that the rate of return to capital is constant; the short-run wage effects can be obtained by adding −3.2 to any statistic reported in the table.

should be obvious that the short-run wage impact for any specific group can be obtained by subtracting 3.2 percent from any statistic in the table.

The simulation, of course, shows that the wage effect on the *average* pre-existing worker in each education group is the same regardless of the value of the elasticity. If the elasticity is less than infinity, however, there is a distributional effect within each education group, with immigrants being relatively harder hit by the supply shock. Note, however, that the wage of native-born high school dropouts falls (in the long run) by between 2 and 3 percent regardless of the value of the elasticity. In other words, even an elasticity σ_{MN} "as low" as 20 has roughly the same operational consequences as the assumption that equally skilled immigrants and natives are perfect substitutes.

Are "High School Equivalents" Equivalent?

The aggregation of workers into a manageable number of skill groups is a crucial step in any empirical analysis of the labor market impact of immigration. In the United States, immigration has disproportionately increased the size of specific education groups, such as high school dropouts and workers with post-college degrees. Hence, the literature has focused on estimating the impact of immigration on those particular groups. In contrast, much of the wage structure literature found it convenient to discuss trends in the returns to skills by examining the wage gap between two broadly defined education classifications, "high school equivalents" (defined as an aggregation of high school dropouts and high school graduates), and "college equivalents" (defined as an aggregation of workers who have more than a high school diploma). A number of recent studies argue that the high school equivalents–college equivalents classification should also be adopted in the immigration literature.[18]

Of course, whether such an adoption is warranted is an empirical question, depending partly on the value of the elasticity of substitution between high school dropouts and high school graduates.[19] Equation (5.2) defined the Armington aggregator giving the total number of efficiency units supplied in the labor market as $L_t = [\sum_e \theta_{et} L_{et}^\beta]^{1/\beta}$, where the index e distinguishes the five education groups ($e = 1, \ldots, 5$). The notion that high school dropouts and high school graduates may be easily substitutable can be captured by specifying yet another level in the nested CES framework. In particular, the aggregator in equation (5.2) is replaced by the two-equation system:

$$L_t = \left[\theta_{HS,t} L_{HS,t}^\beta + \theta_{3t} L_{3t}^\beta + \theta_{4t} L_{4t}^\beta + \theta_{5t} L_{5t}^\beta \right]^{1/\beta},$$
$$L_{HS,t} = \left[\mu_t L_{1t}^\rho + (1 - \mu_t) L_{2t}^\rho \right]^{1/\rho}, \tag{5.14}$$

where $L_{HS,t}$ gives the efficiency units provided by high school equivalents; and $\rho = 1 - 1/\sigma_{HS}$, with σ_{HS} being the elasticity of substitution between high school dropouts and high school graduates ($-\infty < \rho \le 1$).[20] The marginal productivity conditions then imply that the relative demand function for high school graduates/dropouts is given by:

$$\ln \left(\frac{w_{2t}}{w_{1t}} \right) = \mu_t^* - \frac{1}{\sigma_{HS}} \ln \left(\frac{L_{2t}}{L_{1t}} \right), \tag{5.15}$$

where $\mu_t^* = \log[(1 - \mu_t)/\mu_t]$. Note that national-level data provide only one observation per year to estimate σ_{HS}. This limited variation implies that one cannot control for the demand shifter μ_t^* by simply including a vector of year fixed effects; additional assumptions about the nature of the trend are required.

Most studies in the wage structure literature use the annual Current Population Surveys (CPS) to estimate elasticities of substitution across (aggregated) education groups. The early studies in this literature assumed that the demand shifter—in the context of the wage gap between high school equivalents and college equivalents—could be approximated by a linear trend that differed between the two groups. More recent studies, however, argue that that there was a slowdown in demand growth for more skilled workers after 1990. Goldin and Katz (2010) adopt this framework, and add a post-1992 spline to the linear trend, to specifically estimate σ_{HS}, the elasticity of substitution between high school dropouts and high school graduates.

Borjas et al. (2012) used the Goldin-Katz CPS data on relative wages and employment for the 1963–2005 period to evaluate the robustness of estimates of σ_{HS}. Table 5.5 summarizes the results. The first coefficient reported in the table gives the elasticity σ_{HS} estimated using the "preferred" spline specification.[21] The estimated coefficient is −0.135 (0.023), rejecting the hypothesis that the two groups are perfect substitutes. The implied elasticity σ_{HS} is 7.4.

The other rows in Table 5.5 use alternatives to the spline approximation for the demand shifter. It is evident that the estimated σ_{HS} is extremely sensitive to how the regression controls for the unobserved variation in relative demand. Row 2, for example, uses the original linear trend assumption. The estimated elasticity is now equal to 43.5, suggesting that high school dropouts and high school graduates are indeed near-perfect substitutes. The use of a quadratic trend leads to a rejection of the CES framework. The implied elasticity of substitution is statistically significant and sizable, but it has the wrong sign. The use of a cubic trend leads to further instability.

Card (2009) proposed an approach that would seem to avoid the pitfalls inherent in making untestable assumptions about the underlying trends in relative demand. He exploits variation in relative wages and quantities across local labor markets to estimate σ_{HS}. In other words, the value of the elasticity of substitution is inferred from a spatial correlation between relative wages and relative quantities. The comparison of local labor markets leads to the conclusion that the two groups are perfect substitutes. The MSA-level regression reported in Table 5.5 replicates Card's results by using the census-ACS data and defining a cell in terms of metropolitan area r, education e, and time t. Row 5, which includes period fixed effects, shows that the inverse elasticity is −0.024 (0.016), so that the hypothesis that high school dropouts and high school graduates are perfect substitutes cannot be rejected.

Table 5.5 Estimates of inverse elasticity of substitution between high school dropouts and high school graduates $(-1/\sigma_{HS})$

Specification	1. CPS	Census	
		2. MSA level	3. State level
1. Linear trend, post-1992 spline	−0.135 (0.027)	—	—
2. Linear trend only	−0.023 (0.012)	—	—
3. Quadratic trend	0.101 (0.045)	—	—
4. Cubic trend	−0.047 (0.012)	—	—
5. Period fixed effects	—	−0.024 (0.016)	−0.069 (0.025)
6. State/MSA effects × linear trend	—	−0.037 (0.026)	−0.119 (0.011)
7. State/MSA effects × post-1992 spline	—	0.141 (0.074)	−0.152 (0.028)
Includes state or MSA fixed effects	—	Yes	Yes
Number of observations	43	1071	306

Source: Borjas et al. (2012, p. 203).

Notes: Robust standard errors are reported in parentheses, and are clustered at the MSA or state level in the last two columns. The unit of observation is a calendar year in rows 1–4, and a region-year cell in rows 5–7. The dependent variable gives the difference in the mean log wage between high school graduates and high school dropouts in a particular labor market at a point in time. The independent variable gives the corresponding difference in the log total hours supplied. The CPS regressions use the 1963–2005 CPS time series created by Goldin and Katz (2010, p. 306). The regression coefficients reported in the last two columns use data extracts constructed from decennial census and ACS samples. The post-1992 spline uses the definition in Goldin-Katz and is an additional linear trend variable initialized at 1 in 1993. The regressions using the CPS data are unweighted; all other regressions are weighted by the inverse of the variance of the dependent variable.

The benefit of the spatial approach is that it superficially seems to eliminate the need to make arbitrary assumptions about the unobserved demand shifter. Because there are now many observations in each period (for different localities), the regression can include period fixed effects. However, there are likely to be geographic differences in the evolution of relative demand for high school dropouts and high school graduates. Thus, the need arises to make ancillary assumptions about the *MSA-specific* trends in relative demand. Rows 6 and 7 of the table illustrate what happens to the estimated inverse elasticity when the MSA fixed effects are interacted either with a linear trend or with the spline specification. The estimated coefficients are unstable and, in the case of the spline specification, reject the CES framework.

Finally, Table 5.5 also reports the estimated elasticity when the regional labor market is defined at the state level rather than for a metropolitan area. As emphasized in Chapter 4, spatial correlations between wages and immigration are sensitive to the geographic definition of the labor market. As it turns out, so is the estimated elasticity of substitution σ_{HS}. The basic state-level regression reported in row 5 implies an elasticity of 14.5, rejecting the conjecture that high school dropouts and high school graduates are perfect substitutes. Interestingly, the estimated elasticity σ_{HS} becomes numerically larger the smaller the geographic area that defines the labor market: it is 7.4 in the national CPS data (using the spline specification), 14.5 at the state level, and 41.7 at the MSA level. This finding mirrors the finding that wages and supply shifts are more closely linked the larger the size of the geographic labor market.

In short, the available evidence on the elasticity of substitution between high school dropouts and high school graduates is not robust to the assumptions made about the time path of *unobserved* shocks to relative demand. Different assumptions about these demand shifts yield different conclusions about whether high school equivalents are, in fact, equivalent. The sensitivity of the results suggests that the nested CES framework does not provide a particularly useful approach for analyzing the substitutability of labor between these two skill groups.

Nevertheless, it is useful to conduct one last simulation exercise to get a sense of the substantive importance of the value of the elasticity of substitution between high school dropouts and high school graduates. The CES aggregation of education groups in (5.14) implies that equations (5.12) and (5.13) still give the predicted wage effects for foreign- and native-born workers with more than a high school diploma. For workers who are either high school dropouts or high school graduates, the predicted wage impact is now given by:

$$d\log w_{ex}^M = \frac{s_K}{\sigma_{KL}}d\log K + \left(\frac{1}{\sigma_E}-\frac{s_K}{\sigma_{KL}}\right)\bar{m} + \left(\frac{1}{\sigma_{HS}}-\frac{1}{\sigma_E}\right)m_{HS}$$
$$+\left(\frac{1}{\sigma_X}-\frac{1}{\sigma_{HS}}\right)m_e + \left(\frac{1}{\sigma_{MN}}-\frac{1}{\sigma_X}\right)m_{ex} - \frac{1}{\sigma_{MN}}d\log M_{ex},$$

(5.16)

$$d\log w_{ex}^N = \frac{s_K}{\sigma_{KL}}d\log K + \left(\frac{1}{\sigma_E}-\frac{s_K}{\sigma_{KL}}\right)\bar{m} + \left(\frac{1}{\sigma_{HS}}-\frac{1}{\sigma_E}\right)m_{HS}$$
$$+\left(\frac{1}{\sigma_X}-\frac{1}{\sigma_{HS}}\right)m_e + \left(\frac{1}{\sigma_{MN}}-\frac{1}{\sigma_X}\right)m_{ex}.$$

(5.17)

where $m_{HS}=d\log L_{HS}=(s_1\, d\log L_1 + s_2\, d\log L_2)/s_{HS}$; and s_{HS} is the income share accruing to workers who are either high school dropouts or high school graduates. It is again important to emphasize that the extent of substitution between high school dropouts and high school graduates does not affect the mean wage effect of immigration. The mean effect has been predetermined numerically by the Cobb-Douglas assumption.

Table 5.6 summarizes the result of the "generalized" long-run simulation using two alternative values for the elasticity σ_{HS}: 7.4 (the value implied by the Goldin-Katz CPS data), and infinity (the assumption that the two groups are perfect substitutes). The table again uses two alternative values (20 and infinity) for σ_{MN}.

The conjecture that high school dropouts and high school graduates are perfect substitutes has several interesting implications. Most obviously, immigration has a much weaker impact on the wage of low-skill workers. For example, the long-run wage impact on high school dropouts is essentially zero if σ_{HS} is infinity, but −2.1 percent if σ_{HS} is around 7. The weaker impact implied by the assumption that high school dropouts and high school graduates are perfect substitutes arises mechanically. As Borjas et al. (1997) noted, because immigration disproportionately increased the number of high school dropouts in the United States, the identification of high school dropouts as a unique skill group implies that this group experienced a very large supply shock. By pooling all workers with 12 or fewer years of education into "high school equivalents," the relative size of the

Table 5.6 Generalized simulation of the long-run wage impact of the 1990–2010 immigrant influx

		High school dropouts	High school graduates	Some college	College graduates	Post-college	All workers
Percent wage effects, $\sigma_{MN}=20.0$							
$\sigma_{HS}=7.4$	Native born	−0.8	0.6	1.2	0.5	−0.1	0.6
	Foreign born	−4.3	−3.6	−2.7	−4.9	−5.3	−4.2
	All workers	−2.1	0.2	0.9	−0.1	−0.9	0.0
$\sigma_{HS}=\infty$	Native born	1.1	0.2	1.2	0.5	−0.1	0.5
	Foreign born	−2.4	−4.1	−2.7	−4.9	−5.3	−4.0
	All workers	−0.2	−0.2	0.9	−0.1	−0.9	0.0
Percent wage effects, $\sigma_{MN}=\infty$							
$\sigma_{HS}=7.4$	All workers	−2.1	0.2	0.9	−0.1	−0.9	0.0
$\sigma_{HS}=\infty$	All workers	−0.2	−0.2	0.9	−0.1	−0.9	0.0

Source: Elasticities estimated in the male sample of Table 5.1, rows 1 and 2c; Table 5.3, Panel A, data column 1; and Table 5.5, row 1.

Notes: The simulations use the nested CES framework, set $\sigma_X=6.7$, $\sigma_E=5.0$, and assume that the aggregate production function is Cobb-Douglas, implying $\sigma_{KL}=1.0$. The long-run simulation assumes that the rate of return to capital is constant; the short-run wage effects can be obtained by adding −3.2 to any statistic reported in the table.

immigration-induced supply shock on the low-skill workforce becomes much smaller, and the wage impact on low-skill workers gets diluted.

Second, the assumption that high school dropouts and high school graduates are perfect substitutes implies that immigration had little distributional impact. For example, if the elasticity σ_{MN} were infinity, most education groups suffered a negligible (long-run) wage effect. The seemingly unbalanced skill composition of recent immigration does not translate into relative wage effects because the aggregation of high school dropouts and graduates into a single group leads to effective supply shifts that are roughly of the same magnitude for *every* education group.

Finally, the comparison of Tables 5.2 and 5.6 suggests that the traditional separation of the low-skill workforce into high school dropouts and high school graduates leads to predicted relative wage effects that are largely consistent with the value of σ_{HS} implied by the Goldin-Katz CPS data (that is, $\sigma_{HS} = 7.4$). In Table 5.2, for example, immigration is predicted to lower the wage of high school dropouts *relative* to college graduates by 3.0 percentage points. In Table 5.6, the relative wage of high school dropouts falls by 2.0 percent.

It is best to conclude by emphasizing an obvious, but important, lesson. The simulation illustrates the limits to what the nested CES framework can teach us about the labor market impact of immigration. Aggregating or disaggregating education groups can make the estimated wage effects as small or as large as one would like. Yet, there is no convincing evidence on how best to pool.

Descriptive versus Structural Approaches

So what is the "take-away" message from the descriptive and structural approaches to a core question in immigration economics? Specifically, what *is* the effect of an immigration-induced supply shock on the wage structure?

As the discussion in this chapter shows, the nested CES structural approach seems far too sensitive to the imposition of unverifiable (but necessary) assumptions to be of much use in giving a robust and convincing answer. Moreover, the size of the predicted effect on the average wage is driven *entirely* by functional form assumptions about the production technology, rather than estimated from data. At the same time, it is clear that a comprehensive answer requires that we take into account all the cross-effects that occur as immigrants in one skill group influence the productivity of workers in other groups, and this type of systematic cross-accounting is beyond the reach of the descriptive approach.

One potentially fruitful tactic may be to reinterpret the findings from the descriptive approach using the restrictions implied by factor demand theory. A descriptive national-level regression, such as the one specified in equation (4.7), relates the wage of a skill group to the "own" supply shift, and excludes all the other supply shifters. As we saw in Chapter 4, the wage elasticity implied by this approach was -0.37. A straightforward application of the omitted variable bias formula would suggest that this elasticity is obviously measuring not the own wage effect but an amalgam of the own effect and some combination of the cross-effects that have been excluded from the regression. It is easy to illustrate this insight in the simple case where there are 3 skill groups and we observe market conditions for each skill group for a total of T years.

Let y_{it} give the mean log wage of skill group i ($i = A, B, C$) at time t ($t = 1, \ldots, T$); and m_{it} be the relative supply increase experienced by that group ($m_{it} = M_{it}/N_{it}$). Without loss of generality, assume all variables are measured as deviations from the mean. We can describe the structure of the stacked data with the regression model:

$$y_{At} = \beta\, m_{At} + \varepsilon_{AB}\, m_{Bt} + \varepsilon_{AC}\, m_{Ct} + \varepsilon_{BC} \times 0 + \xi_A,$$

$$y_{Bt} = \beta\, m_{Bt} + \varepsilon_{AB}\, m_{At} + \varepsilon_{AC} \times 0 + \varepsilon_{BC}\, m_{Ct} + \xi_B, \qquad (5.18)$$

$$y_{Ct} = \beta\, m_{Ct} + \varepsilon_{AB} \times 0 + \varepsilon_{AC}\, m_{At} + \varepsilon_{BC}\, m_{Bt} + \xi_C,$$

where, by construction, the coefficients are factor price elasticities ($\varepsilon_{ij} = d \log w_i / d \log L_j$). The system of seemingly unrelated equations in (5.18) allows for the supply shock to have both own and cross effects, while building in two important restrictions. The first is that the "own effect," which is measured by the parameter β, is the same for all skill groups. The second is the imposition of a symmetry restriction roughly analogous to that implied by factor demand theory, so that the cross-elasticity of factor price $\varepsilon_{ij} = \varepsilon_{ji}$. This is not precisely the restriction implied by the theory, but I will return to this issue shortly.[22]

It is useful to interpret the descriptive approach as estimating a regression using the stacked data in (5.18), but imposing exclusion restrictions. Specifically, let the variable z denote the first regressor in the system (that is, the first column measuring the own effect). The descriptive regression then infers the wage effect of immigration from the bivariate regression coefficient given by $\hat{\beta} = Cov(z, y)/Var(z)$.[23]

It is well known that $\hat{\beta}$ does not estimate the own wage effect of immigration. An application of the omitted variable bias formula implies that:

$$\text{plim}\hat{\beta} = \beta + [\varepsilon_{AB}\delta_{BA} + \varepsilon_{AC}\delta_{CA}]\frac{\sigma_A^2}{\sigma_m^2} + [\varepsilon_{AB}\delta_{AB} + \varepsilon_{BC}\delta_{CB}]\frac{\sigma_B^2}{\sigma_m^2}$$

$$+ [\varepsilon_{AC}\delta_{AC} + \varepsilon_{BC}\delta_{BC}]\frac{\sigma_C^2}{\sigma_m^2}, \qquad (5.19)$$

where $\delta_{ij} = Cov(m_i, m_j)/Var(m_j)$, the coefficient from an auxiliary regression measuring how an increase in the size of group j changes the size of group i; $\sigma_i^2 = \sum_t m_{it}^2 / T$, and $\sigma_m^2 = \sigma_A^2 + \sigma_B^2 + \sigma_C^2$.

Equation (5.19) has an interesting interpretation. Each of the bracketed terms gives the predicted wage impact of the cross-effects associated with an increase in own supply. For example, the first bracketed term specifically measures the cross-effects associated with an increase in the supply of group A. Such an increase is correlated with a particular increase in the size of groups B and C (as measured by the respective δ's), and each of these supply shifts would have wage effects (as measured by the respective ε's).

The application of the omitted variable bias formula thus indicates that the estimated $\hat{\beta}$ measures an amalgam of the own wage effect plus an "average" of the cross-effects that were excluded from the regression. As a result, the coefficient from the descriptive regression has an economically meaningful interpretation: it is the *total* effect on the wage level resulting from, say, a 10 percent increase in the supply of the own group *and* the associated shift in the supply of all the other groups. Put differently, $\hat{\beta}$ measures the average wage impact of a "generalized" supply shock.

There is one minor caveat. The elegant averaging of cross-effects in equation (5–19) depends crucially on the assumption that factor price cross-elasticities, ε_{ij}, are symmetric. Factor demand theory, however, does not imply this type of symmetry. Instead, factor demand theory implies symmetric cross-elasticities of complementarity, c_{ij}. However, the theory also implies that $\varepsilon_{ij} = s_j c_{ij}$. This proportionality property suggests a simple way for building in the appropriate symmetry restrictions into the stacked system in equation (5.19): Redefine the supply shift variables as $(s_j \times m_j)$ so that the respective coefficient measures only the elasticity of complementarity.[24]

The "trick" of interpreting the descriptive evidence by using insights from factor demand theory has one crucial advantage over the nested CES framework. The estimate of the average wage effect of immigration is inferred directly from observation and is not built in by functional form assumptions. It is certainly the case that the descriptive approach cannot estimate the structure of cross-effects that would allow us to fully predict the impact of any future supply shock, but it is also the case that currently available structural predictions of the average wage effect are not based on any "real world" observation.

6

Labor Market Adjustments
to Immigration

◆

As shown in chapter 4, the magnitude of the correlation between immigration and wages depends on the geographic scope of the labor market where the correlation is estimated. The correlation is negative and small when calculated across cities, and becomes stronger when calculated at the state or national levels. One important reason may be that the various economic agents—specifically, native workers and firms—respond to the economic opportunities (or challenges) created by the supply shock, and these responses may diffuse the impact of immigration into markets that were not directly penetrated by immigrants in the first place.

This chapter explores the determinants and consequences of two distinct types of adjustments. First, native workers may respond to immigration by moving (or *not* moving) to other cities or localities. For example, low-skill workers living in an area that received many low-skill immigrants may escape the worsened economic conditions by moving to locations that immigrants avoided. Similarly, firms may respond to the increased number of low-skill workers by changing their mix of capital investments. Firms can employ more of the now cheaper low-skill workforce, and sidestep making investments in machinery that automates the production process.

It is of interest to determine if these adjustments can "explain" the difference in the measured wage impact of immigration between local and national studies. Such an accounting, however, requires a theoretical framework that identifies which parameters are being estimated under which conditions, and necessarily imposes a lot of structure on the problem. Nevertheless, the available evidence (in the context of the internal migration response) suggests that the observed levels of adjustments are not sufficiently large to explain the bulk of the differences in the estimates from the local and national studies.

Native Internal Migration

The potential link between native internal migration and immigration has attracted wide attention in the U.S. literature. A number of early studies, led by Filer (1992) and Frey (1995a), reported evidence consistent with "demographic balkanization": natives respond to immigration by moving to areas that immigrants did not penetrate. Several subsequent studies, however, including those of Wright et al. (1997) and Card and DiNardo (2000), questioned the empirical relevance of the balkanization effect.[1] It should be noted, however, that the various studies differ greatly in their sample design, methodological approach, and construction of skill groups, making it difficult to determine why the evidence seems so contradictory.

The empirical analysis reported below differs in two crucial ways. First, the analysis is embedded in a theoretical framework that helps us understand precisely what is being measured by correlations between immigration and wages across geographic regions. The theory yields estimable equations that explicitly link the parameters measuring the wage impact of immigration at the national level, the spatial correlation between wages and immigration in local labor markets, and the native migration response. The model implies that the larger the native migration response, the greater will be the difference between the national-level estimates of the wage effect and the spatial correlation. The model also shows that it is possible to use the spatial correlations to retrieve the "true" national impact of immigration as long as one has information on the migration response of native workers.

Second, the approach emphasizes the commonsense notion that income-maximizing natives will respond to immigration only if their economic opportunities are affected. The immigration of one particular skill group will likely affect the earnings of that skill group more than the earnings of other groups, and one would expect a corresponding differential effect on native migration rates. Following the empirical framework presented in earlier chapters, the analysis focuses on how the geographic migration decisions of native workers in a narrowly defined skill group respond to a supply shock that directly targets that skill group. It is partly this more precise delineation of cause and effect that helps to identify the correlation that may have eluded earlier studies.

Before proceeding to a formal discussion, it is instructive to illustrate the relationship—at the state level—between the growth in the size of the native population and immigration for each of the 40 skill groups introduced in earlier chapters. Specifically, I use the 1960–2010 census cross-sections to calculate the size of the male native population in each skill-state-year cell. The scatter diagram in Figure 6.1 relates the within-group change in the log native population to the within-group change in the immigrant share (after removing decade effects).[2] The plot shows a negative correlation, suggesting that (for given skills) the native population grew fastest in those states that were least affected by immigration.

Borjas (2006) proposed to interpret these data through the lens of a simple and estimable model that jointly determines the regional wage structure and the internal migration decision of native workers.[3] Suppose that the inverse labor demand function for workers in skill group h (where h denotes a particular education-experience permutation) and residing in geographic area r at time t is:

$$\log w_{hrt} = \log X_{hr} + \eta \log L_{hrt}, \qquad (6.1)$$

where w_{hrt} is the wage of workers in cell (h, r, t); X_{hr} is a demand shifter; L_{hrt} gives the total number of workers (both immigrants, M_{hrt}, and natives, N_{hrt}); and η is the factor price elasticity (with $\eta < 0$). The total supply of native workers in a particular skill group in the national economy is fixed at $\bar{N}_h$. Note that the elasticity η gives the short-run wage impact resulting from a supply shift in a closed labor market, a labor market where neither capital nor preexisting workers respond to the shock.

To simplify, suppose that the national labor market is in equilibrium prior to the arrival of immigrants, so that the wage has been equalized across regions. At $t = -1$, therefore, $\log w_{hr,-1} = \log w_h^*$ for all regions. Beginning at time 0, however, the labor market receives an inflow of immigrants and this inflow continues in all subsequent periods. To fix ideas, suppose that immigrants do not migrate internally after arriving in the receiving country—they enter region r and remain there.[4] A convenient

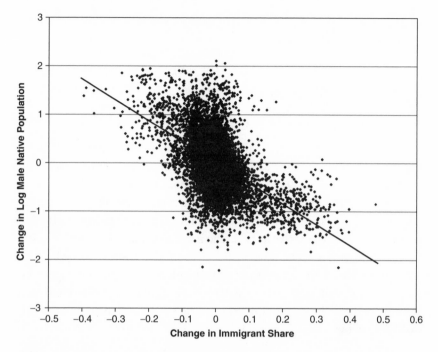

Figure 6.1. Native Population Growth and Immigration, by Skills and States, 1960–2010

Sources: U.S. Census PUMS, 1960–2010; see Appendix B for details.

Notes: The sample consists of persons aged 18–64, who are classified into five education groups and eight experience groups. Each point in the scatter represents a skill-state-year cell, stacked across the 1960–2010 censuses. The "change in log male native population" and "change in immigrant share" variables are residuals from regressions of the log male native population or the immigrant share on vectors of skill-state fixed effects and census year fixed effects. These residuals give the population or the immigrant share in the state-skill-year cell relative to the skill-state group's mean over the sample period, after removing decade effects.

(and obviously restrictive) assumption is that region r receives the same number of immigrants, M_{hr}, in each period. By time t, therefore, the number of immigrant with skills h residing in region r equals $(t+1)M_{hr}$. Similarly, let M_h denote the per-period number of immigrants arriving nationally in skill group h. The variable $(t+1)M_h$ then gives the cumulative number of persons with skills h who have migrated by time t.

The geographic sorting of natives responds to the labor market dislocations created by the supply shock, and region r experiences a net migration of ΔN_{hr1} natives in period 1, ΔN_{hr2} in period 2, and so on. The wage of skill group h in region r at time t is then given by:[5]

$$\log w_{hrt} = \log X_{hr} + \eta \log [N_{hr,-1} + (t+1)M_{hr} + \Delta N_{hr1} + \ldots + \Delta N_{hrt}], \quad (6.2)$$

which can be approximated by:

$$\log w_{hrt} \approx \log w_h^* + \eta [m_{hrt} + v_{hr1} + \ldots + v_{hrt}], \quad \text{for } t \geq 0, \quad (6.3)$$

where $m_{hrt} = (t+1)M_{hr} / N_{hr,-1}$, the total number of immigrants who have settled in region r by time t as a fraction of the initial native stock; and $v_{hrt} = \Delta N_{hrt} / N_{hr,-1}$, the net migration rate of natives at time t.

A key building block of the model is the assumption that the internal migration response of native workers is not instantaneous. In particular, immigrants begin to arrive at $t = 0$. The inverse demand function in equation (6.1) implies that the wage response to immigration is immediate, so that wages fall in the immigrant-penetrated regions. The immigration-induced relocation decisions of natives, however, are not observed until the next period. The supply function describing the native migration decision is given by:

$$v_{hr,t+1} = \sigma(\log w_{hrt} - \log \overline{w}_{ht}), \quad (6.4)$$

where σ is the supply elasticity ($\sigma > 0$), and $\log \overline{w}_{ht}$ is the equilibrium wage (for skill group h) that would be observed throughout the national economy once all migration responses to the immigrant influx that has occurred up to time t have been made.[6] Put differently, the migration decision is made by forward-looking native workers who compare the current wage in region r to the wage that region r will eventually attain. Therefore, native workers are not making migration decisions based on erroneous information (as in the typical cobweb model). Instead, the lags arise because it is costly to change locations immediately.[7]

Assuming that the stability restriction $0 < (1 + \eta\sigma) < 1$ holds, Appendix A shows that the net migration rate and wage of natives in cell (h, r, t) are given by:

$$v_{hrt} = -\eta\sigma m_{ht} + \eta\sigma m_{hrt}, \quad (6.5)$$

$$\log w_{hrt} = \log w_h^* - \eta^2\sigma m_{ht} + \eta(1 + \eta\sigma)m_{hrt}. \quad (6.6)$$

where $m_{ht} = (t+1)M_h / \overline{N}_h$, the relative size of the cumulative supply shock for skill group h as of time t in the national labor market.

The system of equations in (6.5) and (6.6) has several implications for empirical analysis. Note that the parameters can be estimated by stacking data on net migration rates, wages, and immigrant shares across skill groups, regions, and time. Some of the regressors in equations (6.5) and (6.6) can be absorbed by including appropriately defined vectors of fixed effects in the regressions. For example, $\log w_h^*$ is absorbed by a vector of skill fixed effects, whereas m_{ht} is absorbed by a vector of skill-time fixed effects.

The key regressor is the variable m_{hrt}, which gives the cumulative supply shift experienced by skill group h in region r as of time t *relative* to the (initial) number of natives in that skill group and region. The coefficient of this variable in the net migration rate equation measures the product of the factor price and supply elasticities, $\eta\sigma$, and is predicted to be negative. In other words, the greater the (cumulative) supply shock in a particular market, the fewer the relative number of natives who move there. Note that the impact of immigration on the net migration rate will be close to zero if the supply elasticity σ is close to zero.

The variable m_{hrt} is also the key regressor in the log wage equation, and its coefficient is precisely what I defined as the spatial correlation between immigration and wages in Chapter 4. The coefficient is *not* equal to the factor price elasticity η, but instead estimates the amalgam of parameters $\eta(1 + \eta\sigma)$. If the supply elasticity is sufficiently large, therefore, the spatial correlation in wages will be close to zero.

The two coefficients of the variable m_{hrt} in equations (6.5) and (6.6) provide an intuitive interpretation of how the spatial correlation—that is, the impact of immigration on wages that can be estimated by comparing local labor markets—relates to the factor price elasticity η that measures the short-run impact of immigration in a closed economy. Let γ_V be the coefficient of the variable m_{hrt} in the net migration rate equation ($\gamma_V = \eta\sigma$), and γ_W be the respective coefficient in the wage equation ($\gamma_W = \eta(1 + \eta\sigma)$). It is easy to show that:

$$\gamma_W = \eta(1 + \gamma_V). \tag{6.7}$$

The coefficient γ_V can be interpreted numerically as giving the net change in the number of natives in a particular labor market for every immigrant who settles there.[8] The spatial correlation γ_W is then given by the product of the "true" wage elasticity η and an adjustment factor measuring the number of natives who do *not* move per immigrant who enters the locality. To illustrate, suppose that the coefficient γ_V is −0.5, indicating that 5 fewer natives choose to reside in the local labor market for every 10 immigrants entering that market. Equation (6.7) then implies that the spatial correlation will be half the size of the true factor price elasticity.[9]

The model also predicts that the geographic definition of a labor market will influence the magnitude of the measured spatial correlations. In both regressions, the coefficient of the supply shock variable depends on the value of the elasticity σ. It seems sensible to presume that the supply elasticity is larger when migration is less costly, suggesting that σ is larger when the labor market is geographically small. The definitions of γ_V and γ_W then imply that the correlation between the net migration rate and immigration will be more negative when the model is estimated using geographically *smaller* labor markets, and that the correlation between the wage and immigration will be more negative for geographically *larger* labor markets. This mirror-image prediction is an interesting and testable implication of the model.

To estimate the various parameters, I use the data for the 40 skill groups (five education groups and eight experience groups) introduced in earlier chapters. The census data also sometimes report a person's state and metropolitan area of residence 5 years prior to the survey.[10] These data, combined with the information on geographic location at the time of the census, can be used to compute in-, out-, and net-migration rates for native persons in the various skill-region groups. For instance, consider the data available at the state level in a particular census. A native is an out-migrant from the "original" state of residence (that is, the state of residence 5 years prior to the survey) if he lives in a different state by the time of the census. A native is an in-migrant into the current state of residence if he lived in a different state 5 years prior to the census. I define the in-migration and out-migration rates by dividing the total number of in-migrants or out-migrants in a particular skill-state-year cell by the relevant population in the baseline state. The net migration rate is then defined as the difference between the in-migration and the out-migration rate. To minimize the problems associated with the presence of "tied movers" and "tied stayers" (Mincer 1978), the calculation of the net migration rate uses only the sample of men in each of the skill-region groups.[11]

Consider the following empirical counterparts to equations (6.5) and (6.6):

$$v_{hrt} = \phi_H + \phi_R + \phi_T + \phi_{HT} + \phi_{RT} + \phi_{HR} + \theta_V p_{hrt} + \varepsilon, \qquad (6.8)$$

$$\log w_{hrt} = \phi_H + \phi_R + \phi_T + \phi_{HT} + \phi_{RT} + \phi_{HR} + \theta_W p_{hrt} + \varepsilon', \qquad (6.9)$$

where ϕ_H is a vector of skill fixed effects indicating all possible education-experience combinations; ϕ_R is a vector of region fixed effects; ϕ_T is a vector of period fixed effects indicating the census year of the observation.; and p_{hrt} gives the immigrant share. The interacted fixed effects ϕ_{HT} and ϕ_{RT} control for potential changes in the impact of skills and region characteristics over the sample period, and the inclusion of the interactions ϕ_{HR} implies that the coefficients θ_V and θ_W are identified from variation that occurs within skill-region cells.

Table 6.1 summarizes the evidence when the model defines the labor market both at the state and metropolitan area levels. The coefficient of the immigrant share variable in the regression using the state-level net migration rate as the dependent variable is −0.323 (0.099). The regression model, therefore, confirms that there is a numerically sizable and statistically significant negative relation between immigration and native net migration. The coefficient is easier to interpret by calculating the derivative γ_V, which gives the change in the size of the native population when the stock of immigrant workers increases by one. It is easy to show that the derivative of interest is:

$$\gamma_V = \frac{\partial N}{\partial M} = \theta_V (1-p)^2. \tag{6.10}$$

As in earlier chapters, I calculate the derivative in (6.10) at the marginal value of the immigrant supply increase by multiplying the regression coefficient θ_V by 0.7. The regression then implies that 2.3 fewer native workers choose to live in a particular state for every 10 additional immigrants entering that state.[12] In terms of the underlying theory, this derivative equals the product of elasticities $\eta\sigma$.

Table 6.1 also reports that the coefficient θ_V is −0.664 (0.223) when the same regression model is estimated at the metropolitan-area level. This coefficient implies that around 5 fewer native workers choose to reside in a particular metropolitan area for every 10 additional immigrants who enter that locality. As predicted by the theory, the negative impact of immigration on the net migration rate of natives gets numerically larger the smaller the geographic boundaries of the labor market (and the difference is marginally significant).[13] The evidence reported in the table also suggests that the effect of immigration on net migration rates arises both because immigration induces fewer natives to move into the immigrant-penetrated labor markets, and because immigration induces more natives to move out of those markets.

Table 6.1 Immigration and the internal migration of native men

Dependent variable	Geographic definition of regional labor market	
	States	Metropolitan areas
1. Net migration rate of natives	−0.323	−0.664
	(0.099)	(0.223)
2. In-migration rate of natives	−0.159	−0.385
	(0.082)	(0.198)
3. Out-migration rate of natives	0.164	0.278
	(0.049)	(0.070)
4. Log weekly wage of natives	−0.186	−0.058
	(0.029)	(0.018)

Sources: U.S. Census PUMS, 1970–2010; see Appendix B for details. The coefficients reported in row 4 are drawn from Table 4.2, row 1.

Notes: The sample consists of persons aged 18–64, who are classified into five education groups and eight experience groups. The unit of observation is a skill-region-year cell, where a skill group represents an education-experience pairing and the definition of the region varies across the columns. Standard errors are reported in parentheses, and are clustered at the skill-region level. The in- and out-migration rates for each cell are calculated by comparing a person's place of residence at the time of the census with his place of residence 5 years prior, using the entire male population of the cell (including workers and nonworkers). The net migration rate is the difference between these two statistics. The independent variable is the immigrant share for the relevant cell, and is given by the fraction of work hours supplied by all foreign-born workers in that cell (including men and women). All regressions include skill-year, region-year, and skill-region fixed effects. The state-level migration rate regressions use data from the 1970–2000 censuses and have 8,157 observations. The MSA-level migration rate regressions use data from the 1990–2000 censuses and have 21,239 observations.

The last row of Table 6.1 reports the estimates of θ_W. As first documented in Table 4.2, the coefficient of the immigrant share variable in the wage regression is more negative at the state level than at the metropolitan area level. The evidence, therefore, is consistent with the theoretical prediction of a mirror image effect: the correlation between net migration rates and immigration should be more negative the smaller the geographic area, while the correlation between wages and immigration should be more negative the larger the geographic area.

A crucial question remains: Can native internal migration decisions reconcile the very different wage elasticities estimated in the national and local labor market studies? Equation (6.7) summarizes the theoretical implication that the national wage effect of migration and the spatial correlation are linked through a parameter that measures the native migration response. Table 6.2 summarizes the key implications of this synthesis. The first row of the table reports that the wage elasticity at the national level is −0.37 (or the coefficient of −0.529 in Table 4.5 times 0.7). Suppose that the national labor market approximates the concept of a closed economy, so that this elasticity estimates the factor price elasticity η in the model. Row 2 summarizes the estimated effects of immigration on the net migration rate of natives. Specifically, this row reports the value of the derivative $\gamma_V = \partial N / \partial M$. Similarly, row 3 reports the estimated local wage effects of immigration (or θ_W again multiplied by 0.7). These elasticities give the value of γ_W.

Using the multiplicative property derived in equation (6.7), I can now determine whether it is possible to retrieve the "true" value of the factor price elasticity from the estimated parameters. The answer is a definite no. The last row of the table uses the formula to predict the factor price elasticity η using only the information provided by the spatial correlation and the native migration response. At the state level, the spatial correlation is "blown up" to −0.17 after correcting for the native migration response, while at the MSA level, the predicted η is still only −0.08.[14] In other words,

Table 6.2 Theory-based synthesis of wage and migration effects

	State	Metropolitan area
1. Estimate of factor price elasticity in national labor market (η)	−0.370	−0.370
2. Estimate of migration effect (γ_v)	−0.226	−0.465
3. Wage elasticity actually estimated at local level (γ_w)	−0.130	−0.041
4. Predicted factor price elasticity ($\hat{\eta}$)	−0.168	−0.077

Source: Regression coefficients are estimated in the male sample and reported in Table 4.5, row 1; and Table 6.1, rows 1 and 4.

Notes: The synthesis is based on the interpretation of the regression coefficients implied by equation (6.7). The regression coefficients in rows 1–3 have been multiplied by 0.7 to convert them into elasticities.

the native migration response, though measurable and statistically significant, is not sufficiently large to explain a major part of the difference between the measured wage impact of immigration at the national and local labor market levels. It is important to emphasize, however, that this interpretation of the evidence relies heavily on the use of a very restrictive (and functional-form dependent) theoretical framework, and it is unclear if the use of a more general approach would lead to a different inference.

Firm Responses

Changes in the geographic settlement of native workers will not be the only behavioral response to immigration. Firms will also respond to the supply shock. As shown in Chapter 3, immigration increases the relative returns to capital, encouraging firms to expand their use of capital and machinery. Similarly, firms could themselves engage in internal migration: firms that make intensive use of low-skill workers, for example, could perhaps increase their profits by resettling in areas most penetrated by low-skill immigrants. Finally, the firm can adjust the type of capital it employs to better reflect the new opportunities created by the presence of foreign-born workers in specific skill groups.

The frequent assumption of constant returns to scale in factor demand models of immigration is responsible for the theoretical prediction that firms will employ more capital until the value of the aggregate capital/labor ratio returns to its pre-immigration equilibrium.[15] Because of measurement difficulties, however, there has not been any systematic testing of this theoretical insight. Such evidence would obviously allow us to evaluate whether the impact of immigration on the average wage level disappears after a "short" period, or if it takes decades for the labor market to digest the immigration-induced supply shock. Similarly, even though it is obvious that capital has an incentive to flow to areas with lower labor costs, there has not yet been a study of whether immigration-induced changes in the regional wage structure encouraged some firms to resettle in different regions.

Instead, the empirical analysis of the firm's response to immigration has focused on easier-to-observe adjustments. One particularly interesting approach is inspired by the well-known fact that automation machinery and low-skill workers are highly substitutable. This substitutability, in fact, is related to the conjecture that the information revolution stimulated skill-biased technical change, where the new technology had a relative beneficial effect on the marginal product of high-skill workers. If this conjecture

were true, the entry of large numbers of low-skill immigrants should induce a shift in the *type* of capital used by the firm. Specifically, an increase in the supply of low-skill workers reduces the firm's incentives to
invest in machinery that performs automated tasks. After all, there would
now be a vast supply of cheap low-skill workers who can perform those
same tasks.

It is instructive to examine this insight in the context of the closed economy model examined in Lewis (2011).[16] The workforce consists of low-skill
workers (L_U) and high-skill workers (L_S). For concreteness, the low-skill
workforce consists of high school dropouts, while the high-skill workforce
consists of everyone else. The aggregate production function in a particular labor market (that is, a specific region) is given by:

$$Q = (K + L_U)^\alpha L_S^{1-\alpha}. \tag{6.11}$$

Equation (6.11) builds in the fact that low-skill workers and machines are
highly substitutable—in fact, they are perfect substitutes. The production
function also builds in the fact that high-skill workers and machines are
complements.

To further simplify, ignore the migration adjustments that may take
place as a result of a supply shock, both in terms of the internal migration
of native workers moving to markets were wages are higher and the internal migration of firms seeking markets where wages are lower. The input
market for all factors is assumed to be competitive, so that each wage
equals the respective value of marginal product. In the short run, the
number of machines in the market is fixed at $\bar{K}$; in the long run, the rate
of return to machines r is fixed. It is easy to show that the long-run adjustments to the firm's capital stock induced by the supply shock are given by:

$$d\log K = \frac{(\gamma_K - 1)}{\gamma_K} d\log L_U + \frac{1}{\gamma_K} d\log L_S, \tag{6.12}$$

where $\gamma_K = K/(K + L_U)$.

Equation (6.12) implies that an immigration-induced increase in the
number of high school dropouts leads to a *decline* in the number of machines, encouraging the firm to use the abundant low-skill workers and
escape the investments required for mechanization and automation. In
one sense, the immigration of low-skill workers retards the process of
technological growth as firms choose *not* to become automated. In contrast, equation (6.12) shows that the immigration of high-skill workers increases the firm's incentives to use more of the automation machinery.

Not surprisingly, the technological consequences of low-skill immigration may alter the wage structure. If the capital stock were fixed, it follows that:

$$\left.\frac{\partial \log w_U}{\partial \log L_U}\right|_{dK=0} < 0, \quad \left.\frac{\partial \log w_S}{\partial \log L_U}\right|_{dK=0} > 0. \tag{6.13}$$

Even though the wage of high school dropouts falls, the wage of high-skill workers rises. In the long run, however, all wage effects disappear:

$$\left.\frac{\partial \log w_U}{\partial \log L_U}\right|_{dr=0} = \left.\frac{\partial \log w_S}{\partial \log L_U}\right|_{dr=0} = 0. \tag{6.14}$$

Full capital adjustment completely attenuates the wage impact of immigration. In the current context, "capital adjustment" can occur without factor flows across geographic labor markets. The firm's endogenous adjustment in production technologies to the supply shock can help to neutralize the wage impact. Put differently, the wage effect weakens as the firm disinvests in automation machinery.

This family of factor demand models has an obvious, but important, implication about the link between the observed impact of immigration on the wage structure and the firm's choice of production technique. If we observe a change in the firm's production technique, this provides prima facie evidence that there must have been a wage impact in the short run. In the absence of any wage impact, the firm would have no incentive to incur the costs required to change its technology. It is certainly the case, of course, that once the firm fully adjusts its technique, the wage effect vanishes. As with the case of native internal migration, however, it may be that adjustments in production techniques are not instantaneous and are not complete, so that the observed spatial correlation will generally understate the short-run wage impact.

Few empirical studies examine the type of adjustment in the capital stock suggested by equation (6.12). Nevertheless, the available evidence suggests that such adjustments do, in fact, take place. Much of the evidence is anecdotal, but the anecdotal evidence has important lessons for the wave of regression-based studies that are now beginning to appear. For the most part, the anecdotal evidence describes capital adjustments in the agricultural sector, and it illustrates the difficulty of measuring the rate of adjustment resulting from immigration-induced supply shocks even within a single industry. Calvin and Martin's (2010) survey of the trends in mechanization in agriculture is instructive:

> Growers can mechanize the harvest if there is an economical alternative to hand labor. Some growers of raisin grapes, processing oranges, and baby lettuce have mechanized their harvests. Developing a viable mechanized harvest system usually depends on breakthroughs in three areas: machinery, varieties, and cultural practices. Results from all three lines of research may not emerge at the same time. For example, the DOV [dried-on-the-vine] harvest system for raisin grapes was not successful until an earlier-maturing grape variety was developed . . . Most large or extended-season producers of baby lettuce already use mechanical harvesters, but other lettuces do not yet have economical mechanical harvesters. The apple, fresh-market orange, strawberry, and asparagus industries do not yet have mechanical harvesters either. (p. 42)

A key insight is that the technology required for mechanizing agricultural production varies dramatically from crop to crop: different technologies are required to mechanize the production of even different types of lettuce. There is little reason to believe that this heterogeneity is specific to agriculture. The difficulties associated with measuring the rate of capital adjustment across seemingly homogeneous product lines even within a narrowly defined industry raises a red flag for interpreting findings from regression-based studies that compare the behavior of many different types of firms. More likely than not, the sample of firms in surveys that would be used in regression-based studies—even if they were all in the same industry—produce different products that have very different technological requirements if they wish to adopt automation techniques.

Lewis (2011) exemplifies the newer wave of regression-based studies, using data drawn from the 1988 and 1993 Surveys of Manufacturing Technology.[17] These surveys, conducted in a random sample of firms in the manufacturing industry, collected information on a firm's planned and actual use of various types of mechanization technologies, such as "pick-and-place robots" and "automated storage and retrieval systems." The empirical analysis essentially compares the investment decisions of firms located in regional markets that received large numbers of low-skill immigrants with those of firms in markets that received fewer immigrants.

Table 6.3 summarizes the evidence linking a firm's adoption of automation technologies to changes in the (relative) number of low-skill workers in the metropolitan area. The dependent variable in the regression reported in the top row of the table is the number of automation technologies a particular firm *actually* adopted between 1988 and 1993. The key independent variable is the change in the fraction of high school dropouts in the low-skill workforce in the metropolitan area where the firm is located. An increase in the number of high school dropouts in the region would presumably lower the local wage of high school dropouts, and the firm would have fewer incentives to invest in automation technologies. Over time, the *non*-adoption of these technologies in areas that received low-skill immigrants raises the demand for high school dropouts in that area relative to other localities, pushing up the local wage and eventually helping to equate the wage of high school dropouts across metropolitan areas.

The empirical analysis indeed documents a negative relation between the number of automation technologies adopted by firms and the concurrent change in the relative number of high school dropouts in the metropolitan area. Moreover, the magnitude of the coefficient implies that the capital adjustment is numerically important. Consider, for instance, the OLS regression coefficient of −3.0. In 1988 the mean number of automation technologies used by firms in the sample was 6.0, and the mean change in the fraction of dropouts to low-skill workers over the period was 0.3. The

Table 6.3 The impact of low-skill immigration on the number of automation technologies

Dependent variable	OLS	IV
1. Number of automation technologies firm added between 1988 and 1993	−3.02 (1.67)	−11.44 (4.42)
2. Number of automation technologies firm planned to add	1.71 (1.03)	4.79 (2.40)

Source: Lewis (2011, p. 1052).

Notes: Standard errors are reported in parentheses and are clustered at the metropolitan area level. The independent variable is the change in the ratio of the number of workers who are high school dropouts to the number of workers who are high school equivalents in the MSA. The instrument used in the IV regressions approximates a lagged measure of the number of foreign-born high school dropouts in the locality. All regressions include a vector of industry fixed effects.

supply shift in the number of high school dropouts, therefore, accounts for a decline of around 20 percent in the number of automation technologies used. Because the sorting of high school dropouts across metropolitan areas is likely to be endogenous, Lewis (2011) also uses an IV specification of the regression model, with the instrument, as usual, roughly based on the lagged number of foreign-born high school dropouts in the metropolitan area. The IV specification also shows a negative relation between immigration and the adoption of labor-saving production techniques.

The second row of the table reports the regression coefficient when the dependent variable is the number of automation technologies the firm *planned* to adopt between 1988 and 1993, rather than the actual number adopted. The planned adoption is positively correlated with the subsequent change in the number of high school dropouts. Put differently, the entry of low-skill immigrants clearly altered the firm's plans in a way consistent with factor demand theory as long as low-skill workers and automation technologies are highly substitutable.

It is important to emphasize, however, that the anecdotal evidence from the agricultural industry raises an important caveat for interpreting the results in Table 6.3. To adjust for firm heterogeneity, Lewis includes a vector of industry-specific fixed effects in the regression (defined at the four-digit SIC industry level). These fixed effects, however, cannot properly control for the fact that firms, even at the four-digit SIC level, produce very different product lines. For example, one of the four-digit codes (code 0100) is "Agricultural Production, Crops." As the Calvin and Martin (2010) study shows, not all crops are equal, with farmers having an easier time mechanizing some crops, but a much harder time mechanizing others. Any correlation between these intra-industry variations in product lines and the employment of immigrants inevitably contaminates the estimated adjustment.

Finally, it is of interest to examine in more detail the implications of this type of firm adjustment for the spatial correlations between immigration and wages typically reported in the literature. Equations (6.13) and (6.14) summarize the predictions of the model for the wage structure. In the short run, low-skill immigration lowers the wage of high school dropouts and raises the wage of more skilled workers. In the long run, *all* wages return to their pre-immigration equilibrium. If the shift from the "short run" to the "long run" is not instantaneous, however, the spatial correlation in wages does not estimate any structural parameter of interest. This point can be easily illustrated by using an approach analogous to the one used earlier to model the internal migration of native workers. In particular, suppose that the inverse labor demand function for high school dropouts is:

$$\log w_{r0} = \log X + \eta m_r, \qquad (6.15)$$

where w_{r0} gives the wage of high school dropouts in region r at time 0; log X represents the pre-immigration equilibrium wage for this skill group; and m_r gives the relative number of immigrants in the low-skill workforce that entered the local labor market at time 0. Assume that the immigrant influx continues indefinitely. As long as machinery and low-skill workers are substitutable, firms will respond by changing the production techniques, affecting the marginal product of workers *and* the intercept of the inverse demand function in (6.15).[18] In the presence of adjustment costs, the firm's response in its capital adjustment at time t can be summarized by the lagged supply function:[19]

$$\Delta \log X_{rt} = \rho(\log \overline{w}_{t-1} - \log w_{r,t-1}), \qquad (6.16)$$

where $\Delta \log X_{rt}$ gives the shift in the intercept of the inverse demand function for firms in region r that reflects the change in the capital stock between times $t-1$ and t; $\log \overline{w}_{t-1}$ is the equilibrium wage the market will eventually attain after digesting the immigrant influx; and ρ is the supply elasticity of capital, with $\rho > 0$. Equation (6.16) implies that if a particular labor market gets hit by a relatively large supply shock (so that $\log \overline{w}_{t-1} > \log w_{r,t-1}$), local firms respond by disinvesting in capital and raising the marginal product of low-skill labor in the process. Assuming that the stability restriction $0 < (1-\rho) < 1$ holds, Appendix A shows that the log wage of low-skill workers in region r at time t can be written as:

$$\log w_{rt} = \log X^* + \eta(1-\rho)m_{rt}, \qquad (6.17)$$

where $m_{rt} = (t+1)m_r$, or the fraction of the total number of foreign-born high school dropouts who have entered region r as of time t relative to the native baseline.

The regression of the log wage in the locality on the local immigrant share, therefore, does not estimate the factor price elasticity η. Instead, it again estimates a mix of parameters involving both the factor price elasticity and a supply elasticity. The true short-run wage impact could be retrieved if the value of ρ were known. Unfortunately, there do not exist any credible measures of the immigration-induced rate of adjustment in production techniques or in the capital stock at the firm level.

In fact, most adjustments are not well documented, even though it is almost certainly the case that local labor markets adjust to supply shocks and that this adjustment helps the local labor markets converge to a new equilibrium. Moreover, the adjustments that economists can observe (or even think of) are probably a small subset of the adjustments available to the affected agents, who have the most incentive to look for ways in which they can take advantage of the changed opportunities. Because adjustments are costly, *any* response on the part of firms and workers represents evidence that immigration had at least a short-run impact on the wage structure. Two important details are yet to be filled out: Exactly how do markets adjust, and how long does it take for the local labor markets to return to their pre-immigration equilibrium (or converge to a new equilibrium)?[20]

Even though the process of convergence across local labor markets in response to supply shocks has not been studied carefully, there exists a parallel literature that documents the rate of adjustment to *demand* shocks. The classic study by Blanchard and Katz (1992, p. 40) examined wage convergence across states in the United States, and concluded that a demand shock that reduced employment by 1 percent in a particular state had measurable effects on the manufacturing wage in that state even 10 to 20 years after the shock.[21] Moreover, almost all of the cross-state wage convergence resulted from the internal migration of workers. However, several recent studies document that there was a halt in this type of wage convergence after 1990, and there is now growing evidence of a "Great Divergence," where regions that are hit by positive or negative demand shocks may remain wealthier or poorer for decades (Moretti 2012; Ganong and Shoag 2012). Of course, there may be (unknown) asymmetries in the way that firms and workers respond to supply and demand shocks, so the Blanchard-Katz and related evidence on regional wage convergence may have little relevance in the immigration context.[22]

Nevertheless, the central lesson of the discussion is clear. If firms and/or workers adjusted instantaneously to supply shocks, we should never observe a negative correlation between wages and immigration across local labor markets. The fact that such a correlation is, in fact, often observed implies that immigration does indeed alter economic opportunities. As a result, the numerical magnitude of the correlation between immigration and wages across local labor markets is an amalgam of two core parameters: the factor price elasticity and the rate of adjustment, both among workers and firms. It is impossible to isolate the wage effect unless we have a fuller understanding of exactly how and how fast this convergence occurs.

7

The Economic Benefits
from Immigration

———————————————◆———————————————

THIS CHAPTER USES a simple theoretical framework to describe how and why natives benefit from immigration and to provide a back-of-the-envelope calculation of these gains. A central lesson of economic theory is that the net gains from immigration depend directly on its distributional impact: the greater the loss in wages suffered by native workers, the greater the net gains to the receiving country.

The discussion also reveals an important insight: the canonical model of a competitive labor market cannot be manipulated into generating numerically sizable estimates of the net benefits for a country like the United States. At most, an increase in labor supply of even 15 percent would increase native income by only 0.2 or 0.3 percent of GDP. At the same time, however, there seems to be a potential for a huge increase in world GDP if countries stopped being countries and workers were free to move to whichever part of the world offered them higher wages—with the (crucial) caveat that whatever it is that makes workers much more productive in the developed countries remains intact after the influx of hundreds of millions, if not billions, of immigrants.

The Immigration Surplus with Homogeneous Labor

It is instructive to again start the discussion with the assumption of homogeneous labor.[1] Suppose the production technology for the good produced in the receiving country can be summarized by a linear homogeneous aggregate production function with two inputs, capital (K) and labor (L), so that output $Q=f(K, L)$. The workforce contains N native and M immigrant workers, and all workers are perfect substitutes in production ($L=N+M$). Natives own the entire capital stock in the host country and, initially, the supply of capital is perfectly inelastic. Finally, the supplies of both natives and immigrants are also perfectly inelastic.[2]

Each factor price equals the respective value of marginal product in a competitive labor market. The rental rate of capital in the pre-immigration equilibrium is $r_0=f_K(K, N)$ and the price of labor is $w_0=f_L(K, N)$, where the price of the output is the numeraire. The aggregate production function exhibits constant returns, so that the entire output is distributed to the owners of capital and to workers. In the pre-immigration regime, the national income accruing to natives, Q_N, is then given by:

$$Q_N=r_0 K+w_0 N. \tag{7.1}$$

Figure 7.1 illustrates this initial equilibrium. Because the supply of capital is fixed, the area under the marginal product of labor curve (f_L) gives the economy's total output. The national income accruing to natives Q_N is given by the trapezoid ABN0. The entry of M immigrants shifts the supply curve and lowers the wage to w_1. The area in the trapezoid ACL0 gives national income in the post-immigration economy. Part of the increase in national income is distributed directly to immigrants (who get $w_1 M$ in labor earnings). The area in the triangle BCD gives the increase in national income that accrues to natives, or the *immigration surplus*.

The area of BCD is given by $\frac{1}{2}\times(w_0-w_1)\times M$. As a fraction of national income, the immigration surplus then equals:[3]

$$\left.\frac{\Delta Q_N}{Q}\right|_{dK=0}=-\frac{1}{2}s_L \varepsilon_{LL} p^2, \tag{7.2}$$

where s_L is labor's share of national income ($s_L=wL/Q$); ε_{LL} is the elasticity of factor price ($\varepsilon_{LL}=d \log w/d \log L$); and p is the immigrant share ($p=M/L$).

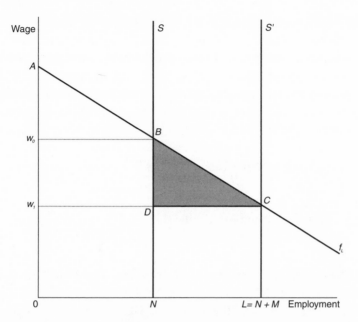

Figure 7.1. The Immigration Surplus, Assuming Homogeneous Labor and Fixed Capital

Equation (7.2) gives a very simple formula for conducting a "back-of-the-envelope" calculation of the net gains from immigration to a receiving country. In the United States, the share of labor income is about 70 percent, and the fraction of immigrants in the workforce is around 15 percent. If the aggregate production function were Cobb-Douglas, we know that the elasticity ε_{LL} is -0.3. The U.S. immigration surplus, therefore, is on the order of 0.24 percent of GDP.

This result implies that in 2013 the entire stock of foreign-born persons in the United States added around $35 billion to the fruits accruing to natives in a $15 trillion economy. Needless to say, this estimate depends on the many assumptions that underlie the model. Nevertheless, as Borjas (1995b) first noted, it says something that is useful and surprising: It is mathematically impossible to manipulate the canonical model of the competitive labor market so as to yield a huge net gain from immigration to the United States, even after immigration has increased labor supply by 15 percent.

Equation (7.2) shows that the immigration surplus is proportional to ε_{LL}. The net gains from immigration to the host country, therefore, are intimately linked to the wage losses suffered by workers. Ironically, the receiving country gains more the greater the drop in the wage of workers who compete with immigrant labor.[4] Of course, the losses suffered by native workers do not disappear into thin air. Immigration redistributes income from labor to capital. In terms of Figure 7.1, native workers lose the area in the rectangle $w_0 BD w_1$, and this quantity plus the immigration surplus accrues to capitalists. Expressed as fractions of national income, the net changes in the incomes of native workers and capitalists are approximately given by:

$$\left.\frac{\text{Change in Native Labor Earnings}}{Q}\right|_{dK=0} = s_L \, \varepsilon_{LL} \, p(1-p), \qquad (7.3)$$

$$\left.\frac{\text{Change in Income of Capitalists}}{Q}\right|_{dK=0} = -s_L \, \varepsilon_{LL} \, p\left(1-\frac{p}{2}\right). \qquad (7.4)$$

Consider again the U.S. context. If the wage elasticity is −0.3, native-born workers lose about 2.7 percent of GDP, while native-owned capital gains about 2.9 percent of GDP. The $15 trillion GDP implies that workers lose on aggregate $402 billion while capitalists gain $437 billion. The small immigration surplus of $35 billion masks a sizable redistribution from workers to the users of immigrant labor.[5]

The derivation of the immigration surplus in equation (7.2) assumed that the host country's capital stock is fixed. However, the rise in the return to capital will encourage capital inflows until the rental rate is again equalized across markets. For expositional convenience, assume that the additional capital stock either originates abroad and is owned by foreigners, or is owned by the immigrants themselves. As we saw in Chapter 3, the assumption of a linear homogeneous production function implies that the immigration-induced capital expansion reestablishes the pre-immigration capital/labor ratio in the host country. In the end, immigration does not alter the price of labor or the returns to capital, and natives neither gain nor lose from immigration. In the long run, therefore, the immigration surplus must be zero.

There is one conceptual point regarding the calculation of the immigration surplus that, although obvious, is worth emphasizing. Natives benefit and lose from immigration in many ways. Immigrants may increase the demand for goods and services; they may make some workers more productive and others less productive; immigrant entrepreneurs may open up firms and increase the demand for labor; and so on. To actually compute the net economic gains from immigration, we would need to list, observe, and measure all the possible channels through which immigration transforms the host economy and compare the resulting national income to the counterfactual income that would have been observed had immigrants never entered the country.

Obviously, this sort of accounting is a very difficult, if not impossible, task. This difficulty explains why "estimates" of the economic benefits from immigration are not estimates in the sense that the researcher used actual data and computed the various gains and losses, but rather they are the result of a calibration exercise of some economic model. As an example, the widely used calculation of economic benefits in the United States that relies on equation (7.2) uses very little immigration-related *evidence* other than the fact that immigration increased labor supply by around 15 percent. The only number in the formula that could be drawn from an empirical study of the economic impact of immigration is the value of the elasticity ε_{LL}. However, as we have seen, the -0.3 value typically used for this elasticity is built in by the assumption that the aggregate production function has a Cobb-Douglas functional form and is not the implication of an empirical analysis that measures the impact of immigration on the average wage level. Put bluntly, there is actually very little data underneath the so-called estimates of the economic benefits from immigration.[6]

Heterogeneous Labor

Suppose there are two types of workers in the host country's labor market, skilled (L_S) and unskilled (L_U). It is analytically convenient to define each of these quantities in terms of the fraction of the native and foreign-born workforce that belongs to each skill group. The linear homogeneous aggregate production function can then be written as:

$$Q = f(K, L_S, L_U) = f[K, bN + \beta M, (1-b)N + (1-\beta)M], \qquad (7.5)$$

where b and β denote the fraction of skilled workers among natives and immigrants, respectively. The production function is continuous and twice differentiable, with $f_i > 0$ and $f_{ii} < 0$ ($i = K, L_S, L_U$). The price of each factor of production, r for capital and w_i ($i = S, U$) for labor, is determined by the respective marginal productivity condition.

As we have seen repeatedly, the economic impact of immigration depends crucially on what happens to the capital stock when immigrants enter the country. Consider initially the case where the supply of capital is perfectly elastic. We can determine the impact of immigration on the wages of skilled and unskilled workers by differentiating the respective marginal productivity conditions, and imposing the long-run capital adjustment implied by $dr=0$. It can be shown that the wage effects of immigration are given by:

$$\frac{\partial \log w_S}{\partial \log M}\bigg|_{dr=0} = \frac{s_S}{c_{KK}}\left[c_{SS}c_{KK}-c_{SK}^2\right]\frac{(\beta-b)}{\pi_S\,\pi_U}(1-p)p, \tag{7.6}$$

$$\frac{\partial \log w_U}{\partial \log M}\bigg|_{dr=0} = \frac{-s_U}{c_{KK}}\left[c_{UU}c_{KK}-c_{UK}^2\right]\frac{(\beta-b)}{\pi_S\,\pi_U}(1-p)p, \tag{7.7}$$

where s_i is the share of income accruing to factor i; π_S and π_U give the shares of the workforce that are skilled and unskilled, respectively; and $p=M/(M+N)$, the immigrant share. The algebra underlying the derivation of equations (7.6) and (7.7) and the calculation of the immigration surplus in this framework is tedious, and is relegated to Appendix A.

We can always write a linear homogeneous production function with inputs (X_1, X_2, X_3) as $Q=X_3\,g(X_1/X_3, X_2/X_3)$. Suppose that the function g is strictly concave, so that the isoquants between any pair of inputs have the conventional convex shape. The concavity assumption also implies that $c_{11}c_{22}-c_{12}^2>0$. Equations (7.6) and (7.7) then indicate that the impact of immigration on the wage structure depends entirely on how the skill distribution of immigrants compares to that of natives. If immigration is balanced (in the sense that natives and immigrants have the same skill distribution), then $\beta=b$ and immigration has no impact on the wage structure of the host country. If immigrants are relatively unskilled ($\beta<b$), the unskilled wage declines and the skilled wage rises. If immigrants are relatively skilled ($\beta>b$), the skilled wage declines and the unskilled wage rises.

The immigration surplus in this model is defined by:

$$\Delta Q_N\big|_{dr=0} = \left(bN\frac{\partial w_S}{\partial M}+(1-b)N\frac{\partial w_U}{\partial M}\right)M. \tag{7.8}$$

By substituting the wage effects in equations (7.6) and (7.7), it follows that the immigration surplus as a fraction of national income can be written as:

$$\frac{\Delta Q_N}{Q}\bigg|_{dr=0} = \frac{-s_S^2}{2c_{KK}}\left[c_{SS}c_{KK}-c_{SK}^2\right]\frac{(\beta-b)^2}{\pi_S^2\,\pi_U^2}(1-p)^2\,p^2\geq 0. \tag{7.9}$$

An important implication of equation (7.9) is that the immigration surplus is zero when immigration is balanced and positive when it is not (and $\beta \neq b$). In other words, the receiving country gains from immigration in the long run only if the skill composition of immigrants differs from that of natives.

Equation (7.9) can be used to think about how a receiving country should set the parameters of immigration policy *if* the goal of the policy were to maximize the immigration surplus. Let β^* be the value of β that maximizes the surplus. By partially differentiating equation (7.9) with respect to β, we obtain:[7]

$$
\begin{aligned}
&\beta^* = 1, &&\text{if } b < 0.5, \\
&\beta^* = 0 \ \text{ or } \ \beta^* = 1, &&\text{if } b = 0.5, \\
&\beta^* = 0, &&\text{if } b > 0.5.
\end{aligned}
\tag{7.10}
$$

Suppose that $b = 0.5$. There is no immigration surplus if half of the immigrant flow is also composed of skilled workers. The immigration surplus is maximized when the immigrant flow is either exclusively skilled or exclusively unskilled. Either policy choice generates a foreign-born workforce that is most different from the native workforce.

The incentives for moving to a particular tail of the skill distribution arise when the native workforce is relatively skilled or unskilled. Suppose the native workforce is relatively unskilled ($b < 0.5$). Admitting skilled immigrants, who most complement native workers, would then maximize the immigration surplus. If the native workforce is relatively skilled, the host country should admit unskilled immigrants to maximize the gains. Note that it is in the host country's long run interests to *always* move to an extreme value of β when setting the policy parameter. In the long run, there is no economic point to welcoming an immigrant influx with heterogeneous skills.

Heterogeneous Labor and Inelastic Capital

The results regarding the optimal skill mix of the immigrant influx summarized in (7.10) are sensitive to the assumption that the supply curve of capital is perfectly elastic. Suppose instead that the capital stock is perfectly inelastic with $K = \bar{K}$, and is owned by natives. The short-run immigration surplus is then defined by:

$$\Delta Q_N \big|_{dK=0} = \left(\bar{K} \frac{\partial r}{\partial M} + bN \frac{\partial w_S}{\partial M} + (1-b)N \frac{\partial w_U}{\partial M} \right) M. \tag{7.11}$$

By differentiating the relevant marginal productivity conditions to derive the set of factor price elasticities and substituting those equations in the derivatives in (7.11), it can be shown that:

$$\frac{\Delta Q_N}{Q} \bigg|_{dK=0} = -\left(\frac{s_S^2 c_{SS} \beta^2 p^2}{2\pi_S^2} + \frac{s_U^2 c_{UU} (1-\beta)^2 p^2}{2\pi_U^2} \right.$$

$$\left. + \frac{s_S s_U c_{SU} \beta(1-\beta) p^2}{\pi_S \pi_U} \right) > 0. \tag{7.12}$$

The quadratic form in (7.12) is necessarily positive.[8] If the capital stock is fixed, therefore, natives will gain from immigration even if the skill distribution of immigrants is the same as that of natives.

It is of interest to again determine the optimal value of β if the goal of immigration policy were to maximize the *short-run* gains. To illustrate the opposing forces facing the social planner, let V be the immigration surplus defined in (7.12) and consider the special case where $\pi_S = \pi_U = 0.5$. The first and second derivatives of the immigration surplus are proportional to:

$$\frac{\partial V}{\partial \beta} \propto -s_S^2 c_{SS} \beta + s_U^2 c_{UU} (1-\beta) - s_S s_U c_{SU} (1-2\beta), \tag{7.13}$$

$$\frac{\partial^2 V}{\partial \beta^2} \propto -s_S^2 c_{SS} - s_U^2 c_{UU} + 2 s_S s_U c_{SU}. \tag{7.14}$$

The choice between skilled and unskilled immigration now depends on the relative magnitude of the various factor price elasticities. Suppose that $c_{SS} < c_{UU}$, which implies that $\varepsilon_{SS} < \varepsilon_{UU}$ and the demand for skilled labor is more inelastic than the demand for unskilled labor. The available evidence supports this assumption about the ranking of own factor-price elasticities across skill groups (Hamermesh, 1993). A relatively inelastic demand for skilled labor implies that they have fewer substitutes than unskilled labor, or conversely, that skilled workers are more complementary with other factors of production, particularly capital. In other words, the ranking of elasticities $\varepsilon_{SS} < \varepsilon_{UU}$ reflects the capital-skill complementarity hypothesis.[9] Appendix A shows that the first derivative in equation (7.13) is then positive at $\beta = 1$, and the second derivative is positive everywhere, so that equation (7.12) is convex.

Evaluating the immigration surplus in equation (7.12) at $\beta = 0$ or $\beta = 1$ (and using the convexity restriction) implies that the short-run immigration surplus is maximized when $\beta = 1$ and the immigrant influx is exclusively skilled. Put differently, capital-skill complementarity "breaks the tie" between the choice of an exclusively skilled or an exclusively unskilled immigrant flow when the native population is 50 percent skilled—and it breaks the tie in favor of skilled immigrants. The complementarity between native-owned capital and skills provides *the* economic rationale for admitting high-skill immigrants in the canonical model of a competitive labor market.

This conclusion, of course, may change if the native workforce is predominantly skilled ($b > 0.5$). There then exist two sets of conflicting incentives. On the one hand, unskilled immigrants most complement the relatively skilled native workforce. On the other hand, skilled immigrants most complement the native-owned capital.

Finally, comparing equations (7.9) and (7.12) yields:

$$\left. \frac{\Delta Q_N}{Q} \right|_{dK=0} - \left. \frac{\Delta Q_N}{Q} \right|_{dr=0} = -\frac{1}{2c_{KK}} \left(s_S c_{SK} \frac{\beta}{\pi_S} + s_U c_{UK} \frac{1-\beta}{\pi_U} \right)^2 p^2 > 0, \quad (7.15)$$

so that the immigration surplus is larger in the short run than in the long run. As with the wage impact of immigration, the net benefits from immigration are attenuated over time as capital adjusts to the changed economic environment.

Estimating the Benefits from Immigration

Several studies use the family of heterogeneous labor models presented above to simulate the impact of immigration on the U.S. labor market.[10] Even in the "simple" case of two labor inputs, the exercise requires far more information about the responsiveness of wages to supply shifts than the estimate of the immigration surplus in the homogeneous labor model.

Most important, the simulation requires the aggregation of workers into *two* skill groups. I adopt a simple classification: the high-skill group consists of workers with more than a high school degree; all other workers are, by definition, low-skill. Not surprisingly, Hamermesh's (1993) survey of the labor demand literature reveals a lot of uncertainty in the estimates of the relevant factor price elasticities, and the uncertainty has not narrowed in the past two decades (suggesting that the resulting "estimates" of the net benefits should be interpreted judiciously). The simulation uses the following values for the vector $(\varepsilon_{SS}, \varepsilon_{UU})$: $(-0.5, -0.3)$ and $(-0.9, -0.6)$, a range that covers many of the estimates in the literature. The evidence also suggests that the cross-elasticity ε_{SU} is small, so I set it to 0.05.[11] I use the education-specific data employed in the impact simulations reported in Chapter 5 to calculate the values of the other relevant parameters. Specifically, $\pi_S = 0.614$; $\beta = 0.489$; $s_S = 0.501$; and $s_U = 0.199$.[12] Finally, the exercise assumes that the immigrant share in the workforce is 15 percent.

Table 7.1 reports the simulation results. Despite the additional complexity, the immigration surplus remains small. The 2000 census reveals that 48.9 percent of the immigrants were high-skill according to the definition used in the simulation. This influx generates an immigration surplus of around 0.2 to 0.5 percent of GDP when capital is perfectly inelastic and around 0.03 percent when capital is perfectly elastic.

Table 7.1 Simulated immigration surplus in a heterogeneous labor model with two skill groups

	Short run		Long run	
	Percent change in GDP	Dollar gain	Percent change in GDP	Dollar gain
Assume $(\varepsilon_{SS}, \varepsilon_{UU})$ $= (-0.5, -0.3)$				
$\beta = 0.489$	0.24	35.6	0.02	2.6
$\beta = 0.0$	0.45	67.6	0.42	62.4
$\beta = 1.0$	0.75	112.1	0.16	24.7
Assume $(\varepsilon_{SS}, \varepsilon_{UU})$ $= (-0.9, -0.6)$				
$\beta = 0.489$	0.50	74.7	0.03	4.8
$\beta = 0.0$	0.90	135.2	0.77	115.8
$\beta = 1.0$	1.35	201.8	0.31	45.8

Notes: The high-skill group consists of workers with more than a high school education; all other workers are in the low-skill group. The parameter β gives the fraction of the immigrant workforce that is high-skill and takes on a value of 0.489 in the 2000 census. All simulations assume that $\varepsilon_{SU} = 0.05$; $\pi_S = 0.614$; $s_S = 0.501$; $s_U = 0.199$; the immigrant share is 15 percent; and GDP is \$15 trillion.

The exercise also suggests that the size of the *short-run* surplus would not increase dramatically if immigration policy were to switch from one that only admitted unskilled workers ($\beta = 0$) to one that only admitted skilled workers ($\beta = 1$). The short-run surplus increases by $50 to $70 billion, regardless of the value of the elasticities ε_{SS} and ε_{UU}. Moreover, the size of the long-run surplus would actually *decline* if immigrants were exclusively high-skill. The reason is simple. The long-run adjustments to the capital stock reduce the value of the capital-skill complementarities, and the native-born workforce, which is relatively high-skill, would be better off with low-skill immigration. Intriguingly, there is a conflict between the types of immigration policies that a host country with a relatively high-skill workforce should pursue in the short run and in the long run if the objective were to maximize the net economic gains.

In sum, the two-factor generalization reinforces the conclusion of the homogeneous labor model. The net gains from immigration (and *even* from high-skill immigration) to an economy as large as the United States cannot be numerically substantial, *as long as* the analysis remains within the confines of the canonical model of a competitive labor market.[13]

The Case of the Nested CES

It is possible that the small surpluses reported in Table 7.1 are an inevitable, but erroneous, conclusion resulting from the artificial—*and totally arbitrary*—aggregation of many diverse groups of workers into two skill groups. It should be obvious, however, that the difficulty of calculating the immigration surplus increases exponentially in a framework that had more than two types. The large number of numerical speculations and guesses about the relevant elasticities would lead to a numerical exercise that had little plausibility. As with the analysis of the wage impact of immigration, therefore, estimating the immigration surplus in a general model of heterogeneous labor requires a reduction in the dimensionality of the problem. The easiest and most tractable approach is again to rely on the nested CES framework.

To illustrate how this particular functional form assumption affects the calculation, consider the simplest two-level nesting:

$$Q = [\alpha K^{\delta} + (1 - \alpha)L^{\delta}]^{1/\delta} \tag{7.16}$$

$$L = \left[\sum_i \theta_i L_i^\beta \right]^{1/\beta},$$ (7.17)

where L gives the aggregate number of workers in efficiency units, and L_i gives the number of workers in skill group i. It is easy to incorporate the possibility that each of the L_i's is itself determined by an aggregation of subgroups, but the key implication of the framework is transparent in the two-level nesting.

The aggregate production function in equation (7.16) implies that the immigration surplus is again given by the shaded triangular area in Figure 7.1 that represents the surplus in the simplest model with homogeneous labor. The "efficiency units approach" homogenizes different kinds of workers into equivalent productive units, and hence all that needs to be done is to redefine what "L" represents. In the homogeneous labor model, L represents the number of workers; in the nested CES framework, L represents the number of efficiency units. The immigration surplus, therefore, is again given by the simple formula in equation (7.2), with the caveat that the supply shock variable p now represents the immigrant share in the total number of efficiency units, rather than the immigrant share in the total number of workers.

As first noted in Chapter 3, there is no need to estimate any additional parameters to calculate the size of the supply shift in efficiency units; this quantity is easy to calculate using available data. In particular, let $m_i = dL_i/L_i$ give the immigration-induced percent shift in the number of workers in group i. The percent shift in the number of efficiency units is $\bar{m} = d\log L = \sum_i s_i m_i / s_L$, where s_i is the share of income accruing to labor input i, and s_L is the share of income accruing to all workers. The immigration surplus in the nested CES framework is then given by:

$$\frac{\Delta Q_N}{Q} = -\frac{1}{2} s_L \varepsilon_{LL} \bar{p}^2,$$ (7.18)

where the factor price elasticity ε_{LL} would *still* be equal to -0.3, since the aggregate production function in (7.16) is typically assumed to be Cobb-Douglas; and $\bar{p} = \bar{m} / (1 + \bar{m})$.

Interestingly, the only difference between the calculation of the immigration surplus in a homogeneous labor model and in a heterogeneous labor model with a nested CES functional form is the definition of the supply shift. In the homogeneous labor model, the aggregate supply shift is given by a simple "body count." In the nested CES model, the supply shift is a weighted average of the body counts, with the weight equal to the relative income share accruing to skill group i. Note that this calculation does not use *any* information on the presence or absence of complementarities among the various skill groups. The observed income shares are a "sufficient statistic" and incorporate all the information that is empirically relevant.

It is also obvious that accounting for heterogeneous labor through a nested CES approach would lead to an even *lower* estimate of the short-run immigration surplus in the U.S. context. After all, the largest percent supply shifts in terms of body counts occurred for the least-skilled groups (high school dropouts). But these groups also happen to have the lowest income shares and, as a result, would matter much less in the calculation of the supply shift $\bar{m}$. In fact, the predicted immigrant share declines by about 1 percentage point if the group-specific supply shocks are weighted by income rather than population shares.[14] Throughout the discussion, I assumed that the immigrant share in the workforce was 15 percent. The income-share weighting would reduce it to around 14 percent. Equation (7.18) then implies that the immigration surplus is 0.21 percent of GDP. Accounting for heterogeneous labor in a nested CES framework, therefore, reduces the estimated surplus from $35 to $30 billion, around a 15 percent reduction.

The Global Gains from Open Borders

It is interesting to extend the analysis to a global context. In particular, what types of gains would accrue to the world's population if countries suddenly decided to remove all legal restraints to international migration and workers moved to those countries that afforded them the best economic opportunities? In contrast to the immigration surplus calculated for the receiving country's native population in the previous sections, it turns out that the "global immigration surplus" is huge and seemingly could do away with much of world poverty in one fell swoop.

An influential study by Hamilton and Whalley (1984) provided the first attempt at using a simple economic model to try to measure the global gains from unrestricted international migration.[15] To easily illustrate the main idea, consider the nature of the gains in a setting where there are two regions, the North (N) and the South (S). The North is a highly industrialized region with relatively few workers, while the South has a large population and lags behind the North in economic development. Initially, the wage in the North, w_N, exceeds the wage in the South, w_S.

The two regions have downward-sloping labor demand curves that, for expositional convenience, are initially assumed to have the same slope. The two demand curves, however, may have different intercepts. The difference between the intercepts measures the economic value of the different infrastructures, with the North's infrastructure allowing any specific worker to have a higher value of marginal product in the North than in the South. Note that the "infrastructure" should be broadly defined and includes not only the existing capital stock but also the set of political, social, economic, and cultural institutions that regulate behavior and economic interactions in the two regions. As is typically done in this type of exercise, I consider a short-run situation where the infrastructure is fixed in each region, so that the height of each labor demand curve is fixed. It will quickly become evident that this is *not* a trivial assumption in the current context. Finally, assume that all labor is homogeneous and supplied inelastically in each of the regions, with supply curves S_N and S_S, respectively.

Figure 7.2 illustrates the initial labor market equilibrium. Because of the supply imbalance between the two regions and because of the gap in the value of marginal product for any specific worker, the wage in the North is substantially higher than the wage in the South. Income-maximizing workers in the South wish to move to the North to take ad-

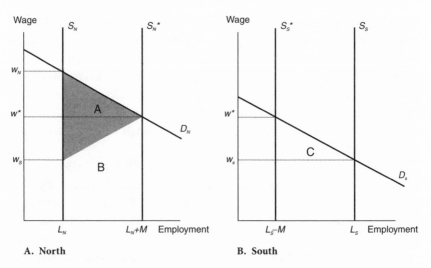

Figure 7.2. The Global Gains from Open Borders

vantage of the higher wage. Immigration restrictions, however, prevent this type of mobility.

Suppose now that all restrictions are lifted *and* that migration from the South to the North is costless. Workers will flow from the low-wage to the high-wage region as long as any wage difference exists, and the flow will stop only when the wage in the two regions is equalized at w^*. As illustrated in Figure 7.2, this new equilibrium is reached when a total of M persons have left the South and entered the North's labor market.

The exit of the M workers from the South generates a loss in the South's GDP equal to the area of the trapezoid C. At the same time, the entry of the M workers in the North (where they are now free to enjoy the higher productivity provided by the North's infrastructure) increases the North's GDP by the size of the area of the trapezoid $A + B$.

It is trivial to show that the area of the trapezoid giving the North's gain exceeds the area of the trapezoid giving the South's loss. In particular, note that the South's loss in GDP is also given by the (mirror-image) trapezoid B in the graph illustrating conditions in the North's labor market. The global immigration surplus, therefore, is given by the triangle A.[16]

It is instructive to carry out a simple back-of-the-envelope calculation of the global gains from unimpeded labor mobility. Suppose the inverse labor demand functions in the two regions are given by:

$$\log w_N = \alpha_N + \eta \log L_N, \tag{7.19a}$$

$$\log w_S = \alpha_S + \eta \log L_S. \tag{7.19b}$$

These demand functions incorporate the key assumption that the factor price elasticity η is the same in both regions (with $\eta < 0$). The hypothesis that the North's infrastructure makes workers more productive implies that $\alpha_N > \alpha_S$.

Table 7.2 summarizes demographic and economic conditions in various broadly defined regions. In 2011, world GDP was around $70 trillion, and 1.1 billion persons lived in the high-income countries, while 5.9 billion persons lived in developing regions. The table also documents the huge differences in (PPP-adjusted) per capita GDP across regions: from $3,300 in South Asia, to $11,900 in Latin American, to over $38,000 in the high-income countries. In short, per capita income easily quadruples or quintuples by moving from some of the developing regions to the developed countries. Of course, per capita GDP differences are not identical to the wage differences that determine the migration decision in the canonical income-maximization

Table 7.2 Differences between high-income and developing regions, 2011

Region	Population (millions)	Labor force (millions)	Per capita GDP (PPP adjusted, current U.S. dollars, thousands)
High income	1,135.0	554.6	38.3
Developing regions			
East Asia and Pacific	1,974.2	1,129.5	7.3
Europe and Central Asia	408.1	190.4	15.0
Latin American and Caribbean	589.0	283.4	11.9
South Asia	1,656.5	652.1	3.3
Sub-Saharan Africa	874.8	347.2	2.3
World	6,974.2	3,264.7	11.6

Source: World Bank (2013).

model. Nevertheless, there is ample evidence that wage differences between developed and developing countries are similarly large, so that a single worker could easily triple his wage if he were to move from many developing countries to the United States.[17]

Suppose that the wage ratio between the North and the South is given by $R = w_N/w_S$. The data in Table 7.2 and the functional form assumptions about the labor demand functions in equation (7.19) provide all the information that is needed to get a back-of-the-envelope estimate of the global gains from migration. The calculation consists of 3 steps:

STEP 1:   Calculate the values of the intercepts α_N and α_S consistent with world conditions prior to the relaxation of immigration restrictions by solving for these two unknowns in the two-equation system:

$$R = \frac{w_N}{w_S} = \left(\frac{\alpha_N}{\alpha_S}\right)\left(\frac{L_N}{L_S}\right)^{\eta}, \tag{7.20}$$

$$Y = \int_0^{L_N} \alpha_N L^{\eta} dL + \int_0^{L_S} \alpha_S L^{\eta} dL = \frac{\alpha_S}{1+\eta}\left[\frac{\alpha_N}{\alpha_S} L_N^{1+\eta} + L_S^{1+\eta}\right], \tag{7.21}$$

where Y gives the value of world GDP prior to the relaxation of immigration restrictions. Equation (7.20) follows directly from the assumed functional form of the two labor demand functions. For given numerical values of R, the factor price elasticity η, and the workforce ratio L_N/L_S, it allows us to solve numerically for the value of the ratio (α_N/α_S). Equation (7.21) defines world GDP as the sum of the relevant areas under the value of marginal product curves for both regions, and uniquely identifies the specific value of the constants α_N and α_S that are consistent with the preexisting numerical value (Y) of world GDP.

STEP 2: Calculate the size of the migrant flow M that will equalize wages across regions. The variable M is implicitly defined by:

$$\frac{\alpha_N(L_N+M)^{\eta}}{\alpha_S(L_S-M)^{\eta}} = 1. \tag{7.22}$$

STEP 3: Calculate the gains to world GDP. These gains are defined by:

$$\Delta Y = \int_{L_N}^{L_N+M} \alpha_N L^{\eta} dL - \int_{L_S-M}^{L_S} \alpha_S L^{\eta} dL \tag{7.23}$$

$$= \frac{\alpha_N}{(1+\eta)}\left[(L_N+M)^{1+\eta} - L_N^{1+\eta}\right] - \frac{\alpha_S}{(1+\eta)}\left[L_S^{1+\eta} - (L_S-M)^{1+\eta}\right]$$

The first integral in (7.23) gives the increase in GDP in the North resulting from the influx of M workers, while the second integral gives the decline in GDP in the South resulting from the exit of M workers.

Table 7.3 reports the results from the numerical exercise, assuming that 600 billion people work in the North and 2.7 billion people work in the South in the pre-migration regime (as suggested by Table 7.2), and that the factor price elasticity η is -0.3. The various columns of the table use alternative assumptions about the value of the wage ratio R. Suppose that the wage in the developed countries is twice as large as the wage in the developing countries (an assumption that probably provides a lower bound for the true value of R). The model then suggests that 1.7 *billion* workers, or over half of the workforce in the developing countries, would need to move in order to equalize wages across the two regions. If the value of R were higher, say 4, the simulation implies that 2.6 billion

Table 7.3 Simulated global gains from unrestricted international migration

	Value of R (w_N/w_S)				
	2	3	4	5	6
1. Number of migrant workers that will equalize wages (in billions)	1.7	2.4	2.6	2.6	2.7
2. Number of migrants as percent of South's workforce	62.3	87.3	94.8	97.5	98.6
3. Net gain in world GDP (in trillions of dollars)	9.4	25.4	40.1	52.3	62.4
4. Net gain as percent of world GDP	13.4	36.3	57.2	74.7	89.1
5. Percent wage change in the North	−33.0	−38.0	−39.3	−39.7	−39.8
6. Breakeven per-person migration costs (in 1,000s of dollars)	50.9	98.7	143.2	181.8	214.4

Notes: The simulations assume that world GDP is $70 trillion in the premigration regime; 600 million persons work in the North; 2.7 billion persons work in the South; and the factor price elasticity is −0.3. The breakeven cost calculation in row 6 gives the per-person (rather than the per-worker) cost of moving. It assumes that the total number of people moving is the emigration rate given in row 2 times the South's population, assumed to be 5.9 billion people, and uses a 5 percent discount rate to calculate the present value of the global gains.

workers, or 95.0 percent of the workforce in the developing region, will need to move.

It is not surprising that a greater fraction of the South's workforce needs to move as the initial wage disparity between the North and the South rises. What is surprising and tends to be underemphasized (and sometimes unmentioned) is that even the lower-bound estimates of the wage ratio R trigger the movement of *billions* of people.[18] This result reflects the simple fact that the North's labor demand curve, for whatever reason, lies far above that of the South. Absent the transferability of the conditions that make a specific worker much more productive in the North, a sufficiently high wage gap essentially implies that some places in the world are so inefficient at production that their equilibrium outcome is to be "economically empty" in a world with free mobility.[19]

As in the original Hamilton-Whalley (1984) study, the exercise reveals that the gains to world income are huge. If $R = 2$, for example, world GDP would rise by $9.4 trillion, a 13.4 percent increase over the initial value of $70 trillion. If $R = 4$, world GDP would increase by $40 trillion, almost a 60 percent increase. In fact, if R were to equal 6, which may be near the upper bound of the range of plausibility suggested by the available data, world GDP would rise by $62 trillion, a near doubling! Note, moreover, that these gains would be accrued *each year* after the migration occurs, so that the present value of the gains would be astronomically high.[20]

Of course, these huge gains are associated with a substantial redistribution of wealth, and the L_N native workers in the North are at the losing end of the deal. As Figure 7.2 shows, the influx of M workers reduces the North's wage from w_N to w^*. The implied percent wage change is given by:

$$\frac{w^* - w_N}{w_N} = \left(\frac{L_N + M}{L_N} \right)^{\eta} - 1. \tag{7.24}$$

Row 5 of Table 7.3 reports the wage change predicted by equation (7.24). Regardless of the value of R, the earnings of the North's native workforce drop by 30 to 40 percent.

The huge global gains typically found in these types of numerical calibrations have led a number of economists to emphasize that the "gains from globalization" resulting from the decades-long effort to ease trade restrictions pale in comparison to the gains that are there for the taking if countries simply removed all existing restrictions on international migration.[21] Even putting aside the political difficulties in enacting such a policy, this argument in favor of unrestricted international migration glosses over two conceptual obstacles.

First, the calculation assumes that people can somehow start at a specific latitude-longitude coordinate and end up at a different coordinate *at zero cost*. Unfortunately, even the seemingly simple transporter used by *Starship Enterprise* personnel, which is able to instantaneously move people across vast distances, is not costless. The absence of legal restrictions prohibiting the movement of people from one country to another does not circumvent the fact that it would be very costly to move billions of workers.

As noted in Chapter 1, large wage differences across regions can persist for a very long time simply because *many people choose not to move.* In a world of income-maximizing agents, the stayers are signaling that there are substantial psychic costs to mobility, perhaps even on the order of hundreds of thousands dollars per person, and that they are willing to leave substantial wage gains on the table. Kennan and Walker (2011 p. 232), for instance, estimate that it costs $312,000 to move the average person from one state to another within the United States.[22] Similarly, Artuc et al. (2010) report that average moving costs are nearly 8 times the annual salary for workers who move from one industry to another as they try to escape the adverse consequences of industry-specific trade shocks.

Although these costs seem implausibly high, moving costs *must be* around that order of magnitude to be consistent with the observed fact that people do not move as much as they should given the existing regional wage differences. If moving costs were indeed in that range, it is easy to show that the huge global gains from migration become substantially smaller and may even vanish after taking moving costs into account.

Suppose, for instance, that $R = 4$, so that the global gain is around $40 trillion *annually* when 2.6 billion *workers* move from the South to the North. Assuming a 5 percent rate of discount, the present value of these gains is $800 trillion! The 2.6 billion worker-migrants will, more likely than not, bring their families, so the actual number of *people* moving would be around 5.6 billion (or the 95 percent migration rate times the South's population of 5.9 billion people). The "breakeven" cost of migration given in the last row of Table 7.3 is around $140,000. In short, the entire present value of the global gains is wiped out even if the costs of migration were only half of what is typically reported in existing studies.[23]

Needless to say, the magnitudes involved in this numerical exercise are mindboggling and should be taken with more than the proverbial grain of salt. But they do teach us an important lesson: the global gains from "free migration" need to be contrasted with the costs of moving billions of people, many of whom do not wish to move, if the exercise is to be taken seriously.

It is also important to emphasize that the gains reported in Table 7.3 depend crucially on the assumption that the intercepts of the labor demand curves in the North and South are fixed. However, the North's demand curve lies above the South's demand curve, not simply because that is just the way things are, but because of very specific political, economic, institutional, and cultural factors that *endogenously* led to the development of different infrastructures in the two regions, with the Northern infrastructure allowing similarly skilled workers to attain a higher value of marginal product.

As the important work of Acemoglu and Robinson (2012) suggests, "nations fail" mainly because of differences in political and economic institutions. For immigration to generate substantial global gains, it must be the case that billions of immigrants can move to the industrialized economies without importing the "bad" institutions that led to poor economic conditions in the source countries in the first place. It seems inconceivable that the North's infrastructure would remain unchanged after the admission of billions of new workers. Unfortunately, remarkably little is known about the political and cultural impact of immigration on the receiving countries, and about how institutions in these receiving countries would adjust to the influx.

In a general equilibrium framework, it seems reasonable to imagine that the integration of the two regions could easily result in the dilution of whatever unique set of circumstances allowed the North to enjoy such a large productive advantage.[24] A "modest" relaxation of immigration restrictions— say, one that only allows 10 percent of the optimal number of immigrants into the developed countries—would still imply migration flows of more than half a billion people, including the related family members, when $R = 4$. This limited migration flow would still be almost three times as large as the number of international migrants that now exist. The magnitude of even these limited flows would likely lead to different results in partial and general equilibrium calibrations: As the North adapts to its new political and demographic reality, the gains implied by the partial equilibrium simulation may begin to dissipate.

8

High-Skill Immigration

⸻

THE CANONICAL MODEL of a competitive labor market predicts that the net economic benefits from immigration to the receiving country are relatively small. In the U.S. context, for example, it is unlikely that the gains from a supply shock that increases the number of workers by 15 percent would generate net gains far exceeding 0.3 percent of GDP in the short run, and those gains would be even smaller in the long run.

Even an influx composed exclusively of high-skill workers would not dramatically increase the gains as long as we maintain the typical set of assumptions of the canonical model. Certainly, the presence of capital-skill complementarities ensures that the gains from immigration are larger for a high-skill than for a low-skill supply shock in the short run, but the differential gain between the two extremes is not large. Moreover, the gains resulting from capital-skill complementarities would also dissipate over time.

The widespread perception that high-skill immigration can be hugely beneficial must then rely on a crucial departure from the textbook model: high-skill immigrants generate human capital externalities. The presence of high-skill immigrants exposes us to new forms of knowledge, increases our human capital, and makes us more productive. In fact, the foundation of modern theories of economic growth is the assumption that such externalities are prevalent and strong (Lucas 1988; Romer 1986). This chapter examines the recent literature that attempts to determine if immigration creates these types of human capital externalities and tries to quantify their magnitude. The evidence suggests that productivity spillovers can indeed be empirically important. The evidence also suggests, however, that widespread spillovers are not necessarily a universal consequence of high-skill immigration.

A Model of Immigration and Human Capital Externalities

Modern theories of economic growth emphasize how human capital externalities alter the productivity of specific workers. A worker suddenly surrounded by many high-skill workers will himself become more productive by being exposed to new ideas and concepts. This productivity spillover, however, must coexist with the traditional laws of scarcity and diminishing returns that form the core of economic analysis. Following the excellent summary of the literature in Jones and Romer (2010), suppose that the production function depends on the stock of ideas A, the capital stock K, and the number of (high-skill) workers L. It is typically assumed that there are constant returns to K and L. Suppose further that the production function can be written as:[1]

$$Y = A^{\phi}[K^{\alpha} L^{1-\alpha}], \tag{8.1}$$

where ϕ gives the "externalities elasticity," the percent expansion in output associated with a 1 percent increase in the stock of ideas.

It is common in the literature to assume that the stock of ideas is proportional to the number of workers (or, for simplicity, $A = L$). The marginal product of a high-skill immigrant is then given by:

$$MP_{L} = (1 + \phi - \alpha)K^{\alpha}L^{\phi-\alpha}. \tag{8.2}$$

An influx of immigrants simultaneously increases the number of ideas *and* the number of workers. It is instructive to illustrate the implications of the model in two alternative scenarios: the short run and the long run. By definition, capital resources K are fixed in the short run and are fully adjusted in the long run. If the input markets were competitive, additional resources would enter the market until the rate of return r to these resources is again equal to the world rate and the percent change in the capital stock equals the percent change in the size of the workforce. The resulting change in the marginal product of high-skill workers is then given by:

$$d \log MP_L = \begin{cases} (\phi - s_k)m, & \text{if } d\log K = 0, \\ \\ \phi m, & \text{if } d\log K = m. \end{cases} \qquad (8.3)$$

where $m = d \log L$; and s_K gives capital's share of income.

Equation (8.3) clearly illustrates the race between the spillover effect and the law of diminishing returns in the short run. If the elasticity ϕ is sufficiently large, the value of marginal product of high-skill workers rises. Otherwise, the impact on the marginal product of workers will be negative in the short run. Equation (8.3) also shows that the marginal product of high-skill workers *must* rise in the long run after the capital stock fully adjusts to the high-skill supply shock. In the words of Jones and Romer (2010, p. 231): "In the long run, the benefits of a larger population which come from an increase in the stock of available ideas decisively dominates the negative effects of resource scarcity."

The Labor Market for Doctorates

A number of recent empirical studies attempt to measure the net effect of high-skill immigration in specific contexts where it would seem likely *a priori* that human capital spillovers could be observed. The labor market for workers with doctoral degrees in the United States, examined in Borjas (2009), may provide such an environment.

In fact, the sizable influx of foreign students into the U.S. doctoral labor market provides a near-ideal research setting for measuring the wage impact of high-skill immigration. The labor market for these high-skill workers is certainly national (and perhaps even international) in scope. It would make little sense to compare the earnings of doctorates in Boston and Denver to determine the impact of a high-skill supply shock on the wage of these workers.

It is also unlikely that the "internal migration" of doctorates across disciplines plays an important role in helping this high-skill labor market adjust to the supply shocks. A doctoral education in science and engineering is a highly specialized endeavor, requiring the investment of a lot of time and effort, and the training is very specific.[2] An exogenous supply shock in a particular discipline at a particular time may affect the career decisions of future generations of students, but it is unlikely that there is much mobility between the disciplines of computer science and chemistry as workers in those fields reassess the changed opportunities.

Finally, the National Science Foundation (NSF) conducts frequent and detailed surveys that provide reliable information on the number and earnings of doctorates in science and engineering. For example, the Survey of Earned Doctorates (SED) provides a population census of all persons who received doctorates in 22 distinct fields of science and engineering from a U.S. institution, and identifies whether the doctoral recipient is native- or foreign-born. Similarly, the Survey of Doctoral Recipients (SDR) is a biennial longitudinal file that provides a 7 percent sample of persons who obtained their doctoral degrees in the United States in science or engineering, and contains detailed information on a worker's employment history and earnings. The analysis of labor market outcomes reported below uses all four SDR panels conducted between 1995 and 2001.

It is well known that the immigrant share in the number of doctoral degrees awarded each year in the United States has risen dramatically: it was 17.5 percent in 1968, peaked at 39.7 percent in 1994, and then fell to 34.8 percent by 2000 (Borjas 2009b, p. 136). In addition, many of the foreign students remain in the country after receiving their doctoral degree, so that the foreign student influx had a significant impact on the supply of high-skill workers.[3]

Consider the population of persons who are granted a doctorate in calendar year c and discipline d. As usual, define the foreign-born share in this particular cohort-discipline cell by $p_{cd} = M_{cd}/(M_{cd} + N_{cd})$, where M_{cd} and N_{cd} give the number of immigrants and natives in cell (c, d), respectively. Figure 8.1 illustrates the trend in the immigrant share by cohort and discipline for the five largest disciplines. The nature of the supply shock differs substantially across disciplines both in terms of the size and the timing of the shock. For example, the immigrant share in electrical engineering rose rapidly in the 1970s, from about 19 percent in 1970 to about 50 percent in 1985, and then remained stable at that level through 1998. In contrast, the immigrant share in biological sciences declined throughout the 1970s, from 15 percent in 1970 to 12 percent in 1982, rose rapidly until 1996 to 35 percent, and then began to decline again.

It is possible to exploit the differences in the size and timing of the foreign student supply shock across the 22 doctoral disciplines to estimate the

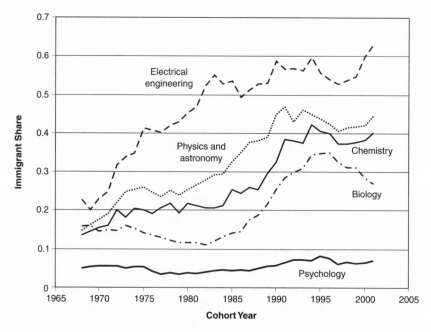

Figure 8.1. The Immigrant Supply Shock in the Doctoral Labor Market, Selected Disciplines

Source: Borjas (2009, p. 140).

Notes: The immigrant share gives the fraction of doctorates awarded to foreign-born persons in each of the disciplines in a particular year. The five disciplines illustrated in the figure produced the largest number of doctorates between 1968 and 2000.

impact of immigration on the earnings of native-born doctorates. Consider the regression model:

$$\log w_{cd}(t) = \phi_c + \phi_d + \phi_t + \phi_{ct} + \phi_{dt} + \theta p_{cd} + \varepsilon, \qquad (8.4)$$

where $\log w_{cd}(t)$ gives the mean annual earnings at time t of workers who obtained their doctorate in calendar year c and in discipline d; and ϕ_c, ϕ_d, and ϕ_t are vectors of fixed effects indicating the cohort year, the discipline of study, and the calendar year in which earnings are observed, respectively. The interactive fixed effects ϕ_{ct} and ϕ_{dt} allow for the possibility that wages are changing over time for a particular cohort (capturing any aging effects) as well as changing differentially in different disciplines.

Workers who received their doctoral degree in the same discipline at roughly the same time are more likely to influence each other's labor market opportunities than workers who are in the same discipline but graduated at very different times. It is easy to capture the (within-discipline) similarity across workers who have the same years of experience by aggregating the doctoral degree recipients into 3-year cohort intervals, indicating if the worker earned his doctorate between 1968 and 1970, 1971 and 1973, 1974 and 1976, and so on. The analysis is restricted to persons who received their doctoral degrees between 1968 and 2000, so there are eleven 3-year cohorts in the data (per discipline). I can then calculate the immigrant share for each of these cohort-discipline cells, and this is the key independent variable p_{cd} used in the regression model in equation (8.4).

Table 8.1 reports the estimates of the coefficient θ. There is a numerically sizable and significant negative relation between the mean earnings of doctorates in a particular cohort-discipline cell and the supply shock. The coefficient of the immigrant share variable is −0.409 (with a standard error of

Table 8.1 The wage impact of immigration on the doctoral labor market

Definition of Immigrant Share	Men	Men and women
1. Includes all foreign students to calculate share	−0.409	−0.378
	(0.150)	(0.155)
2. Includes only intended stayers to calculate share	−0.535	−0.502
	(0.164)	(0.169)

Source: Adapted from Borjas (2009, p. 144).

Notes: The unit of observation is a cohort-discipline-year cell. A cohort is defined by 3-year groupings of the calendar year in which the doctoral degree was awarded (between 1968 and 2000). The earnings data are available in the biennial waves of the Survey of Doctoral Recipients conducted between 1995 and 2001. Standard errors are reported in parentheses and are clustered at the cohort-discipline level. The dependent variable is the mean log annual earnings of workers in a cohort-discipline-year cell, while the independent variable is the immigrant share in the respective cohort-discipline cell. The calculation of the immigrant share used in row 2 uses only those foreign students who intended to stay in the United States at the time they received their doctoral degree. The regression includes vectors of cohort-year and discipline-year fixed effects. The regressions are weighted by the sample size used to calculate the dependent variable and have 892 observations.

0.150). As in our earlier discussion, it is easier to interpret the coefficient by converting it into an elasticity that gives the percent change in earnings associated with a percent change in labor supply. The implied wage elasticity is −0.24.[4] The second row of the table shows that the implied wage elasticity is somewhat larger if the immigrant share is calculated only using the sample of foreign-born doctorates that intend to stay in the United States. The elasticity estimate increases to −0.31.[5]

It is important to note that the negative wage effects documented in Table 8.1 do not necessarily imply that human capital externalities are unimportant. As suggested by the theoretical framework presented in the previous section, the negative wage effects could be reflecting the fact that the resource constraints represented by the law of diminishing returns swamp the benefits resulting from having large numbers of high-skill foreign workers in the doctoral labor market. Put differently, the negative wage effects could have been even larger in the absence of the spillovers.

High-Tech Immigration

In addition to the high-skill influx provided by the enrollment of large numbers of doctoral foreign students in American universities, the United States also uses the H-1B visa program to grant temporary visas to skilled immigrants in "specialty occupations."[6] In practice, these occupations tend to require specialized knowledge, usually in science, engineering, and computer-related jobs. Not surprisingly, almost all H-1B visa recipients have at least a college education.

The H-1B temporary visa is noteworthy not only because it has been a key source of high-skill immigration to the United States in the past two decades, but also because it creates a binding contract between a particular employer and a particular worker. Specifically, the sponsoring firm files an application for a prospective employee, and that worker is typically tied to the sponsoring firm for a number of years if the visa is granted.[7] If at the end of the visa period (usually 6 years), the worker is unable to adjust his visa status into one that allows permanent residence in the United States, the H-1B visa holder must leave the country.

Since 1990 the United States has capped the number of H-1B visas that are granted each year. The annual cap has fluctuated over the years, and the policy debate typically focuses on whether the cap should be increased. Figure 8.2 illustrates the changes in the annual cap as well as the trend in the total number of H-1B visa holders residing in the country. The initial

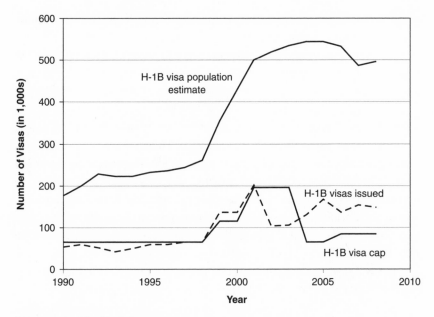

Figure 8.2. The H-1B Program

Source: Kerr and Lincoln (2010, p. 483).

Notes: The H-1B program grants temporary visas to workers in "specialty occupations." The number of H-1B visas issued each year may differ from the mandated cap because of various exemptions in the legislation.

cap of 65,000 visas was increased to 115,000 in 1999, and increased further to 195,000 in 2001, before being reset to its initial value of 65,000 in 2004. Because of the various policy changes, the number of H-1B visa holders residing in the United States rose from 261,000 in 1998 to over 500,000 by 2006.

Several recent studies exploit the changes in the H-1B cap to measure the impact of the program on various outcomes in the high-skill labor market. Kerr and Lincoln's (2010) inventive and careful study examined trends in the rate of innovation (as measured by the number of patents granted), employment, and wages in the high-skill workforce. The study exploits the fact that H-1B visa holders cluster in a relatively small number of locations in the United States. For example, in 2001–2002, employers in the San Francisco area filed 8.3 H-1B applications per every 1,000 workers in the local workforce; Seattle employers filed only 3.4 applications per 1,000 local workers. This variation provides a city-specific index of "H-1B dependency." The Kerr-Lincoln study then proceeds to estimate spatial correlations that relate the outcomes for high-skill workers in the local labor market to the presumably exogenous increases in the size of the local H-1B workforce induced by the changing cap.

Suppose y_{it} measures a particular outcome variable of interest in city i at time t. The generic regression model can be written as:

$$y_{it} = \phi_i + \phi_t + \theta\,(D_i \times N_t) + \varepsilon, \tag{8.5}$$

where ϕ_i gives a vector of region fixed effects or city-specific variables; ϕ_t is a vector of year fixed effects; D is the city's H-1B dependency rate; and N is the (log) number of H-1B visa holders nationwide. The interaction $(D_i \times N_t)$ roughly predicts the "effective" number of H-1B visa holders that city i can expect to employ at time t. The reduced-form coefficient θ then measures the spatial correlation between labor market outcomes and the high-skill supply shock and is interpreted as giving the "impact" of the H-1B program on the outcome variable.

Table 8.2 summarizes some of the results from the Kerr-Lincoln study. The outcomes of interest include the number of patents granted to innova-

Table 8.2 The impact of the H-1B visa program

Dependent variable	Specification	
	(1)	(2)
1. Log number of patents by persons with Indian surnames	0.339	0.142
	(0.048)	(0.043)
2. Log number of patents by persons with Chinese surnames	0.390	0.174
	(0.061)	(0.061)
3. Log number of patents by persons with Anglo-Saxon surnames	0.056	0.023
	(0.028)	(0.029)
4. Log number of total patents	0.074	0.048
	(0.028)	(0.029)
5. Change in labor force participation rate of native science-engineering workers	—	0.004
		(0.004)
6. Change in log wage of native science-engineering workers	—	−0.010
		(0.013)
Includes city characteristics, region/time fixed effects	No	Yes

Source: Kerr and Lincoln (2010, pp. 492, 494).

Notes: The data consist of a panel where an observation represents a particular city-year combination (in rows 1–4), or state-year combination (in rows 5–6). Standard errors are reported in parentheses and are clustered at the city or state level. The independent variable is the interaction between the local labor market's "dependency rate" on H-1B employment and the log size of the national H-1B population.

tors in the city, and the local employment and earnings of science and engineering workers. It is well known that two ethnic groups, Indians and Chinese, dominate the national origin mix of the H-1B visa holders, making up at least half of the population. The table shows a strong positive correlation between the patenting rate of persons with either Indian or Chinese surnames in the city and the effective size of the local H-1B workforce.

Although it is not possible to determine if the actual patent holder is an H-1B visa holder, it is likely that some of the patents granted to persons in these ethnic groups were granted to the visa recipients themselves. After all, the number of patents granted to innovators with "Anglo-Saxon" surnames is independent of local H-1B employment. Put differently, the positive correlation seems mainly attributable to innovation produced by the H-1B visa holders, rather than "spillover innovation" by their local co-workers. Finally, note that the impact of the visa program on the overall patenting rate in the city, although positive, is only marginally significant after the regression controls for region-time fixed effects. The sensitivity of the evidence to the inclusion of these fixed effects suggests that part of the "raw" spatial correlation between patenting and the H-1B program could be measuring concurrent changes in local demand for scientists and engineers.[8]

Finally, the table reports the impact of the program on the labor force participation rate and wage of native-born workers. There is little correlation between these variables and increases in the effective number of H-1B visa holders. These results may indicate that the human capital externalities offset the competitive effects induced by the laws of supply and demand. Alternatively, as with the discussion of spatial correlations in earlier chapters, they could imply that some of the actors in the local labor market reacted to the inflow of H-1B visa holders, and that these reactions, however they manifest themselves, attenuated the impact on the locality.[9]

Case Studies of High-Skill Immigration

There is little doubt that high-skill immigration increases the number of innovators in a host country's economy. In the U.S. context, this increase can be easily documented by simply counting the many patents awarded to high-skill immigrants, the number of successful high-tech companies founded by these immigrants, or the disproportionately large number of Nobel Prizes awarded to foreign-born Americans (Hunt and Gauthier-Loiselle 2010). Nevertheless, the study of large-scale supply shifts in the doctoral labor market or in the high-tech workforce does not provide a resounding endorsement for the view that high-skill immigration also generates substantial (net) human capital externalities for the native population.[10] In recent years, a new genre of research has intensified the search for the presence of such spillovers by conducting case studies that compare the productivity of the preexisting workforce in specific disciplines—and even in narrowly defined *fields* within a discipline—before and after a supply shock.

Nazi Germany

Waldinger (2010) represents a pioneering example of this type of research methodology. Specifically, he examined the productivity of the doctoral students who were left behind when many renowned Jewish mathematicians left Nazi Germany.

In 1933, shortly after Hitler secured power in Germany, the Nazi government enacted the notorious Law for the Restoration of the Professional Civil Service. A key provision of the law was that "civil servants who are not of Aryan descent are to be placed in retirement." A subsequent implementation degree clarified: "Anyone descended from non-Aryan, and in particular Jewish, parents or grandparents, is considered non-Aryan. It is sufficient that one parent or one grandparent be non-Aryan." Most university professors in Germany at the time were civil servants, and therefore they were subject to the law and German universities began to systematically dismiss their Jewish faculty. Nearly 15 percent of university researchers, and 18 percent of mathematics professors, were dismissed in 1933 and 1934.

Because German mathematics played a central role in the world mathematical community at the time, many of the dismissed professors had little trouble finding employment outside Germany. Most of them, in fact, emigrated, with the main destination countries being the United States, England, Turkey, and Palestine. A small minority were unable to leave Germany, and some of those perished in the Holocaust.

Waldinger's study exploited this natural experiment to evaluate the impact of the dismissals on the quality of the doctoral students produced by the mathematics departments in German universities. The econometric identification of the impact of the supply shock follows from the fact that the dismissals did not affect all mathematics departments equally. Some of the departments lost few mathematicians, while other departments dismissed half of their faculty. In general, the best mathematics departments were the ones hardest hit. The two leading German mathematics departments at the time were those at the University of Göttingen and the University of Berlin. The dismissed professors at these two departments included such eminent mathematicians as John von Neumann, Richard Courant, and Richard von Mises.

Using archival records from German universities, Waldinger examined the professional careers of doctoral students who were enrolled in German universities before and after the dismissals. The departure of many leading mathematicians should presumably affect the output produced by the doctoral students (as measured, for example, not only by the number of publications in the students' career, but also by the number of citations that those publications received). In fact, the existence of strong human capital externalities would imply that post-1933 students graduating from the departments that suffered a serious decline in quality (for instance, the departure of von Neumann) should have lower lifetime productivity than the students who graduated from those same departments just prior to 1933.

Figure 8.3 summarizes the key results from this fascinating case study. The top panel in the figure shows the impact of the dismissals on student productivity. In particular, Waldinger examined the careers of the students who obtained their doctorates in each of the German university departments and calculated the probability that a student's research output had received at least one lifetime citation. The figure shows the mean probability of one lifetime citation for each cohort of students in two types of departments: departments where no dismissals occurred and departments where high-quality professors were dismissed.[11] It is obvious that students enrolled in the departments that suffered the heaviest losses experienced a relative decline in their productivity, as measured by their subsequent influence in the mathematics profession. The relation between student productivity and departmental quality, therefore, suggests the presence of human capital spillovers. The departure of Jewish mathematical luminaries depressed the future contribution of students who were deprived of their mentorship.

In more recent work, Waldinger (2012) extended the analysis to other scientific disciplines, including physics. About 14 percent of German physics professors were also dismissed after the Nazi edict, including Albert Einstein. As with mathematics, the dismissals did not affect all departments equally. The bottom panel of Figure 8.3 illustrates the impact of these dismissals, not on the doctoral students left behind, but on the *colleagues* of the dismissed physicists. In other words, the analysis now attempts to

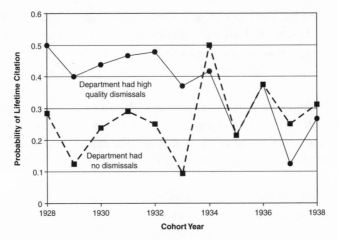

A. Impact on Output of Doctoral Students, Mathematics

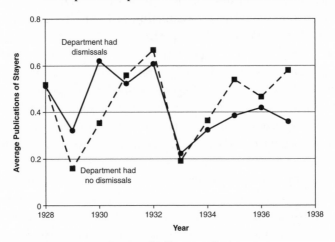

B. Impact on Output of Colleagues, Physics

Figure 8.3. The Productivity Impact of the Dismissal of Jewish Professors in Nazi Germany

Sources: Waldinger (2010, p. 813) and Waldinger (2012, p. 852).

Notes: In Panel A, the department had high-quality dismissals if the average quality of the dismissed scientists (as measured by the number of pre-1932 citations) was above the department mean. The output of the doctoral students is measured by the probability that they had at least one lifetime citation to their work. Panel B examines the impact on the productivity of the colleagues "left behind" by comparing their average number of publications in departments that had and did not have dismissals.

detect the existence of "peer effects"—the possibility that human capital externalities affect the productivity of one's peers in the workplace. Figure 8.3 shows that no such peer effects exist, at least in this particular natural experiment. The trend in the publication rate of the colleagues of Albert Einstein and others who left Germany after the Nazi edict is essentially the same as that of physicists employed by departments that had no dismissals.

In sum, the Waldinger case studies of the dismissal of Jewish professors by the Nazi regime reveal an interesting insight: an exodus of high-skill workers seems to have a strong effect on the productivity of the students they directly interact with (that is, the students they mentor), but has no impact on the productivity of their geographically close colleagues.[12]

The Collapse of the Soviet Union

Soon after the collapse of the Soviet Union in 1992, over 1,000 Soviet mathematicians (or roughly 10 percent of the stock) left the country, with around one-third eventually settling in the United States.[13] To understand the nature of this supply shock, it is helpful to describe the chasm that separated the Soviet and Western mathematical communities throughout much of the twentieth century. A key event cementing the separation was the "Luzin affair." In 1936, Nikolai Luzin, a mathematician at Moscow State University and a member of the USSR Academy of Sciences, became the target of a political witch hunt. The allegations included not only the generic charge of promoting anti-Soviet propaganda, but also the specific accusation that Luzin saved his best theorems for publication in foreign outlets. The impact on Soviet mathematics was swift and dramatic, with Soviet mathematicians quickly grasping that they should publish only in Soviet journals.

To varying degrees between 1922 and 1992, the Soviet government imposed restrictions on which scientists could communicate with Western peers, the parameters of scientific travel, the acceptable outlets for publication, and access to Western materials. In addition, although translations of Soviet journals eventually became available, many American mathematicians exhibited a "home country bias," being far less familiar with Soviet mathematical developments. Just as speakers of one language, when separated geographically for many generations, eventually develop separate and different dialects, so Soviet and Western mathematicians began to specialize in very different fields within the discipline of mathematics.[14]

Table 8.3 summarizes some of the differences in specialization between Soviet and American mathematicians across the nearly 70 fields that make up the discipline of mathematics. The two most popular Soviet fields were partial differential equations and ordinary differential equations, and these two fields accounted for 17.8 percent of the Soviet publications. The two most popular American fields were statistics and operations research, and these two fields accounted for 15.6 percent of the American publications.

Using archival information from the American Mathematical Society, Borjas and Doran (2012) constructed a data set that reports the number of papers published by every mathematician since 1939, by field and year. These fields are very narrowly defined—for example, algebraic topology, partial differential equations, and abstract harmonic analysis. Given the very different research interests of American and Soviet mathematicians prior to the collapse of the Soviet Union, these field classifications can help determine whether

Table 8.3 Main fields of mathematical publications in the Soviet Union and the United States, 1984–1989

Field	Share of papers published in the Soviet Union	Share of papers published in the United States
Top fields in the Soviet Union		
1. Partial differential equations	0.104	0.033
2. Ordinary differential equations	0.074	0.019
3. Quantum theory	0.068	0.059
4. Probability theory and stochastic processes	0.061	0.039
5. Global analysis, analysis on manifolds	0.048	0.039
Top fields in the United States		
1. Statistics	0.016	0.085
2. Operations research, mathematical programming	0.044	0.071
3. Quantum theory	0.068	0.059
4. Computer science	0.015	0.045
5. Numerical analysis	0.043	0.043

Source: Adapted from Borjas and Doran (2012, p. 1149).

Notes: The fields listed in the table represent the five "most popular" fields in mathematics in the Soviet Union and the United States, respectively, just prior to the collapse of the Soviet Union.

the exposure to new knowledge in a very narrow specialization generates sufficiently strong human capital externalities for the preexisting workers.

There are, in fact, reasons to suspect that these spillovers could be unusually strong. Before 1992 the average (future) émigré had published 10 more papers and received 66 more citations than the typical Soviet who remained in the Soviet Union (Borjas and Doran 2012, p. 1163). After 1992 the émigrés' productivity in the United States far surpassed that of the preexisting American mathematicians. In short, the Soviet émigré supply shock was composed of (very) positively selected mathematicians.

The net productivity effect of the influx can be measured by comparing the productivity of (preexisting) American mathematicians who had worked on problems where the Soviets could offer assistance and/or competition with that of mathematicians who had worked on problems that the Soviets knew little about. To quantify the degree of exposure, Borjas and Doran calculated an index that reflects the field "overlap" between the pre-1990 publication record of *each* preexisting American mathematician and that of the Soviets. Let a_{ij} be the share of papers that mathematician i published in field j, and let s_j be the share of all Soviet papers published in field j before the collapse of the Soviet Union. The commonly used index of similarity is defined by:

$$D_i = 1 - \frac{1}{2} \sum_j \left| a_{ij} - s_j \right|. \tag{8.6}$$

The index of similarity equals one when there is a perfect overlap in the relative field distributions between American mathematician i and the Soviet research program, and zero when there is total dissimilarity. The mean index of similarity in the sample of preexisting American mathematicians is 0.058; the 25th percentile value is 0.016 and the 75th percentile value is 0.077.

The data used to measure the net impact of the Soviet influx consist of a panel where an observation gives the output of each (preexisting) American mathematician in each year from 1978 to 2008. Let $y_i(t)$ be the number of papers published by mathematician i in year t. The regression model is then given by:

$$y_{it} = \phi_i + \phi_t + X_i(t)\, \gamma + \theta\,(T \times D_i) + \varepsilon, \tag{8.7}$$

where ϕ_i is a vector of individual fixed effects; ϕ_t is a vector of year fixed effects; X is a vector of standardizing variables that includes the mathematician's years of work experience; and T is a dummy variable indicating if the year for the particular observation is 1992 or beyond.

The coefficient θ measures whether the productivity of mathematicians who had pursued a Soviet-style research agenda changed after 1992, when the Soviet ideas began to be disseminated to a wider audience in the United States, and Soviet mathematicians began to publish their ideas in the same journals and compete for jobs in the same institutions as American mathematicians. Table 8.4 shows that the coefficient θ is negative and the effect is sizable. An increase in the index of similarity from the 25th to the 75th percentile reduces the number of annual publications by 0.09 (or -1.5×0.06). The regression, therefore, predicts a relative decline of about 1.5 published papers (or 0.09×17) over the 1992–2008 period for the "exposed" mathematician. The average mathematician published around 6.8 papers during that period, so that the Soviet supply shock reduced productivity by around 20 percent. It is evident, therefore, that the externalities, even in the unique context of an influx of mathematical "superstars," were not sufficiently strong to swamp the competitive forces unleashed by the law of diminishing returns.

Table 8.4 The impact of the Soviet supply shock on the productivity of American mathematicians

Specification	Number of papers
1. Sample period: 1978–2008	−1.523
	(0.113)
2. Sample period: 1978–1999	−1.056
	(0.111)
3. Sample periods: 1978–1991 and 2000–2008	−1.930
	(0.150)

Source: Borjas and Doran (2012, p. 1170).

Notes: The data consist of a panel where each observation represents a mathematician-year permutation, and the sample is restricted to American mathematicians whose first publication appeared prior to 1990. Standard errors are reported in parentheses and are clustered at the individual level. The dependent variable gives the number of papers that a mathematician published in a given year. The table reports the coefficient of the interaction between a post-1992 indicator variable and the "index of similarity" measuring the resemblance between a mathematician's pre-1990 research interests and the Soviet research program. All regressions include a vector of individual fixed effects, year fixed effects, and the mathematician's years of experience (introduced as a fourth-order polynomial).

It is easy to illustrate graphically the impact of the supply shock on the productivity of American mathematicians with overlapping research agendas. Suppose we classify mathematicians whose index of similarity is in the upper quartile of the distribution as "most exposed," while the group in the bottom quartile is "least exposed." The raw trends shown in Figure 8.4 are revealing. Prior to 1990 the most exposed group had a slight upward trend in the average number of papers published annually, while the least exposed group had a slight downward trend. After 1990 there is a precipitous decline in the publication rate of the group whose research agenda overlaps most with that of the Soviets.[15]

Table 8.4 also presents regressions that specifically examine the question of whether the spillover effects are more apparent in the long run. In row 2, the empirical analysis is limited to the years 1978–1999, so that the regressions measure the short-run productivity effect, while the regressions reported in row 3 include the years 1978–1991 and 2000–2008, so that the productivity impact is measured roughly 10 to 15 years after the Soviet influx occurred. If anything, the long-run effect is *more negative* than the short-run effects. It is typically very difficult for academics to reenter the publications market once they have taken some years off from successful active research.

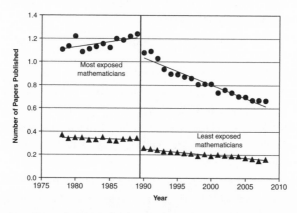

Figure 8.4. Trends in the Publication Rate of American Mathematicians

Source: Borjas and Doran (2012, p. 1172).

Note: The sample consists of American mathematicians whose first publication appeared prior to 1990. The least exposed mathematicians are in the bottom quartile of the distribution of the index of similarity between their published work and the pre-1990 Soviet research program, while the most exposed mathematicians are in the top quartile of the distribution.

As noted earlier, the preexisting American mathematicians would find it very difficult to avoid the competitive effects of the Soviet supply shock by switching disciplines and becoming physicists or computer scientists overnight. Nevertheless, there are other margins along which knowledge producers can adjust to escape the adverse effects. For example, mathematicians who are conducting research on a particular set of questions can respond to supply shocks by shifting their efforts and resources to a different set of questions. Borjas and Doran (2014) introduce the concept of "cognitive mobility" to measure the transition from one location to another in the *space of ideas*. In other words, American mathematicians working in partial differential equations or statistics could shift their research interests and start working on different mathematical topics to take advantage of the changed opportunities.

It is easy to describe the mechanism generating these cognitive mobility flows. Let MP_{iS} and MP_{iA} denote the marginal product of mathematician i in Soviet- and American-style fields, respectively. An income-maximizing mathematician who decided to conduct research in Soviet-dominated fields prior to the collapse of the Soviet Union must have satisfied the inequality $MP_{iS} > MP_{iA}$. Let ρ_i measure the net effect of the supply shock on the mathematician's productivity in Soviet-style research. After the supply shock, a Soviet-style mathematician engages in cognitive mobility and switches to American-style research only if:

$$MP_{iS} + \rho_i < MP_{iA} - C_i, \tag{8.8}$$

where C_i gives the costs of cognitive mobility (such as retooling skills). The preshock revealed preference of mathematician i implies that a Soviet-style mathematician will switch to American-style research only if $\rho_i < -C_i$. Because mobility costs are positive, a Soviet-style mathematician responds to the supply shock by switching to American-style research only if the net effect ρ_i is strongly negative.

Consider instead the cognitive mobility decisions of mathematicians who are initially conducting American-style research. These mathematicians satisfy the inequality $MP_{iA} > MP_{iS}$ and switch to Soviet-style research after the supply shock only if:

$$MP_{iS} + \rho_i - C_i > MP_{iA}. \tag{8.9}$$

Because these mathematicians had an initial advantage in conducting American-style research, the observation of cognitive mobility to Soviet-style fields implies that $\rho_i > C_i$. Cognitive mobility from American-style to

Soviet-style research implies the presence of strong positive externalities. In short, the direction of flows of cognitive movers provides *independent* information about the relative importance of human capital spillovers. As people "vote with their minds" in search of the best research opportunities, they reveal private information about changes in relative productivities in different locations of idea space.

In fact, the most exposed preexisting American mathematicians engaged in a substantial amount of cognitive mobility in the aftermath of the Soviet supply shock. Figure 8.5 illustrates the key trends based on whether the mathematician wrote a Soviet-style or an American-style

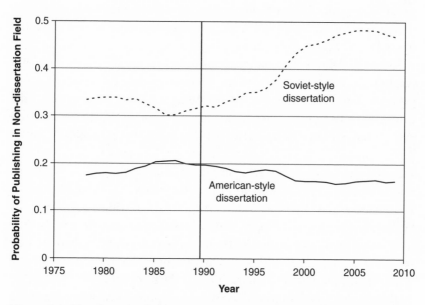

Figure 8.5. Trends in the Cognitive Mobility Rate of American Mathematicians

Source: Borjas and Doran (2014, fig. 1A).

Notes: The sample consists of American mathematicians whose first publication appeared prior to 1992. A field is defined to be "Soviet-style" if it was one of the top 10 fields of publication in the Soviet Union prior to 1990; all other fields are defined as "American-style" fields. A mathematician is then classified as having written a Soviet-style or an American-style dissertation based on the field of his first publication. The cognitive mobility rates give the probability that a preexisting American mathematician who wrote a Soviet-style (American-style) dissertation subsequently writes an American-style (Soviet-style) paper. The trend is smoothed by using a 3-year moving average of the rate of cognitive mobility centered on the middle year in the interval.

dissertation.[16] In the 1980s, before the collapse of the Soviet Union, American mathematicians who wrote their dissertations on American-style topics had about a 20 percent probability of writing in a Soviet-style field in subsequent papers. This probability declined slightly after 1992, suggesting that the presence of the Soviet influx made it a bit less likely that the Americans would "try out" research in Soviet-style fields.

In contrast, before the collapse of the Soviet Union, American mathematicians who wrote their dissertations on Soviet-style topics had a 30 to 35 percent probability of writing on a non-Soviet topic in each of their later papers. But this probability began to increase rapidly after the Soviet influx. In other words, American mathematicians who wrote a Soviet-style dissertation responded to the influx by moving to a new location in idea space that received *fewer* immigrants. The evidence, therefore, suggests that the net spillover effect must be strongly negative.

Although the recent literature seems to be generating a confusing set of results regarding the practical value of human capital externalities, it is important to emphasize that the various studies are attempting to detect the externalities along very different dimensions. Some of the studies measure externalities within a collaborative network (such as the students of Jewish mathematicians in Nazi Germany); other studies measure them within a narrow geographic area (such as the departmental colleagues of the Jewish scientists or the high-skill workers in areas that receive a large supply of H-1B visa holders); and still other studies measure them within a discipline or field (such as the impact of supply shocks in particular disciplines in the doctoral labor market or in particular mathematical fields).[17] There is little reason to presume that spillovers remain equally strong regardless of the economic distance between the donor and the recipient of the externality.

There is also a sense in which case studies of specific disciplines may "miss the point" in their efforts to detect the externalities. For example, even if the average American mathematician published less as a result of the Soviet supply shock, it could easily be that mathematics as a whole is better off. In the long term, the contributions to overall mathematical knowledge made by the Soviet émigrés could outweigh the short-run cost imposed on preexisting American mathematicians. Although this is certainly a plausible argument, it is also problematic, particularly in the context of mathematics. Mathematical proofs that are true are true forever. As a result, there is an opportunity cost to unpublished proofs. A complete cost-benefit analysis would require a comparison of the long-term value of the proofs that were proven by the Soviet émigrés (or inspired by their work) with the proofs that would have been proven by the displaced American mathematicians.

Finally, it is notable that much of the research focuses on the knowledge production function in a very specific (and peculiar) institutional setting: academia. Deep-rooted features like tenure and relatively inelastic demand in university departments constrain the nature of the productivity effects that supply shocks can generate in the academic marketplace. Moreover, the academic market is unforgiving in one important sense: it is very difficult to "escape" the short-term effects of a supply shock by temporarily moving outside the academy and returning to a university job at a later point in life. It is not hard to imagine that the same flows of high-skill immigrants could have had very different productivity repercussions if filtered through a competitive setting.

9

The Second Generation

———————————————◆———————————————

THE ULTIMATE IMPACT of immigration on a host economy depends not only on what happens during the life cycle of the immigrant population, but also on the rate of assimilation across generations. Because of the surge in international migration, the population share of second-generation persons (that is, of persons born in the host country with at least one foreign-born parent) will grow rapidly in the next few decades. In the United States, for example, the fraction of second-generation persons in the population is predicted to rise from 9.7 percent in 1990 to over 15 percent by 2050, with the third-generation making up an additional 11 percent of the population by the end of the century (Edmonston and Passel 1992, p. 471).

This chapter summarizes the evidence on economic assimilation across generations. The data reveal that the sizable inequality in economic outcomes across national origin groups observed in the immigrant population tends to narrow across generations, although there seems to be more "stickiness" than is typically found in studies that correlate the earnings of parents and children. This stickiness suggests that ethnicity may play an independent role in intergenerational mobility.

Income Mobility in Immigrant Families

At least in the U.S. context, it is widely believed that the socioeconomic performance of the children of immigrants far surpasses that of their parents. Much of this perception can be traced back to the early studies of Chiswick (1977) and Carliner (1980). Both of these studies compared the earnings of various generations of workers in the United States at a particular point in time, specifically the 1970 decennial census. Table 9.1 summarizes the available evidence in the United States for three such cross-sections: the 1940 census, the 1970 census, and the pooled 1996–2005 Current Population Surveys (CPS), which, for convenience, I will refer to as the "2000" cross-section.[1]

Table 9.1 Wage differentials across generations (relative to the third generation)

	1940	1970	2000
A. Age-adjusted log weekly wage			
First generation	0.079	0.015	−0.233
	(0.008)	(0.003)	(0.004)
Second generation	0.214	0.158	0.086
	(0.008)	(0.002)	(0.007)
B. Age- and education-adjusted log weekly wage			
First generation	0.132	0.026	−0.135
	(0.008)	(0.002)	(0.004)
Second generation	0.227	0.131	0.039
	(0.007)	(0.002)	(0.006)

Sources: U.S. Census PUMS, 1940, 1970, and the pooled 1996–2005 CPS (which forms the "2000 cross-section"); see Appendix B for details.

Notes: The first generation consists of men (aged 25–64) born abroad, while the second generation consists of men born in the United States with at least one parent born abroad. All other men are in the residual third generation. Standard errors are reported in parentheses. The wage differences reported in the table are obtained from individual-level regressions estimated separately in each cross-section. The dependent variable gives the worker's log weekly wage, and the regressors include variables indicating the worker's generation and a third-order polynomial in the worker's age (and years of education in Panel B). The regressions using the pooled CPS also include a vector of year fixed effects indicating the survey from which the observation is drawn. There are 50,253 observations in the 1940 regressions, 1,046,095 in the 1970 regressions, and 378,234 in the 2000 regressions.

Each of these cross-section data files allows the precise identification of two generations of Americans: the immigrant generation (persons born abroad) and the second generation (persons born in the United States who have at least one parent born abroad). The generation of the remaining persons in the sample (those who have American-born parents and were themselves born in the United States) cannot be determined, but they are typically referred to as "third-generation" Americans. It is worth noting, however, that the residual group of the third generation contains individuals who are both grandchildren of immigrants as well as descendants of the Mayflower Pilgrims.

For each of the available cross-sections, Table 9.1 reports the (age-adjusted) log weekly wage of first- and second-generation workers relative to that of the baseline third generation. The calculation uses the sample of working men aged 25–64 who are not enrolled in school.[2] In 1970, for example, immigrant men earned 1.5 percent more than workers in the third generation, while the second-generation earned 15.8 percent more than the baseline. Put differently, second-generation workers in 1970 earned more than both the immigrants and than the subsequent generations. In fact, Table 9.1 reveals this same pattern in every cross-section snapshot. In 1940, second-generation men earned 21.4 percent more than the baseline third generation, while immigrants earned only 7.9 percent more. Finally, in 2000, second-generation men earned 8.6 percent more than the baseline, while immigrants earned 23.3 percent less.

The wage superiority of second-generation workers in each cross-section seems to imply—and has been interpreted as implying—that second-generation Americans earn more than both their parents and their children. One story used to justify this inference is that the children of immigrants are "hungry" and have the drive and ambition that ensures success in the U.S. labor market—but this hunger is lost once the immigrant household becomes fully Americanized by the third generation.

The discussion of economic assimilation at the beginning of this book emphasized that the strong positive correlation between earnings and years-since-migration found in cross-section studies says nothing about the actual earnings gain experienced by specific immigrant cohorts. Ironically, I now return to the same technical point at the end of the journey.

In particular, the cross-section snapshots summarized in Table 9.1 do not necessarily provide any valuable information about the rate of income mobility in immigrant households. After all, the family ties among the three generations identifiable in any cross-section of data are very tenuous. It is unlikely that most working-age second-generation persons enumerated in a particular cross-section are the direct descendants of the immigrants enumerated at the same time. For instance, working-age immigrants enumerated in 2000 (most of whom arrived in the 1980s and 1990s) typically cannot have American-born children who are also of working age by the year 2000. Second-generation Americans of working age are the descendants of immigrants who have been in the country for at least three or four decades. Because there are skill differences across immigrant cohorts, and because some of these differences could easily be transmitted to their children, the wage gap between first- and second-generation workers in a cross-section does not correctly portray the income mobility that occurs across generations.

To calculate the improvement in economic status between the first and second generations, one must link the economic performance of parents and children, rather than compare the economic performance of workers belonging to different generations at a point in time. Although the decennial censuses do not allow an exact matching of parents and children across censuses, it is possible to conduct a rough intergenerational comparison by "tracking" the immigrant population across the decades.[3]

The 1970 census provides information on the economic performance of the immigrants present in the United States at that time. Many of these immigrants are, in fact, the parents of the second-generation workers enumerated in the 2000 cross-section. Similarly, the 1940 census provides information on the economic performance of immigrants in 1940. These immigrants, in turn, are probably the parents of the second-generation workers enumerated at the time of the 1970 census. It is only by comparing the economic performance of immigrant workers in 1940 with the economic performance of second-generation workers in 1970—or the economic performance of immigrants in 1970 with that of the second-generation in 2000—that we can better assess the economic progress experienced by the children of immigrants.

Consider again the relative wage information summarized in Table 9.1. If we (incorrectly) used only the information provided by the 2000 cross-section, we would conclude that because second-generation workers earn 8.6 percent more than the baseline third generation and first-generation workers earn 23.3 percent less than the baseline, second-generation workers earn about 32 percent more than first-generation workers. A longitudinal calculation, however, reveals much less income mobility. The typical immigrant in 1970 earned 1.5 percent more than the typical third-generation worker. And the typical second-generation worker in 2000 (who is presumably the descendant of the immigrants enumerated in 1970) earns 8.6 percent more than the baseline. In short, the true intergenerational growth in wages was only on the order of 7 percent—rather than the 32 percent implied by the 2000 cross-section.

Similarly, the 1970 census snapshot seems to suggest that the children of immigrants earn 14.3 percent more than their parents (or 15.8 percent minus 1.5 percent). But the economic status of the parents of these second-generation workers can only be observed in the 1940 census, where the immigrants had a relative wage advantage of 7.9 percent. The intergenerational wage improvement between 1940 and 1970 is then on the order of 7.9 percent (or .158 − .079). Note, however, that the roughly 8 percent intergenerational wage growth between the first and second generations still represents a substantial improvement in economic opportunities.

The bottom panel of Table 9.1 reports the wage differentials among the various generations after adjusting for differences in educational attainment across workers. The adjusted wage differentials reveal that much of the longitudinal income mobility found in the "raw" data disappears in the adjusted data. In other words, much of the intergenerational progress observed between the first and second generations (which leads to the 8 percent wage increase) can be explained by the changes in educational attainment that occur between these two groups, as the native-born children of immigrants go through the American education system.

The evidence summarized in Table 9.1 reveals a second interesting empirical pattern. Given the discussion in Chapter 2, it is not surprising that the relative wage of immigrants has declined steadily since 1940. The table also reveals, however, a concurrent decline in the relative wage of second-generation workers. In 1940 the typical second-generation worker earned 21.4 percent more than baseline workers. By 1970 the wage advantage had fallen to 15.8 percent, and by 2000 it had fallen to 8.6 percent. In short, the relative economic status of second-generation workers has been declining over time—just like that of the foreign-born workforce—but with a lag.[4]

The Persistence of Ethnic Wage Differentials

The melting pot metaphor vividly captures the traditional view of the intergenerational mobility experienced by immigrant households: Immigrants are molded from a collection of diverse national origin groups into a homogeneous native population in a relatively short time, perhaps two generations. Although some sociologists have questioned the relevance of the melting pot hypothesis for understanding the experience of many ethnic groups in the United States, the metaphor has a magnetic and intuitive resonance that confounds the detractors.[5] As a result, the "assimilationist" perspective has long dominated the thinking of many observers of the immigrant experience.

As we saw in Chapter 1, there is a large variance in earnings across the national origin groups that make up the immigrant population. Not surprisingly, there also exists a large variance in earnings across the ethnic groups that make up the second-generation workforce. Some ethnic groups do quite well in the U.S. labor market, while other ethnic groups fare much worse. To determine how much of the ethnic earnings differences in the immigrant generation persist into the second generation, consider a regression model that relates the mean relative wage of a second-generation ethnic group to the mean wage of their first-generation counterpart:

$$\log \overline{w}_{i2} = \alpha + \beta \log \overline{w}_{i1} + \varepsilon, \tag{9.1}$$

where $\log \overline{w}_{ig}$ gives the mean log earnings of workers in ethnic group i in generation g ($g = 1, 2$) relative to the wage of the baseline third generation. The coefficient β measures the rate at which the mean earnings of different ethnic groups converge across generations, and measures the "rate of mean convergence"—with a higher β, of course, implying a lower rate of convergence.

This regression model, of course, is inspired by the voluminous literature that measures the correlation in earnings between parents and children at the *individual* level. The generic regression in the individual-level studies is given by:

$$\log w_{\ell 2} = a + b \log w_{\ell 1} + \varepsilon', \tag{9.1'}$$

where $w_{\ell 1}$ gives the earnings of worker ℓ and $w_{\ell 2}$ gives the earnings of his child. The coefficient b is often called the "intergenerational correlation" between parents and children.

Until the 1980s it was generally believed that the intergenerational correlation b in the United States was around 0.2.[6] Put differently, if there were a 30 percent wage gap between any two randomly chosen fathers, the expected wage gap between their children would be only around 6 percent (or 30 percent × 0.2). If the intergenerational correlation were constant across generations, the expected wage gap among the grandchildren would be only 1.2 percent (or 30 percent × 0.2 × 0.2). An intergenerational correlation of 0.2, therefore, implies that there is a great deal of income mobility in the population because the economic status of workers in the parental generation is essentially uncorrelated with that of their grandchildren.

Beginning with Solon (1992), a number of studies have shattered this consensus.[7] The revisionist literature argues convincingly that the intergenerational correlation in the United States is much higher, perhaps as high as 0.4 (Lee and Solon, 2009). The problem can be traced to the presence of a substantial amount of measurement error in parental skills. When workers are asked about the socioeconomic status of their parents, the responses regarding parental education and earnings are probably not very precise. This measurement error weakens the estimated correlation between parents and children in equation (9.1′). The revisionist studies have shown that the estimated coefficient b often doubles in size after netting out the impact of measurement error. If the intergenerational correlation were indeed around 0.4, it would imply that a 30 percent wage gap between two parents translates into a 12 percent expected wage gap between the children and a 5 percent wage gap between the grandchildren. Skill and income differences across households, therefore, would be more persistent across generations.

A critical distinction between the models that examine the rate of wage convergence across ethnic groups in equation (9.1) and the models that estimate the correlation between parents and children in equation (9.1′) is that the former use group-level data, while the latter use individual-level data. The aggregation of the data at the ethnic group level should wash out the measurement errors in parental skills emphasized by Solon, so that estimates of the parameter β should be similar to those of b after the latter are adjusted for measurement error.

Figure 9.1 illustrates the dispersion in the group-level data and the regression line that links the mean earnings of ethnic groups in the United States between the first and second generations.[8] In particular, the horizontal axis gives the age-adjusted log weekly wage of immigrant workers in 1970, while the vertical axis gives the log wage of the second generation in 2000 (each relative to the respective third generation). There is obviously a large variance in relative earnings across ethnic groups in both the first and second generations. There is also a positive correlation between the average skills

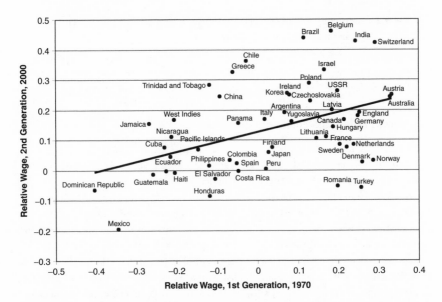

Figure 9.1. Income Mobility between First and Second Generations, 1970–2000

Sources: U.S. Census PUMS, 1970, and the pooled 1996–2005 CPS (which forms the "2000 cross-section"); see Appendix B for details.

Notes: Each point in the scatter diagram gives the age-adjusted log weekly wage of a foreign-born national origin group in 1970 and of the respective second-generation ethnic group in 2000 (each relative to the residual third generation in the relevant cross-section). The notes to Table 9.2 describe the construction of the relative wage data for each group in each generation. The sample is restricted to the 54 largest national origin groups.

of workers in the two generations; the national origin groups that did well in the first generation also did well in the second.

Table 9.2 reports the estimates of the parameter β over both the 1940–1970 and the 1970–2000 periods. The intergenerational correlation is 0.49 in the earlier period and 0.59 in the latter. It is notable that the estimated rate of mean convergence in earnings across ethnic groups is somewhat higher than the "consensus" estimate of the intergenerational correlation between the earnings of parents and children (which is somewhere between 0.3 and 0.4). The reasons for the relatively higher "stickiness" in the mean earnings of ethnic groups will be discussed at length later in this chapter.

The estimates of the coefficient β suggest two interesting conclusions.[9] First, about half of the wage differential between any two national origin

Table 9.2 Intergenerational correlation between first and second generations in the mean wage of ethnic groups

	1940–1970	1970–2000
1. Age-adjusted relative wage	0.485	0.592
	(0.085)	(0.115)
2. Age- and education-adjusted relative wage	0.312	0.371
	(0.051)	(0.061)

Sources: U.S. Census PUMS, 1940, 1970, and the pooled 1996–2005 CPS (which forms the "2000 cross-section"); see Appendix B for details.

Notes: The unit of observation is an ethnic group. The regressions use the 30 largest groups in 1940–1970 and the 54 largest groups in 1970–2000. The dependent variable is the relative log weekly wage of the second-generation ethnic group, and the independent variable is the relative log weekly wage of the respective first-generation group thirty years earlier (with the baseline being the residual third generation); see the notes to Table 9.1 for the definition of the generations. Robust standard errors are reported in parentheses. All regressions are weighted by the sample size of the ethnic group in the second generation. The relative wages are the coefficients of the ethnic group fixed effects from individual-level log weekly wage regressions estimated separately for the first and second generation in each census year, after adjusting for a third-order polynomial in age (and education in row 2). The first-stage regressions estimated in the pooled CPS also include a vector of year fixed effects indicating the survey from which the observation was drawn.

groups in the first generation persists into the second. If the average wage of two ethnic groups is 30 percentage points apart in the first generation, the expected wage of the two groups is expected to be about 15 percentage points apart in the second. There is some mobility, but ethnicity remains an important determinant of labor market outcomes in the second generation.

Second, although the point estimates suggest more intergenerational stickiness in recent decades, the difference between the 1940–1970 and 1970–2000 intergenerational correlations is not statistically significant. As noted by Card et al. (2000), the data indicate that the process linking the earnings of first- and second-generation ethnic groups was roughly similar during the last half of the twentieth century, despite the major changes in economic and social conditions, as well as in immigration policy, over the period.

The bottom panel of Table 9.2 reports the estimated coefficients after the earnings data are adjusted not only for age differences across the groups, but for differences in educational attainment as well. The estimates of β are smaller after the data control for differences in educational attainment. The rate of convergence in mean earnings drops by nearly half to 0.31 in the 1940–1970 period and to 0.37 in the 1970–2000 period. Nevertheless, the intergenerational correlation is still sizable. In other words, ethnicity seems to matter even after adjusting for differences in educational attainment across the ethnic groups.

Let me conclude the discussion of mean convergence by noting a potentially important data problem that can seriously contaminate measures of intergenerational mobility. The definition of the ethnic group for a first- or second-generation worker is well defined: someone has to be born in a particular country in order for a worker to be classified into one of those groups. Suppose, however, that we wish to examine intergenerational mobility beyond the second generation and must now rely on a person's self-identification of ethnic status (for example, some category of Hispanic or Asian ancestry). In a series of important papers, Duncan and Trejo (2011, 2014) document that a person's self-reported ethnicity is endogenous and the resulting selection bias can easily contaminate observed measures of intergenerational mobility.

In particular, the "ethnic label" that an objective observer would choose for a person based on the birthplace of his parents or grandparents need not be the same as the label that person chooses to self-identify in a census survey. In fact, the combination of selective intermarriage and endogenous self-identification opens the way for a wide array of possibilities. As a result, the persons who opt into or opt out of particular ethnic groups are not a random sample of the potential members of that group. In the case of persons of Mexican ancestry, for example, Duncan and Trejo show that persons who have a well-defined Mexican heritage and have lower levels of socioeconomic achievement are more likely to self-identify as Mexicans than persons who have an equally well-defined Mexican heritage but have higher levels of achievement. This negative selection effectively hides some of the intergenerational progress experienced by persons of Mexican ancestry, because the sample of "Mexicans" in higher-order generations excludes those persons who, in fact, experienced the most upward mobility.

The measurement problems introduced by the endogeneity of ethnicity are likely to intensify as the number of second- and third-generation workers increases rapidly in the next few decades. Because the selection likely differs across different ethnic groups, however, it may prove difficult to establish how endogenous ethnic self-identification affects the measured rate of mean convergence.

Ethnic Capital

The estimated intergenerational correlation between the average earnings of ethnic groups reported in Table 9.2 is somewhat higher than would be expected given the value of the correlation in earnings between parents and children. To explain this discrepancy, some studies have examined the possibility that ethnicity *per se* may play an independent role in the intergenerational transmission process in immigrant families. Borjas (1992), for example, argued that ethnicity may act as an externality in the production of human capital. In particular, the skills of the next generation depend not only on parental inputs, but also on the overall quality of the ethnic environment in which parents make their investments, or "ethnic capital." The introduction of ethnic capital into an economic model of intergenerational mobility has one important implication: if the external effect of ethnicity is sufficiently strong, ethnic differences in skills observed in this generation may persist for several generations.

To illustrate, consider a one-person household in generation t. This person has a human capital stock that can either be sold to the marketplace at constant price R or used in the production of the human capital of his children. To simplify further, suppose that workers do not invest in their own human capital, so that the human capital stock of workers in generation $t+1$ is completely determined by the actions of generation t. Finally, suppose that the household has only one child.

The parent has a CES utility function defined over the child's quality, which is given by the human capital stock of the child, k_{t+1}, and own consumption C_t:

$$U_t = [\delta_1 k_{t+1}^\rho + \delta_2 C_t^\rho]^{1/\rho}, \tag{9.2}$$

where $\rho \leq 1$, and $\sigma = 1/(1-\rho)$ is the elasticity of substitution between consumption and child quality.

As noted above, the parent can either sell his human capital to the marketplace or devote a fraction π_t to the production of the child's human capital. Setting the price of C_t as the numeraire yields the budget constraint:

$$R(1-\pi_t) k_t = C_t. \tag{9.3}$$

Finally, suppose that the average human capital stock of the ethnic group in the parental generation, $\bar{k}_t$, or ethnic capital, acts as an externality in the production of the human capital of children. The production function for child quality is then given by:[10]

$$k_{t+1} = (\pi_t k_t)^{\beta_1} (\overline{k}_t)^{\beta_2}. \tag{9.4}$$

where $0 < \beta_1 < 1$ and $0 \leq \beta_2 < 1$. It turns out that the value of the sum $\beta_1 + \beta_2$ determines the extent to which skill differentials across ethnic groups converge over time.

The production function in (9.4) has two important properties. First, the specification uses the neutrality assumption introduced by Ben-Porath (1967) in his classic analysis of human capital accumulation. In particular, the parent's human capital stock (k_t) does not play an independent role in the production of the children's human capital. Second, the specification implies that parental time and ethnic capital are complements in the production of child quality. It is not only the case that persons who grow up in high-quality ethnic environments are exposed to social and economic factors that increase their eventual productivity, but also a given level of parental inputs is more productive in environments with higher-quality ethnic capital. This complementarity underlies some of the theoretical results that follow.

The maximization of the utility function in (9.2), subject to the budget constraint and the production technology, generates the household's supply function for time allocated to investing in the human capital of children, $\pi_t = \pi(k_t, \overline{k}_t)$. It is easy to show that the elasticities of π_t with respect to k_t and $\overline{k}_t$ are:

$$\frac{\partial \log \pi_t}{\partial \log k_t} = \frac{\rho(\beta_1 - 1)(1 - \pi_t)}{(1 - \pi_t)(1 - \rho\beta_1) + \pi_t(1 - \rho)}, \tag{9.5a}$$

$$\frac{\partial \log \pi_t}{\partial \log \overline{k}_t} = \frac{\rho\beta_2(1 - \pi_t)}{(1 - \pi_t)(1 - \rho\beta_1) + \pi_t(1 - \rho)}. \tag{9.5b}$$

The hypothesis of utility maximization does not generate unambiguous predictions about how the fraction of time devoted to investments in children varies with either the parental human capital stock or ethnic capital. The first ambiguity arises because increases in k_t generate both income and substitution effects, and these effects work in opposite directions. An increase in k_t raises the demand for child quality (because of the income effect), but also makes child quality more expensive. The CES functional form implies that parental time decreases with k_t when the elasticity of substitution between consumption and child quality is greater than one ($\rho > 0$), and increases otherwise.

The variable π_t also varies with respect to the amount of ethnic capital. Equation (9.5b) indicates that π_t and ethnic capital are positively correlated as long as the elasticity of substitution between consumption and child quality is greater than one. Intuitively, as long as C_t and k_{t+1} are easily substitutable, the household takes advantage of the complementarity in production between the parent's human capital and ethnic capital by devoting more time to their children in advantageous ethnic environments.

Despite the fact that the time devoted by parents to human capital investments in their children depends ambiguously on both parental human capital and on ethnic capital, the relation between child quality and these variables is unambiguous. In particular, it is easy to show that:

$$\frac{\partial \log k_{t+1}}{\partial \log k_t} = \frac{\beta_1(1-\rho)}{(1-\pi_t)(1-\rho\beta_1)+\pi_t(1-\rho)} > 0, \qquad (9.6a)$$

$$\frac{\partial \log k_{t+1}}{\partial \log \bar{k}_t} = \frac{\beta_2(1-\rho\pi_t)}{(1-\pi_t)(1-\rho\beta_1)+\pi_t(1-\rho)} > 0. \qquad (9.6b)$$

There is a positive relationship between child quality and both parental human capital and ethnic capital regardless of the value of the elasticity of substitution between own-consumption and child quality.

To analyze the evolution of the human capital stock across generations for a particular ethnic group, and hence to determine whether the dispersion in human capital across ethnic groups narrows over time, it is useful to consider the special case where all parents in the ethnic group have the same human capital, so that $k_t = \bar{k}_t$. The elasticity of (average) child quality with respect to $\bar{k}_t$ is then given by:

$$\frac{\partial \log \bar{k}_{t+1}}{\partial \log \bar{k}_t} = \frac{\beta_1(1-\rho)+\beta_2(1-\rho\pi_t)}{(1-\pi_t)(1-\rho\beta_1)+\pi_t(1-\rho)}. \qquad (9.7)$$

The average human capital stock of different ethnic groups will converge or diverge across generations depending on whether the elasticity in equation (9.7) is less than or greater than one. It is easy to show that:

$$\frac{\partial \log \bar{k}_{t+1}}{\partial \log \bar{k}_t} \begin{cases} <1, & \text{if } \beta_1+\beta_2<1, \\ =1, & \text{if } \beta_1+\beta_2=1, \\ >1, & \text{if } \beta_1+\beta_2>1. \end{cases} \qquad (9.8)$$

If the externality introduced by ethnic capital leads to constant returns in the human capital production function, ethnic inequality will persist indefinitely. In other words, sufficiently strong externalities can generate human capital growth paths where relative differences in skills among ethnic groups do not change over time. A key insight of the model is that the external effects of ethnicity can greatly retard the process of mean convergence.

Empirical Evidence on Ethnic Capital

The relevance of the ethnic capital model, of course, depends on whether the parameter β_2 is sufficiently positive in the "real world." The estimation of the model, however, imposes stringent data requirements. In particular, a regression analysis requires information not only on the matched skills of parents and children, but also on the ethnic background of a particular worker. These needs greatly limit the number of data sets that can be used to test the ethnic capital hypothesis. Borjas (1992, 1995c) estimated the model using data from the National Longitudinal Surveys of Youth (NLSY).[11]

The NLSY forms a panel of 12,686 young men and women who were first surveyed in 1979 when they were 14 to 22 years old. The data report both the respondent's and the father's educational attainment and occupation, as well as the respondents' earnings once they entered the labor market. A person's ethnicity is determined by the response to a question that asks: "What is your origin or descent?" The regressions use two alternative dependent variables to measure human capital: a person's educational attainment and the person's hourly wage rate. The father's wage is imputed by using information on the average earnings in the father's occupation.

The regression model implied by the ethnic capital hypothesis is:

$$y_{ij} = \gamma_1 x_{ij} + \gamma_2 \bar{x}_j + \varepsilon_{ij}, \tag{9.9}$$

where y_{ij} measures the skills of worker i in ethnic group j; x_{ij} gives the skills of his father; and $\bar{x}_j$ gives the average skills of the ethnic group in the father's generation.

Table 9.3 reports the coefficients estimated from alternative specifications of the regression model. The coefficient from a simple regression of a child's education on the father's education is 0.25, which is in the range of those reported in the literature. The addition of the ethnic capital variable to the regression shows that ethnic capital has a positive and significant impact both on the educational attainment and log earnings of the children. In

Table 9.3 Estimates of ethnic capital model

	Specification		
	(1)	(2)	(3)
A. Education			
Parental education	.246	0.240	0.175
	(.035)	(0.067)	(0.072)
Ethnic capital	—	0.200	0.038
		(0.047)	(0.029)
B. Log hourly wage			
Parental log wage	.381	0.377	0.250
	(.034)	(0.037)	(0.042)
Ethnic capital	—	0.319	0.046
		(0.156)	(0.133)
Includes neighborhood fixed effects	No	No	Yes

Source: Adapted from Borjas (1995c, p. 383).

Notes: The regressions use a random effects specification and the standard errors are reported in parentheses. The ethnic-capital variable gives either the mean-educational attainment (in Panel A) or the mean-log wage (in Panel B) of the ethnic group in the parental generation.

particular, a 1-year increase in the average schooling level of an ethnic group increases the schooling of the next generation by 0.2 years. Note that the coefficients of the ethnic capital and the parental skills variables have roughly similar magnitudes. Ethnic capital seems to play as important a role as the father's human capital in determining the skills of the next generation.

It is easy to show the link between the parameters estimated by the ethnic capital model in (9.9) and the intergenerational coefficients estimated using aggregate census data in the previous section. Aggregating equation (9.9) within ethnic groups leads to:

$$\bar{y}_j = (\gamma_1 + \gamma_2)\bar{x}_j + \bar{\varepsilon}_j, \qquad (9.10)$$

The regressions estimated in aggregate census data, therefore, estimate $\gamma_1 + \gamma_2$. This sum yields precisely the transmission coefficient relevant for determining the rate of mean convergence.[12] The estimates reported in Table 9.3 imply that the rate of mean convergence is between 0.4 and 0.7, similar to the regression coefficients reported earlier in this chapter that correlated the mean earnings of national origin groups across generations. The evidence, therefore, suggests that about half of the correlation in the mean skills of ethnic groups across generations is due to the external effects of ethnicity.

Although the ethnic capital model provides an interesting (and potentially important) interpretation of the intergenerational "stickiness" in ethnic outcomes, the measured impact of ethnic capital may also arise spuriously if parental skills are measured with error. To illustrate, suppose that the model that correctly captures the intergenerational mobility process is given by:

$$y = \delta x + \varepsilon, \tag{9.11}$$

where y gives the skills of children, x gives the skills of parents (with variance σ_x^2), and subscripts for individuals and ethnic groups are suppressed. The error term ε is i.i.d. and independent of x. Note that ethnic capital does *not* enter the "true" model.

Observed parental skills, x_1, are an imperfect measure of x. In particular, $x_1 = x + v_1$, where the random variable v_1 is i.i.d., with mean zero and variance σ_1^2. In addition, v_1 is independent of x and ε. The traditional errors-in-variables formula obviously implies that the least-squares regression of y on x_1 inconsistently estimates the parameter δ. Suppose, however, that a different measure of parental skills, x_2, is available, where x_2 gives the average skills of parents in the ethnic group, or ethnic capital. By construction, $x_2 = x + v_2$, where v_2 is i.i.d., with mean zero, variance σ_2^2, and is independent of ε and v_1. Note, however, that v_2 is not independent of x, because high values of parental skills imply lower values of v_2 within ethnic groups.[13] Using this notation, the ethnic capital regression model can be written as:

$$y = \theta_1 x_1 + \theta_2 x_2 + \varepsilon'. \tag{9.12}$$

Borjas (1992) shows that the OLS estimates of the parameters in (9.12) have the properties:

$$\text{plim}\,\hat{\theta}_1 = \frac{\pi h}{1 - h(1 - \pi)}\delta, \tag{9.13a}$$

$$\text{plim}\,\hat{\theta}_1 = \frac{1 - h}{1 - h(1 - \pi)}\delta, \tag{9.13b}$$

where $h = \sigma_x^2 / (\sigma_x^2 + \sigma_1^2)$, and $\pi = \sigma_2^2 / \sigma_x^2$. Equations (9.13a) and (9.13b) indicate that the estimated coefficients of parental capital and ethnic capital are each inconsistent estimates of the "true" transmission parameter δ. Equally important, the measurement error in parental skills will make it seem as if ethnic capital "matters." In fact, the coefficient of the ethnic capital variable will be larger, the greater the errors in measuring parental skills. In addition:

$$\text{plim}(\hat{\theta}_1 + \hat{\theta}_2) = \delta, \tag{9.14}$$

so that the sum of the two estimated coefficients of the ethnic capital model identifies the true intergenerational parameter δ even though ethnic capital does *not* play an independent role in the intergenerational mobility process.[14]

The fact that measurement error generates a spurious correlation between children's skills and ethnic capital suggests that it is important to go inside the "black box" of the ethnic capital variable in order to understand what it is that generates the external effect. It turns out that the ethnic capital effect is intimately linked with the residential segregation exhibited by ethnic groups in the United States. This residential segregation provides the environmental opportunity for ethnicity to matter and to generate the externalities that are at the core of the ethnic capital model.

Ethnicity and Residential Segregation

Ethnic neighborhoods have long been a dominant feature of cities. In fact, segregation by race and ethnicity often creates the invisible line that defines a neighborhood. These neighborhoods insulate people of similar backgrounds, and foster a set of cultural attitudes, social contacts, and economic opportunities that affect workers throughout their lives. The segregation suggests that some of the external effect of ethnicity may "work" through the fact that children are frequently exposed to a particular ethnic environment when they grow up.[15]

The number of data sets that can be used to estimate the ethnic capital model in the U.S. context dwindles even more if one also wishes to analyze the interaction between ethnic capital and residential segregation. In addition to information on parental skills and ethnic background, the analysis now requires the identification of a narrowly defined geographic area, such as a neighborhood, at the time the child was growing up. Borjas (1995c) used a version of the NLSY data that (confidentially) identified the zip code of each respondent in 1979, at the time the survey began.

The expanded NLSY can be used to calculate the probability that other NLSY respondents growing up in the same zip code had the same ethnic background.[16] Not surprisingly, there is strong evidence of residential segregation. For example, the average person of Mexican ancestry lived in a neighborhood that was 50.3 percent Mexican, even though only 4.1 percent of the population has Mexican ancestry. Similarly, the average person of Portuguese ancestry lived in a neighborhood that was 19.7 Portuguese, even though only 0.6 percent of the population is of Portuguese ancestry.

The clustering of particular ethnic groups in specific neighborhoods suggests that part of the ethnic capital effect in equation (9.9) may be capturing the influence of the neighborhood's socioeconomic background on intergenerational mobility. To illustrate, suppose that ethnic groups are completely segregated so that there is one ethnic group per neighborhood. The ethnic capital variable $\bar{x}_j$ would then also represent the mean skills of the neighborhood, and the coefficient γ_2 in (9.9) captures the total impact of the ethnic externality and of the neighborhood's socioeconomic background. The coefficient of ethnic capital would be significant even if ethnicity did not have a direct impact on intergenerational mobility and there were no measurement error in parental skills, but neighborhood characteristics mattered.

Of course, the data do not exhibit this extreme type of segregation. Ethnic groups, however, are likely to cluster by skill level, so that low-skill ethnic groups live together in low-income neighborhoods and high-skill ethnic groups live in high-income neighborhoods. The ethnic capital variable would again be correlated with the skill level of the neighborhood, and the ethnic capital coefficient could be capturing neighborhood effects (that is, the impact of the neighborhood's socioeconomic background), rather than the direct effect of ethnicity. In effect, the ethnic capital model may work because ethnic capital proxies for the relevant neighborhood characteristics that influence the intergenerational transmission process. If ethnicity did not have a direct impact on intergenerational mobility, controlling for the neighborhood characteristics would drive the ethnic capital coefficient down to zero.

Ethnic capital might still matter, *above and beyond neighborhood effects*, if intragroup contacts within a neighborhood are more frequent or more influential than intergroup contacts.[17] Children who belong to ethnic group

j are then exposed to a different set of values, social contacts, and economic opportunities than children who belong to other ethnic groups but who grow up in the same neighborhood. Ethnic capital would then influence the intergenerational mobility process even after controlling for neighborhood effects.

A simple way of determining the extent to which the impact of ethnic capital operates through neighborhood effects is to expand the model in (9.9) to include a vector of neighborhood fixed effects:

$$y_{ijk} = \phi_k + \gamma_1 x_{ij} + \gamma_2 \bar{x}_j + \varepsilon_{ijk}, \qquad (9.15)$$

where y_{ijk} measures the skills of person i in ethnic group j who grew up in neighborhood k; x_{ij} gives the skills of the father; $\bar{x}_j$ gives the average skills of the ethnic group in the father's generation; and ϕ_k is a vector of neighborhood fixed effects.

The coefficients γ_1 and γ_2 measure the *within-neighborhood* impact of parental skills and of ethnic capital. The last column of Table 9.3 reports the estimates of the generalized model in equation (9.15). Note that the introduction of a vector of fixed effects indicating the zip code where a person grew up reduces the parental coefficient in the educational attainment regression to 0.18 and the ethnic capital effect evaporates (the coefficient falls to 0.04 and is now insignificant).

Overall, the evidence suggests that what in the previous section I called the "ethnic capital effect" reflects mainly the impact of neighborhood characteristics (common to all residents of the neighborhood) on the intergenerational transmission process. In view of this result, it is worth asking if ethnicity *per se* plays any role in intergenerational mobility, above and beyond the influence of parents and neighborhoods. Ethnicity is likely to play a more important role among persons who grow up in a highly segregated ethnic environment. After all, these persons will probably experience (and be influenced by) more frequent social and economic intragroup contacts. To determine if ethnicity plays an independent role among workers raised in very segregated neighborhoods, I estimate the regression model after allowing for the ethnic capital coefficient to vary according to the extent of residential segregation in the neighborhood.

In particular, both the ethnic capital variable and the parental skills variable are interacted with a variable indicating the proportion of persons in the neighborhood who share the same ethnic background as the individual. Table 9.4 summarizes the results from the interactive model. The educa-

Table 9.4 Ethnic capital and residential segregation

	Percent of neighborhood's population in same ethnic group		
	<5%	5–33%	>33%
A. Education:			
Parental education	0.207	0.201	0.131
	(0.013)	(0.013)	(0.011)
Ethnic capital	0.049	0.044	0.119
	(0.026)	(0.027)	(0.027)
B. Log hourly wage:			
Parental log wage	0.318	0.329	0.259
	(0.076)	(0.074)	(0.062)
Ethnic capital	0.029	0.015	0.143
	(0.142)	(0.144)	(0.125)

Source: Borjas (1995c, p. 385).

Notes: The regressions use a random effects specification and the standard errors are reported in parentheses. The regression includes a vector of neighborhood fixed effects. The ethnic capital variable gives either the mean educational attainment (in Panel A) or the mean log wage (in Panel B) of the ethnic group in the parental generation. For each dependent variable, the coefficients are drawn from a single regression where both the parental and ethnic capital variables are interacted with fixed effects indicating the extent of segregation in the neighborhood where the person grew up.

tional attainment regressions, for instance, show that (after controlling for neighborhood fixed effects) the ethnic capital coefficient increases from 0.05 for children who grew up in areas where fewer than 5 percent of the neighbors had the same ethnic background to 0.12 for children who grew up in areas where at least 33 percent of the neighbors belonged to the same ethnic group. Ethnicity, therefore, has an independent external effect among children who grow up in highly segregated neighborhoods and are presumably most exposed to the ethnic influences.

It is too early to tell how these ethnic externalities will affect the workings of the melting pot in immigrant-receiving countries over the next century. Nevertheless, the continuing surge in international migration and the rapid growth of thriving ethnic enclaves suggest that ethnic externalities may play an increasingly important role in determining the skill composition of the descendants of current immigrants—*and* the economic impact of current immigration—far into the future.

Conclusion

———————————◆———————————

THE ECONOMIC LITERATURE on immigration came of age in the past three decades and now features a set of models and econometric methods that provide a solid foundation for future work. It is also clear, however, that there remain many questions in immigration economics—even putting aside the increasingly important policy challenges faced by both sending and receiving countries—that will continue to advance the literature. Perhaps the best way to conclude the journey of this book is to briefly summarize some of the key issues that remain to be resolved, rather than just provide a listing of what we already know.

Selection: The question of how immigrants are self-selected from the population of the source countries frames the stage for all that follows. A key problem with the existing set of selection models (and empirical methods) is that they rest upon the assumption that immigrants react to existing differences in wage opportunities across countries, and that this reaction leads to a particular sorting of people into movers and stayers. This approach seems sensible when immigrants compose but a small fraction of the population in both sending and receiving countries. But the partial equilibrium approach can easily fall apart if immigration begins to have a significant influence on the wage structure of the various countries, as it surely would if the migrants make up a sizable fraction of the population in these countries. We do not yet understand the nature of selection in a general equilibrium context.

Economic assimilation: It is obvious, but it bears repeating, that the extent to which immigrants assimilate in a host country will depend on the economic benefits from doing so. If post-migration human capital investments are profitable, such investments will inevitably take place; if the investments are not profitable, they will not. We do not yet understand the factors that can speed up or slow down the rate of economic assimilation in the immigrant generation, but the increasing number of foreign-born persons in many host countries obviously changes the calculus. Moreover, the measurement of the rate of economic assimilation requires identifying assumptions about how changes in macroeconomic conditions change the relative wages of immigrants and natives over time. The worldwide surge in international labor flows implies that these macroeconomic effects are now themselves affected by immigration, further complicating the measurement of the economic progress of immigrants.

The wage impact: We know much more about how to approach the question of measuring the labor market impact of immigration than we did three decades ago, but it is far from clear that we can be sure of the answer we now have. Prudence suggests that we keep an open mind about how to interpret the existing evidence until we have a full understanding of why different approaches lead to radically different results. The search for a synthesis is bound to prove extremely useful and will enhance our grasp of the underlying economics of the problem. In particular, we need to fully understand why different classifications of the same data (such as aggregating the data into different types of geographic regions) can fundamentally change the nature of the results. There is also a need for estimation methods that can better capture the technological interactions among the various skill groups in the workforce, and that lead to estimated wage effects of immigration that are both much more robust and far less dependent on functional form assumptions. Finally, far too little effort has been devoted to examining the economic impact of international migration on sending countries. The outflow of large numbers of workers—and often of high-skill workers—from developing countries alters the wage structure and human capital stock in the sending regions in ways that can have far-reaching economic and social implications.

Adjustments: I suspect many of the puzzles in our current understanding of the economic impact of immigration will be resolved only when we have a fuller accounting of how labor markets adjust to international migration, both in sending and receiving countries. It is obvious that immigration changes economic opportunities differently for different agents, and the various agents have an incentive to react and adjust accordingly. Far too much attention has been paid to only one source of adjustment—the flow of native workers within a country after immigrants settle in particular cities. This myopia has masked the vast array of possible adjustments that natives (and immigrants) will undertake. Such adjustments include the resettlement of firms, the expansion of the capital stock, the decision by firms to change methods of production as well as what it is they produce, the capacity of workers to change occupations and retool their human capital to avoid increased labor market competition, the possibility that knowledge producers change research topics, and a myriad of others. All of these adjustments are costly, and we know little about the magnitude of the adjustment costs that immigration imposes on both workers and firms in sending and receiving countries.

The benefits: The net economic gains from immigration to a host country depend intimately on the parameters that measure the impact on the wage distribution. Given the canonical model of the competitive labor market, these net gains *must* be positive. Although the calibration of models is a standard and useful exercise in economics, it is important to note that there is no evidence showing that the *actual* gains from immigration—as opposed to the theoretically implied gains—are actually positive. For instance, in contrast to the vast literature that examines the impact of immigration on wages, there has been remarkably little study of how immigration affects the firm's profitability or market value. Some of these issues may also be illuminated by the literature that examines the impact of high-skill immigration. Many of these studies are specifically "looking for" external effects that high-skill immigrants may impart on the productivity of the preexisting workforce. Further, the fact that natives adjust to supply shocks and that such adjustments can be costly raises a fundamental welfare question that is yet to be addressed: Under what conditions will the native population be better off after all adjustments take place *and* after all adjustment costs are incurred than they were prior to the supply shock, and are these conditions frequently satisfied?

Policy: The existing research on the economic impact of immigration typically treats the policy parameters that regulate international migration flows as exogenously determined, and then exploits the policy-induced variation in the size, timing, and skill composition of these flows to identify and measure the various economic effects. However, the enactment of a particular set of immigration restrictions in a particular place at a particular time does not come out of thin air. Host countries choose certain policy parameters and change them because it is in their benefit to do so. Remarkably little is known about the political economy calculus that generates the optimal immigration policy and whether the chosen policy, in fact, has the desired outcomes in terms of the size and composition of the immigrant flow. Even less is known about how the endogeneity of policy choices affects the measured costs and benefits in the host country. Our current ignorance suggests that the effects observed in a particular context (for example, the United States in the 2010s) should be interpreted cautiously, as they may provide little insight into the economic impact that similar supply shocks may have in other places and at other times.

The long, long run: Even if all new immigrants were turned away starting tomorrow, the large-scale migration flows that entered the developed countries in the past three decades have already set in motion a series of economic and labor market adjustments that are bound to affect these countries throughout the next century. As a result, it is crucial to find out what will happen to the children and grandchildren of the immigrants, and the extent to which ethnic external effects may or may not delay the economic progress of the descendants. The evidence suggests that ethnicity matters, and that it matters a lot, even in such a socially mobile country as the United States. Nevertheless, we need a far better understanding of the role that these ethnic external effects will play in different economic and social settings. The long-term impact of immigration will hinge crucially on the factors that strengthen or weaken the ethnic externality.

Mathematical Notes

Chapter 1. Stochastic Dominance in the Roy Model

Suppose $f(x, y)$ is a bivariate normal density function, with means (μ_X, μ_Y), variances (σ_X^2, σ_Y^2), and correlation coefficient ρ. The random variable y is truncated from below at a and from above at b. Arnold et al. (1993, p. 473) show that the (marginal) moment generating function of $(x - \mu_X)/\sigma_X$, given the truncation of y, is given by:

$$m(t) = \left[\frac{\Phi(\beta - \rho t) - \Phi(\alpha - \rho t)}{\Phi(\beta) - \Phi(\alpha)} \right] e^{t^2/2}, \tag{A.1}$$

where Φ is the cumulative distribution function of a standard normal random variable; $\alpha = (a - \mu_Y)/\sigma_Y$; and $\beta = (b - \mu_Y)/\sigma_Y$.

A cumulative distribution function $F(u)$ stochastically dominates cumulative distribution function $G(u)$ if $F(u) < G(u)$, for all u. Proposition 4 in Thistle (1993, p. 307) states that this definition of stochastic dominance holds if and only if:

$$m_F(-t) < m_G(-t), \tag{A.2}$$

where m_F is the moment generation function associated with distribution F, and m_G is the moment generating function associated with G.

These results can be easily adapted to show that the distribution function of movers stochastically dominates that of stayers if there is positive selection, and conversely if there is negative selection (assuming that time-equivalent migration costs are constant). In particular, using the notation of the Roy model in Chapter 1, the random variables x and y can be defined as: $x = v_0$, and $y = (v_1 - v_0)$, with correlation coefficient:

$$\rho = Corr(v_0, v_1 - v_0) = \frac{\sigma_1}{\sigma}\left[\rho_{01} - \frac{\sigma_0}{\sigma_1}\right],$$ (A.3)

where σ is the standard deviation of $(v_1 - v_0)$. In the sample of movers, the truncation in the random variable y is from below and implies that $\alpha = k = (\mu_0 - \mu_1)/\sigma$, and $\beta = \infty$. In the sample of stayers, the truncation in the random variable y is from above, and the truncation points are $\alpha = -\infty$ and $\beta = k$. By substituting these properties into equation (A.1), it is easy to show that the moment generating functions for the pre-migration income distribution of movers and stayers are given by:

$$m_M(t) = \left[\frac{1 - \Phi(k - \rho t)}{1 - \Phi(k)}\right]e^{t^2/2},$$ (A.4a)

$$m_S(t) = \left[\frac{\Phi(k - \rho t)}{\Phi(k)}\right]e^{t^2/2},$$ (A.4b)

The correlation ρ will be positive if the movers are positively selected, and negative if the movers are either negatively selected or there is an inverse sorting. Suppose there is positive selection. The comparison of equations (A.4a) and (A.4b) easily shows that $m_M(-t) > m_S(-t)$ if $\rho > 0$. The direction of the stochastic dominance will be reversed if $\rho < 0$.

Chapter 3.

1. Derivation of Averaging Property in Equation (3.20)

To illustrate, consider a two-level CES nesting. The two levels are given by:

$$Q = \left[\alpha_K K^\delta + \alpha_L L^\delta\right]^{1/\delta},$$ (A.5)

$$L = \left[\theta_1 L_1^\beta + \theta_2 L_2^\beta\right]^{1/\beta}.$$ (A.6)

The wage of an efficiency unit in the labor market is given by $w = \alpha_L Q^{1-\delta} L^{\delta-1}$. It follows that labor's share of income is:

$$s_L = \frac{wL}{Q} = \frac{\alpha_L L^\delta}{Q^\delta}.$$ (A.7)

The wage of a worker in skill group j is $w_j = \alpha_L \theta_j Q^{1-\delta} L^{\delta-\beta} L_j^{\beta-1}$. It follows that the income share of group j is:

$$s_j = \frac{w_j L_j}{Q} = s_L \frac{\theta_j L_j^\beta}{L^\beta}. \tag{A.8}$$

A generalized supply shift changes the number of efficiency units by:

$$d\log L = \frac{dL}{L} = \frac{\theta_1 L_1^\beta}{L^\beta}\frac{dL_1}{L_1} + \frac{\theta_2 L_2^\beta}{L^\beta}\frac{dL_2}{L_2} = \sum_j \frac{s_j d\log L_j}{s_L}. \tag{A.9}$$

This property extends to any number of levels in the CES framework.

2. Derivation of Wage Elasticities in Equations (3.40) and (3.41)

I derive the wage effects in the open-economy model using the more general specification of a CES production function, so that $Q = [\alpha K^\delta + (1-\alpha)L^\delta]^{1/\delta}$, and also let the inverse supply function for capital be given by $r = K^\lambda$. The mathematical exercise is greatly simplified by adapting the approach in Kennan (1998). First, note that the value of marginal product condition for labor can be written as:

$$\frac{w}{p} = (1-\alpha)Q^{1-\delta}L^{\delta-1}. \tag{A.10}$$

By substituting the inverse product demand curve in (3.37) into (A.10), it follows that:

$$\log w = \eta \log C + \log (1-\alpha) + (1-\eta-\delta) \log Q + (\delta-1) \log L. \tag{A.11}$$

Differentiating with respect to the immigrant supply shift yields:

$$\frac{d\log w}{d\log L} = \eta\phi + (1-\eta-\delta)\frac{d\log Q}{d\log L} + (\delta-1). \tag{A.12}$$

Next, note that the ratio of input prices in a CES technology can be written as a simple function of the ratio of input quantities. In particular:

$$\frac{w}{r} = \frac{(1-\alpha)L^{\delta-1}}{\alpha K^{\delta-1}}. \tag{A.13}$$

Differentiating the expression in (A.13), while accounting for the supply function of capital $r = K^\lambda$ yields:

$$\frac{d\log K}{d\log L} = \frac{1}{1+\lambda-\delta}\left(\frac{d\log w}{d\log L} + (1-\delta)\right). \tag{A.14}$$

Finally, the CES production function implies that:

$$\frac{d\log Q}{d\log L} = s_K \frac{d\log K}{d\log L} + s_L. \tag{A.15}$$

The substitution of equations (A.14) and (A.15) into (A.12) yields:

$$\frac{d\log w}{d\log L} = \frac{-\lambda(1-\delta-\eta)s_K}{(1+\lambda-\delta)-(1-\delta-\eta)s_K} - \frac{(1+\lambda-\delta)\eta(1-\phi)}{(1+\lambda-\delta)-(1-\delta-\eta)s_K}. \tag{A.16}$$

The wage effects reported in equation (3.40) and (3.41) follow directly by evaluating (A.16) in the case of a Cobb-Douglas production function ($\delta = 0$) and either in the short run ($\lambda = \infty$) or the long run ($\lambda = 0$).

Chapter 6.

1. Internal Migration Model

The labor market is initially in equilibrium. It is useful to start with a simpler version of the immigrant influx, a onetime supply increase. In particular, M_{hr} immigrants in skill group h enter region r at time 0. Native migration will then occur as a response to the impact of immigrants on the wage structure.

The impact of the onetime immigrant supply shock on native migration can be solved recursively using the supply function in equation (6.4). In particular, the supply increase induces $\eta\sigma(m_{hr} - m_h)$ natives to move in period 1, $\eta\sigma(1 + \eta\sigma)(m_{hr} - m_h)$ in period 2, and $\eta\sigma(1 + \eta\sigma)^{t-1}(m_{hr} - m_h)$ in period t. Convergence requires that $0 < (1 + \eta\sigma) < 1$. The *total* (or cumulative) net migration rate of natives at time t is then given by:

$$V_{ijt} = \sum_{\tau=1}^{t} \eta\sigma(1+\eta\sigma)^{\tau-1}(m_{hr} - m_h) \tag{A.17}$$

$$= -[1-(1+\eta\sigma)^t](m_{hr} - m_h).$$

The model can now be extended to the case where the same immigrant influx continues indefinitely. Equation (A.17) gives the (cumulative) net migration rate of natives as of time t induced by a period-0 immigrant supply increase. Consider now what the native response would be to a similarly sized supply increase occurring at $t = 1$. The cumulative (up to time t) migration rate of natives induced by the period 1 migration flow would be $V_{ij,t-1}$. The total net migration of natives in period t attributable to a constant supply increase between periods 0 and $t-1$ is then given by:

$$V_{ijt}^* = \sum_{\tau=0}^{t-1} V_{ij\tau} = -\left[t + \frac{(1+\eta\sigma)}{\eta\sigma}[1-(1+\eta\sigma)^t]\right](m_{hr} - m_h). \qquad (A.18)$$

Equation (6.5) in the text follows directly from (A.18) by differencing and using the approximation $(1+x)^t \approx (1+xt)$. Similarly, the log wage in region r at time t is given by:

$$\log w_{hrt} = \log X_{hr} + \eta((t+1)m_{hr} + V_{ijt}^*). \qquad (A.19)$$

Equation (6.6) in the text follows by substituting (A.18) into (A.19), using the approximation noted above, and assuming t is large so that $(t+1)/t \approx 1$.

2. Capital Adjustment Model

Initially, the labor market for a particular skill group is in equilibrium. At time 0, region r receives a onetime influx of immigrants and the wage in that region falls to:

$$\log w_{r0} = \log X + \eta m_r, \qquad (A.20)$$

where $\log X$ is the equilibrium wage in the pre-migration regime (and the subscript for the skill group is suppressed). The intercept of the demand function in (A.20) depends on the level of capital investments in the region, and will shift as firms change their capital stock. If the capital investments follow the lagged response in equation (6.16), the change in the intercept is $\eta\rho(m-m_r)$ in period 1, $\eta\rho(1-\rho)(m-m_r)$ in period 2, and $\eta\rho(1-\rho)^{t-1}(m-m_r)$ in period t. Convergence requires that $0 < (1-\rho) < 1$.

Suppose now the immigrant influx is permanent (and of constant size). By using a method analogous to that used in deriving equation (A.18), it is easy to show that the total change in the intercept in region r as of time t is:

$$X_{rt}^* = \sum_{\tau=0}^{t-1} \Delta\log X_{r\tau} = -\left[t - \frac{(1-\rho)}{\rho}[1-(1-\rho)^t]\right]\eta(m-m_r)$$
$$\approx -\eta\rho(m-m_r)t. \qquad (A.21)$$

Equation (6.17) follows by substituting this expression into the log wage function.

Chapter 7. Immigration Surplus with Heterogeneous Labor

The concave, linear homogeneous production function is given by:

$$Q=f(K, L_S, L_U)=f(K, bN+\beta M, (1-b)N+(1-\beta)M), \qquad (A.22)$$

where b and β denote the fraction of skilled workers among natives and immigrants, respectively. The wage of each factor of production (capital, skilled workers, and unskilled workers) is determined by the respective marginal productivity condition.

The short-run increase in national income accruing to natives is:

$$\Delta Q_N\big|_{dK=0}=\left(K\frac{\partial r}{\partial M}+bN\frac{\partial w_S}{\partial M}+(1-b)N\frac{\partial w_U}{\partial M}\right)M. \qquad (A.23)$$

Define $\varepsilon_{ij}=\partial \log w_i/\partial \log X_j$ (where $X_j=K, L_S, L_U$). By differentiating the relevant marginal productivity conditions, it can be shown that the changes in the various factor prices are given by:

$$\frac{\partial \log r}{\partial \log M}\bigg|_{dK=0}=\varepsilon_{KS}\frac{(\beta-b)}{\pi_S\pi_U}(1-p)p-\varepsilon_{KK}\frac{1-\beta}{\pi_U}p, \qquad (A.24a)$$

$$\frac{\partial \log w_S}{\partial \log M}\bigg|_{dK=0}=\varepsilon_{SS}\frac{(\beta-b)}{\pi_S\pi_U}(1-p)p-\varepsilon_{SK}\frac{1-\beta}{\pi_U}p, \qquad (A.24b)$$

$$\frac{\partial \log w_U}{\partial \log M}\bigg|_{dK=0}=-\varepsilon_{UU}\frac{(\beta-b)}{\pi_S\pi_U}(1-p)p-\varepsilon_{UK}\frac{\beta}{\pi_S}p. \qquad (A.24c)$$

where π_S and π_U are the shares of the workforce that are skilled and unskilled, respectively. The derivation of equation (A.24) is very tedious and requires using the identities $(\varepsilon_{SS}\varepsilon_{KK}-\varepsilon_{SK}\varepsilon_{KS}) \equiv -(\varepsilon_{SU}\varepsilon_{KK}-\varepsilon_{SK}\varepsilon_{KU})$ and $(\varepsilon_{UU}\varepsilon_{KK}-\varepsilon_{UK}\varepsilon_{KU}) \equiv -(\varepsilon_{US}\varepsilon_{KK}-\varepsilon_{UK}\varepsilon_{KS})$. It is instructive to prove one of these identities, because many of the results rely on similar manipulations. For example, note that the first identity can be rearranged as:

$$\varepsilon_{KK}(\varepsilon_{SS}+\varepsilon_{SU})\equiv\varepsilon_{SK}(\varepsilon_{KS}+\varepsilon_{KU}), \qquad (A.25)$$
$$\varepsilon_{KK}(-\varepsilon_{SK})\equiv\varepsilon_{SK}(-\varepsilon_{KK}),$$

where the substitution in the second equation follows from the fact that $\sum_\ell\varepsilon_{i\ell}=0$.

It is well known that when the derivatives in (A.23) are evaluated at the initial equilibrium, where $L_S=bN$ and $L_U=(1-b)N$, the infinitesimal increase in national income accruing to natives is zero (Bhagwati and Srinivasan 1983, p. 294). To calculate finite changes, evaluate the immigration surplus using an "average" rate for $\partial r/\partial M$, $\partial w_S/\partial M$, and $\partial w_U/\partial M$, where the

average is defined by $\dfrac{1}{2}\left(\left.\dfrac{\partial y}{\partial M}\right|_{L_S=bN} + \left.\dfrac{\partial y}{\partial M}\right|_{L_S=bN+\beta M}\right)$, with $y=r$, w_S, and w_U.

This approximation implies that the finite change in the immigration surplus is half the gain obtained when equation (A.24) is evaluated at the post-immigration level of labor supply.

If we convert the definition of the immigration surplus into percentage terms, evaluate the various derivatives at the "average" point, and use the condition that a weighted average of elasticities of complementarity equals zero, we obtain the immigration surplus defined in equation (7.12), or:

$$V = \left.\frac{\Delta Q_N}{Q}\right|_{dK=0} = -\frac{s_S^2 c_{SS}\beta^2 p^2}{2\pi_S^2} - \frac{s_U^2 c_{UU}(1-\beta)^2 p^2}{2\pi_U^2}$$
$$- \frac{s_S s_U c_{SU}\beta(1-\beta)p^2}{\pi_S \pi_U}. \tag{A.26}$$

The concavity of $f(K, L_S, L_U)$ implies that $f_{SS}\le 0$, $\begin{vmatrix} f_{SS} & f_{SU} \\ f_{US} & f_{UU} \end{vmatrix}\ge 0$, and $\begin{vmatrix} f_{SS} & f_{SU} & f_{SK} \\ f_{US} & f_{UU} & f_{UK} \\ f_{KS} & f_{KU} & f_{KK} \end{vmatrix}\le 0$. The linear homogeneity of the production function implies that the determinant of the three-by-three matrix is zero. We can write the production function in its intensive form as $Q=K\,g(L_S/K, L_U/K)$. Assuming that g is strictly concave implies that $f_{SS}f_{UU} - f_{SU}^2 > 0$, so that $c_{SS}c_{UU} - c_{SU}^2 > 0$. Using this restriction, the quadratic form in equation (A.26) is positive.

Assume $\pi_S = \pi_U = .5$ and differentiate the immigration surplus with respect to β. To prove that $V'(1) > 0$, let $x=-c_{SS}$, $y=-c_{UU}$, and $z=-c_{SU}$. The inequality $xy-z^2 > 0$ implies that $\sqrt{xy} > z$. It is also the case that $(x+y)/2 > \sqrt{xy}$, hence $(x+y)/2 > z$. It follows that $-c_{SS} - c_{UU} + 2c_{SU} > 0$, and c_{SU} exceeds the average of c_{SS} and c_{SU}. The assumption that $c_{SS} < c_{UU}$ then implies $c_{SS} < c_{SU}$. Equation (7.13) shows that the derivative $V'(1)$ is proportional to $(-s_S^2 c_{SS} + s_S s_U c_{SU})$. It follows that $V'(1) > 0$ as long as $s_S > s_U$ (that is, high-skill workers have a higher marginal product than low-skill workers).

The proof that the second derivative, $V''(\beta)$, is positive everywhere proceeds along similar lines. Let $R=s_S/s_U$, with $R>1$. Equation (7.14) implies that the second derivative will be positive if:

$$-R^2 c_{SS} - c_{UU} + 2R c_{SU} > -R c_{SS} - R c_{UU} + 2R c_{SU}. \tag{A.27}$$

The discussion surrounding the sign of the first derivative showed that the term in the right-hand side of the inequality in (A.27) must be positive. Hence, the second derivative is positive everywhere if:

$$-R^2 c_{SS} - c_{UU} > -R c_{SS} - R c_{UU}. \tag{A.28}$$

Let $k = c_{UU}/c_{SS}$, with $k < 1$. The inequality in (A.28) must hold, because $(R-1)(R-k) > 0$.

In the long run, the immigration surplus is defined by:

$$\Delta Q_N \big|_{dr=0} = \left(bN \frac{\partial w_S}{\partial M} + (1-b)N \frac{\partial w_U}{\partial M} \right) M. \tag{A.29}$$

The condition that $r = f_K(K, L_S, L_U)$ is constant implies that the immigration-induced long-run adjustment in the capital stock equals:

$$\frac{\partial K}{\partial M} \bigg|_{dr=0} = -\frac{[f_{KS}\beta + f_{KU}(1-\beta)]}{f_{KK}}. \tag{A.30}$$

The derivation of the wage effects in equations (7.6) and (7.7) and the long-run immigration surplus requires using the adjustment restriction in equation (A.30) as well as identities similar to those in equation (A.25) and $\alpha_S^2 (c_{KK} c_{SS} - c_{SK}^2) = \alpha_U^2 (c_{KK} c_{UU} - c_{UK}^2)$.

Finally, note that $\pi_S = b(1-p) + \beta p$ and $\pi_U = (1-b)(1-p) + (1-\beta)p$. These definitions imply:

$$\frac{\beta}{\pi_S} - \frac{1-\beta}{\pi_U} = \frac{(\beta-b)(1-p)}{\pi_S \pi_U}. \tag{A.31}$$

The relationship between the short- and long-run immigration surpluses in equation (7.15) follows from equation (A.31) and the various identities linking the factor price and complementarity elasticities.

Construction of Data Extracts

Chapters 1 and 2

The data are drawn from the 1960, 1970, 1980, 1990, and 2000 Public Use Microdata Samples (PUMS) of the U.S. Census, and the pooled 2009–2011 American Community Surveys (ACS). The pooled ACS data is referred to as the "2010 census." All data sets were downloaded in June 2013 from the Integrated Public Use Microdata Series (IPUMS) archive maintained at the University of Minnesota. The analysis reported in these chapters uses the 3-year pooled ACS sample (rather than the 5-year pooled sample) to better capture the marginal change in the skills of the most recent immigrant cohorts. Although I do not use the 1960 census until later in the book, it is convenient to describe the construction of the 1960 data extract at this point, because its construction is identical to that of the 1970 extract.

In the 1960 and 1970 censuses, the data extracts form a 1 and 3 percent random sample of the population, respectively. The 3 percent 1970 extract is created by pooling the "Form 1" state, metropolitan area, and neighborhood files. The 1980, 1990, and 2000 data extracts form a 5 percent random sample of the population, and the pooled 2009–2011 ACS forms a 3 percent random sample of the population (and is, for expositional convenience, called the "2010 census"). A person is classified as an immigrant if he is either a noncitizen or a naturalized citizen; all other persons are classified as natives. Sampling weights are used in all calculations. The analysis is restricted to men aged 25–64, who do not reside in group quarters, have positive weeks worked during the year, are not enrolled in school, and have 1–40 years of experience (as defined below). In addition, the immigrant sample is restricted to persons who were at least 18 years old at the time of their migration to the United States.

Weekly earnings: The worker's annual earnings are given by the total earned income variable. In the 1960, 1970, and 1980 censuses, the top-coded annual income is multiplied by 1.5. In the 1960 and 1970 censuses, weeks worked in the calendar year prior to the survey are reported as a categorical variable. I impute weeks worked for each worker as follows: 8.0 weeks for 13 weeks or less, 20.8 for 14–26 weeks, 33.1 for 27–39 weeks, 42.4 for 40–47 weeks, 48.3 for 48–49 weeks, and 51.9 for 50–52 weeks. These imputed values are the mean values of weeks worked in the relevant bracket in the 1980 census. The 2009–2011 pooled ACS report weeks worked only as a categorical variable. I impute weeks worked as follows: 7.4 weeks for 13 weeks or less, 21.3 for 14–26 weeks, 33.1 for 27–39 weeks, 42.4 for 40–47 weeks, 48.2 for 48–49 weeks, and 51.9 for 50–52 weeks. These imputed values are the mean values of weeks worked in the relevant bracket in the 2000–2007 ACS. The worker's weekly wage is then defined by the ratio of annual earned income to weeks worked.

Years since migration: The regressions reported in Chapter 2 use a continuous measure of the number of years the immigrant has resided in the United States. The 1970–1990 censuses, however, provide the year-of-arrival information only as a categorical variable. I impute years-since-migration in these censuses. The vector of imputed values in the 1970 census is: (57, 50, 40, 30, 22, 17, 12, 7, and 2). This vector approximates the variable for the following categories: migrated in 1911–1914, 1915–1924, 1925–1934, 1935–1944, 1945–1949, 1950–1954, 1955–1959, 1960–1964, and 1965–1970. The vector of imputed values in the 1980 census is: (44, 25, 17, 12, 7, 2); the respective categories are: 1949 or earlier, 1950–1959, 1960–1964, 1965–1969, 1970–1974, and 1975–1980. Finally, the vector of imputed values in the 1990 census is: (54, 35, 27, 22, 17, 12, 8.5, 6, 3.5, 1); and the respective categories are: 1949 or earlier, 1950–1959, 1960–1964, 1965–1969, 1970–1974, 1975–1979, 1980–1981, 1982–1984, 1985–1986, and 1987–1990.

Country-specific variables: The per capita GDP variable is drawn from the Penn World Table and gives the (PPP-adjusted) real per capita GDP at the beginning of the 5-year period when the migration took place (Heston et al. 2012). The Penn World Table does not provide information for the earlier years used in the analysis for three countries (Czechoslovakia, Russia, and Yugoslavia). The missing values of the per capita GDP variables are set equal to the 1990 value that the Penn World Table reports for that specific country.

The Gini coefficient is drawn from the World Development Indicators database (World Bank, 2013). I smooth out the noise in the data by averaging all the reported Gini coefficients for each country between 1978 and 2012. The World Bank data is incomplete for a few countries (Barbados, Cuba, Lebanon, Russia, Yugoslavia, and Taiwan). The Gini coefficients for these countries were imputed using the Deininger and Squire (1996) time series. In addition, because almost all of the immigrants residing in the United States from South Africa are white, the Gini coefficient for South Africa is drawn from the South African white wage distribution documented in Hoogeven and Özler (2005).

Freedom House (2011) constructs an index of civil liberties annually for each country in the world. The index ranges from 1 to 7, with higher values being assigned to countries with more oppressive regimes. The variable used in the regression classifies a country as "repressive" if the index is 4 or greater, and is evaluated during the decade when the immigrant cohort arrived.

The size of the national origin group gives the number of immigrants living in the United States who originated in a particular country, but who arrived prior to the immigrant cohort. It is calculated in each census using the entire population of foreign-born persons, regardless of age or gender.

Finally, the distance variable gives the distance from the source country to the United States and was estimated using a country-to-country distance calculator (www.distancefromto.net).

Chapters 4, 5, and 6

The data are drawn from the 1960, 1970, 1980, 1990, 2000 census samples described above, and the pooled 2007–2011 ACS. The pooled ACS data form a 5 percent random sample of the population and are referred to as the "2010 census." The analysis is restricted to persons aged 18–64, who do not reside in group quarters.

Definition of education and experience cells: I categorize persons into five education groups: high school dropouts, high school graduates, persons with some college, college graduates, and persons with more than a college education. The classification uses the information provided by the completed educational attainment variable. I assume that high school dropouts enter the labor market at age 17, high school graduates at age 19, persons with some college at age 21, college graduates at age 23, and persons with more than college at age 24. I then define work experience as the worker's age at the time of the survey minus the assumed age of entry into the labor market. I restrict the analysis to persons who have between 1 and 40 years of experience. Persons are then classified into one of eight experience groups. The experience groups are defined in 5-year intervals (1–5 years of experience, 6–10, 11–15, 16–20, 21–25, 26–30, 31–35, and 36–40).

Immigrant share: The supply of immigrants or natives in each of the 40 skill cells (and for each region, when relevant) is given by the total number of hours worked by persons in a specific education-experience-region group during the relevant year. The annual number of hours worked by a person is given by the product of weeks worked and usual hours worked weekly. The weeks worked variable is imputed as described above when required. The usual hours variable is also defined as a categorical variable in the 1960 and 1970 censuses, and I impute hours worked as follows: 8.7 hours for 14 or fewer hours, 20.9 for 15–29 hours, 31.1 for 30–34 hours, 36.5 for 35–39 hours, 40 for 40 hours exactly, 45.3 for 41 to 48 hours, 51.8 for 49 to 59 hours, and 68.1 for 60 or more hours. These imputed values are the mean values of weeks worked in the relevant bracket in the 1980 census. All workers are included in the calculation of these counts, including men and women, as well as self-employed and salaried workers. The immigrant share in a particular cell is defined by the fraction of all work hours attributable to foreign-born workers.

Mean log weekly wage: To better approximate the price of a skill unit, the worker's earnings are given by his wage and salary income, so the calculation of the mean log weekly earnings in a skill-region cell is restricted to workers employed in the wage and salary sector who are not enrolled in school. As before, the top coded annual income is multiplied by 1.5 in the 1960 and 1970 censuses. Weekly earnings for a worker are defined by the ratio of annual earnings to weeks worked (which are imputed when required). The mean log weekly earnings for a skill-region cell is then defined by the average of a worker's log weekly earnings, weighted by the product of the sampling weight and annual hours worked.

Income shares: The income shares used in the simulations reported in Chapter 5 were calculated using data drawn from the 2000 census. The calculation uses the total earned income of workers not enrolled in school (including men and women, and workers in the wage-and-salary and self-employment sectors). I impose the normalizing restriction that the sum of income shares across all skill groups equals 0.7.

Internal migration rates: Migration rates are calculated only in the male sample and use all persons in the skill-region cell (regardless of whether they worked). A native is an out-migrant from the original region of residence (where the original region is defined as either the state or the metropolitan area of residence 5 years prior to the survey) if he lives in a different place by the time of the census. The native is an in-migrant into the current region of residence if he lived in a different region 5 years prior to the census. I define the in-migration and out-migration rates by dividing the total number of in-migrants or out-migrants in a particular skill-region-year cell by the relevant population of the "baseline" region. The baseline region is either the original region of residence when calculating out-migration rates or the current region of residence when calculating in-migration rates, and the population of the baseline region 5 years prior to the census gives the baseline population. I multiplied the resulting migration rates by 2 to convert them into the "decadal" units implicitly used in the other variables. The net migration rate is defined as the difference between the in- and out-migration rates.

Chapter 9

The data are drawn from the 1940 and 1970 Public Use Microdata Samples of the U.S. Census, and the pooled 1996–2005 (March) Annual Social and Economic Supplements of the Current Population Surveys (CPS). The 1940 census forms a 1 percent random sample, and the 1970 census forms a 3 percent random sample obtained by pooling the "Form 2" state, metropolitan area, and neighborhood files. The 1940 census extract used in the analysis, however, contains only "sample line" observations because the nativity information is available only in this subsample. The analysis is restricted to persons aged 25–64 who do not reside in group quarters, are not enrolled in school, and worked during the survey year.

Weekly earnings: The worker's annual earnings are given by total earned income. The top coded annual income is multiplied by 1.5 in the 1940 and 1970 censuses. Weekly earnings are then calculated as described above.

Generation and ethnicity: The first generation consists of workers born outside the United States. The second generation consists of workers born in the United States, but with at least one parent born abroad. The third generation consists of all other workers. For first-generation workers, ethnicity is defined by the worker's country of birth. For second-generation workers, ethnicity is defined by the mother's country of birth. If the mother is native-born, it is then defined by the father's country of birth.

Notes

1. The Selection of Immigrants

1. Equations (1.1) and (1.2) could be easily reinterpreted as giving the distributions of the present value of the earnings stream in each country. This reformulation would place the model squarely within the human capital investment framework proposed by Sjaastad (1962).

2. Greenwood (1997) surveys the literature examining internal migration in developed countries.

3. These wage differences do not adjust for price differences. Nevertheless, the Penn World Table reports that in 2010 the PPP-adjusted per capita GDP in the United States was almost twice as large as that in Puerto Rico.

4. Several studies construct structural models of migration that, as a by-product, provide an estimate of migration costs. These estimates are usually very large as well. For example, Bertoli et al. (2013) report that the measure of π for the average Ecuadorian immigrant in the United States is around 9 times the worker's salary. Similarly, Kennan and Walker's (2011) study of interstate migration in a sample of young workers in the United States concludes that the migration cost for the average person is $312,000. Finally, related work by Artuc et al. (2010) estimates average moving costs to be around 8 times the annual wage for workers who "migrate" from one sector of the economy to another in response to trade shocks in specific industries.

5. Munshi (2003) documents that a larger ethnic network is associated with a higher probability of employment and higher-paying jobs for new immigrants.

6. Of course, restrictive immigration policies will inevitably reduce the size of migration flows even further; see, for example, Klein and Ventura (2004) and Ortega and Peri (2013). Similarly, it is well known that the cost of entering the United States illegally across the Mexican border depends on the level of border enforcement; see Gathmann (2008).

7. Heckman and Honoré (1990) present a technical discussion of the many implications of the Roy model for the earnings distribution.

8. Johnson and Kotz (1970) summarize the properties of the truncated normal distribution; see also Heckman (1979).

9. The case where Q_0 and Q_1 are both negative is theoretically impossible; it would require that the correlation coefficient ρ_{01} be greater than one.

10. This interpretation of the variances follows directly from the definition of the log wage distribution in the host country in terms of what the population of the source country would earn if the entire population migrated there. The definition effectively holds constant the population distribution of skills.

11. Borjas et al. (2013) first noted the implications of the Roy model for stochastic dominance.

12. Note that the model ignores the restrictive role that immigration and emigration policies play in determining the skill composition of international migrants. As long as these policies do not force persons who find it against their self-interest to move or stay, the migrants would consist of the subset of persons who find it optimal to move and who have the "right" set of qualifications that allow an exit or entry visa to be granted.

13. The discussion initially ignores the model's implication that there should be two-way migration flows between the two countries.

14. This extension of the Roy model to a multi-region framework was first developed in Borjas, Bronars, and Trejo (1992). Dahl (2002) presents an important semiparametric generalization that allows for utility maximization and multiple destinations, as well as develops a correction for sample selection bias in polychotomous choice models.

15. It is important to emphasize that this result treats the distribution of rates of returns to skills across countries as fixed. A general equilibrium approach might have very different implications about the nature of the sorting of workers and countries.

16. It is obvious from Figure 1.2 that the parameters of the country-specific income distributions must satisfy a number of properties in order for the country's population not to be the empty set; see Borjas, Bronars, and Trejo (1992) for details.

17. Borjas and Bratsberg (1996) generalize the model to allow for uncertainty in host country outcomes and show that the correction for initial mistakes reinforces this type of selection. Bartolucci et al. (2013) examine the internal (and

return) migration of workers from the south to the north of Italy and document selection patterns that are consistent with the Roy implications.

18. Note that the wage offers made by employers in country k do not depend on the identity of the worker's source country, suggesting that skills acquired in one country are perfectly transferable to all other countries.

19. For example, suppose the rate of return to skills is 10 percent everywhere, and that low-skill workers earn $30,000 in the rich country and $10,000 in the poor country. The skill wage gap is $3,000 and $1,000 in the two countries, respectively, and the differenced wage gap in equation (1.30) is positive.

20. The introduction of positive mobility costs does not necessarily change this predicted path of migration dynamics. For example, the argument follows analogously if mobility costs were to increase proportionately with income as countries became richer.

21. It is common for many empirical studies in the immigration literature to examine the determination of male earnings, although some of the studies present parallel results for women. The main reason is that the study of female earnings introduces a number of compounding conceptual difficulties. For example, in the current context, the researcher would have to worry not only about the selection that determines the sample of immigrants, but also about the selection that determines which subset of immigrant (and native) women choose to work. Typically, the evidence suggests that the estimation of the models in samples of female workers leads to qualitatively similar (though often weaker) results.

22. The age-adjusted mean wage for each cell is obtained from an individual-level first-stage regression estimated separately in each census of the log weekly wage on age (introduced as a third-order polynomial) and a vector of fixed effects indicating the source country. These fixed effects become the dependent variable in equation (1.31). The age- and education-adjusted mean wage is calculated in the same manner, but the first-stage regression also includes a variable giving the worker's years of schooling.

23. The per capita GDP variable is drawn from the Penn World Table and gives the (PPP-adjusted) real per capita GDP at the beginning of the period when the migration took place (Heston et al. 2012). The Gini coefficient is drawn from the World Development Indicators database (World Bank 2013). To smooth out the noise in the inequality data, I use the average Gini for country k between 1978 and 2012. Although the Gini coefficient is often interpreted as a measure of the returns to skills, a larger Gini may indicate not only that the returns to skills are higher, but also that there is a larger variance in the distribution of skills.

24. The increase in the source country's per capita GDP also signals a change in the "intensity" of selection: fewer persons migrate, and the self-selected

immigrants are more heavily clustered in the respective tail of the skill distribution.

25. Other studies that document the existence of this negative correlation include Cobb-Clark (1993) and Bratsberg (1995). In contrast, Belot and Hatton (2012) report cross-country regressions that analyze the selection of immigrants in OECD countries, and their evidence provides only weak support for the Roy model predictions.

26. Freedom House (2011) constructs an index of civil liberties annually for each country in the world. The index ranges from 1 to 7, with 7 being assigned to the countries with the most oppressive regimes. The variable used in the regression classifies a country as "repressive" if the index is 4 or greater, and is evaluated during the decade when the immigrant cohort arrived.

27. Mattoo et al. (2008) document the presence of differences in the human capital content of a particular level of educational attainment across immigrants belonging to different national origin groups. This variation suggests that immigrants with the same level of education, but originating in different countries, may be selected on the basis of unobserved ability, making educational attainment a particularly poor predictor of immigrant outcomes.

28. A number of studies in other contexts also address related selection issues; see, for example, Abramitzky's (2009) case study of the Israeli kibbutz, which finds some support for the Roy-type predictions; and the McKenzie et al. (2010) analysis of the use of a lottery to allocate permanent visas to Tongans wishing to emigrate to New Zealand.

29. Taylor (1987) provides an early study of selection in the Mexican context. He examined migration from a single rural Mexican village, and concluded that Mexicans who migrated illegally to the United States were less skilled, on average, than the typical person residing in the village.

30. Other studies of the selection of Mexican immigrants include Ambrosini and Peri (2012), Caponi (2011), Ibarrarán and Lubotsky (2007), and McKenzie and Rapoport (2007, 2010). Some of these studies have expanded the selection model to incorporate such factors as migration networks and the distinction between rural and urban migrants (a distinction that seems important in the Mexican context). Fernández-Huertas (2013) surveys the various approaches and findings.

31. Gould and Moav (2011) provide a rare study (in the Israeli context) of how differences in the extent to which specific types of skills are transferable across countries can generate differential returns across the various types of skills.

32. Ramos (1992) and Borjas (2008) test the implications of the Roy model in the Puerto Rican context.

2. Economic Assimilation

1. See Mincer (1974) for the classic derivation of the Mincer earnings function. Heckman et al. (2006) give an excellent overview of the vast literature inspired by the Mincer framework.

2. The related work of Polachek (1975) and Mincer and Polachek (1978) on the determinants of female earnings also extends the Mincer earnings function to account for discontinuities in work experience over the life cycle.

3. Obviously there are other ways of defining the concept of assimilation. For example, assimilation could refer to the rate of convergence between immigrants belonging to a particular ethnic group and natives with that ethnic ancestry (for example, Hispanic immigrants in the United States and the large native-born U.S. Hispanic population). Borjas (1999) discusses potential definitions of assimilation.

4. As an affirmation of the Ecclesiastes axiom that there is nothing new under the sun, Douglas (1919) presented a related discussion of cohort effects in the context of early twentieth-century immigration to the United States. Abramitzky et al. (2013) revisit the issue of measuring aging and cohort effects among the immigrants who arrived during the Great Migration of the early 1900s.

5. The self-selection of return migrants can also generate skill differences among immigrant cohorts. Suppose, for example, that the return migrants are those who fare poorly in a host country. Earlier cohorts will then have higher average wages than the more recent cohorts, because in any given cross-section the earlier cohorts have been "filtered out." This issue is addressed in more detail later in this chapter.

6. See, for example, Glenn (1976) and Heckman and Robb (1985).

7. Friedberg (1992) proposed an interesting extension of the model by noting that equation (2.2a) ignores the role of an immigrant's age at the time of migration. Because age, age-at-migration, and years-since-migration are also related through an identity, the estimation of the age-at-migration effect introduces additional identification problems. The empirical analysis presented below bypasses the issue by focusing on the economic assimilation of immigrants who arrived in the country as adults. Beck et al. (2012) examine the adult outcomes of persons who immigrated to the United States as children; see also Schaafsma and Sweetman (2001).

8. For example, the value of the period effect γ_n can be obtained by estimating the earnings function in the native sample. This estimate can then be used to "solve out" the period effect from the immigrant earnings function.

9. See, for example, Antecol et al. (2006), Aydemir and Skuterud (2005), Baker and Benjamin (1994), Borjas (1985, 1995a), Chiswick (1986), Duleep and Regets

(1997), Edin et al. (2000), Friedberg (2000), Funkhouser and Trejo (1995), Green (1999), LaLonde and Topel (1992), and Schoeni (1997b).

10. Funkhouser and Trejo (1995) show that the changing national origin composition of immigrants accounts for part of the decline in entry wages. Borjas and Friedberg (2009) analyze the uptick in the relative entry wage of the 1995–2000 cohort and conjecture that it may be partly due to the temporary expansion of the high-tech H-1B visa program in the late 1990s.

11. Jasso and Rosenzweig (2009) present a detailed discussion of this point. Studies that examine the post-migration outcomes of immigrants who enter a particular host country using different types of visa categories include Aydemir (2011), Hunt (2011), and Jasso and Rosenzweig (1995).

12. The presence of cohort differences in the rate of economic assimilation, with more recent cohorts having relatively smaller wage growth rates, explains the peculiar finding in Figure 2.1 that the cross-sectional relative earnings profile of immigrants shifted from being strongly concave to slightly convex between 1970 and 2010. Let Z be the vector of variables (X, A) and suppose that all of these variables have the same impact on immigrants and natives. Further, suppose that the years-since-migration effect is described by a quadratic function, so that a pooled cross-section regression of immigrants and natives can be written as:

$$\log w = Z\varphi + \lambda F + \alpha_1 y + \alpha_2 y^2 + \beta C + \theta(Cy),$$

where the variables y and C should be interpreted as being interactions with the foreign-born indicator variable, F. Because $C = T - y$, the cross-section model collapses to:

$$\log w = Z\varphi + (\lambda + \beta T)F + (\alpha_1 - \beta + \theta T)y + (\alpha_2 - \theta)y^2.$$

The quadratic term in years-since-migration turns positive if the growth cohort effects are sufficiently negative.

13. For simplicity, the cohorts that entered the country prior to 1965 are pooled into a single cohort.

14. The 10-year growth in the relative wage of immigrants is calculated by predicting immigrant and native log earnings both at the time of entry, assumed to occur at age 25, and 10 years later.

15. Workers are classified into one of five education groups and into one of eight age groups, for a total of 40 skill groups. The five education groups are: high school dropouts, high school graduates, workers with some college, college graduates, and workers with more than a college education. The eight age brackets are: 25–29, 30–34, 35–39, 40–44, 45–49, 50–54, 55–59, and 60–64.

16. I use the 2000 cross-section as the baseline. The implied price deflator for a specific skill group in cross-section τ is then given by $\phi_{h\tau} = \overline{w}_{h\tau} / \overline{w}_{h0}$, where

$\bar{w}_{h\tau}$ gives the mean weekly wage of native workers in group h in cross section τ and $\bar{w}_{h0}$ gives the mean weekly wage in 2000.

17. See also Barth et al. (2004) and Butcher and DiNardo (2002).

18. To minimize the potential problems caused by outlying or top-coded observations, the bottom 3 and top 3 percentiles are merged into two separate skill groups.

19. The evidence, therefore, suggests a "real" decline in the entry skills of successive cohorts (at least through 1990) as well as a slowdown in the rate of human capital accumulation. In fact, the probability that the most recently arrived cohort as of 1970 had 11 or fewer years of education was 10.0 percentage points higher than that of natives. The respective gap grew to 21.5 by 1990, and remained steady at 22.9 percentage points in 2010. Similarly, newer immigrant waves "pick up" English-language skills at a slower rate (Borjas 2013a). The (age-adjusted) English fluency rate of the cohort that entered in the late 1970s increased from 32.2 to 43.3 percent during their first 10 years in the United States. The respective growth for the late 1990s cohort was from 33.9 to 36.0 percent.

20. Although direct data are not available, it is estimated that the rate of out-migration in the foreign-born population is around 30 percent; see Jasso and Rosenzweig (1990) and Borjas and Bratsberg (1996).

21. Other studies that use longitudinal data include Beenstock et al. (2010) and Duleep and Dowhan (2002); see also Lindstrom and Massey (1994).

22. The special case of relative neutrality is analogous to the neutrality assumption in the Ben-Porath model, where the marginal cost curve of producing human capital is independent of the worker's initial stock.

23. The rate of economic assimilation is given by the difference between $\dot{w}$ and the rate of wage growth experienced by comparable native workers.

24. Some studies examine the assimilation process by measuring the volume of human capital investments (rather than the rate of wage convergence), mostly in terms of acquiring fluency in the host country's language; see, for example, Lazear (1999), Chiswick and Miller (1999, 2005) and Isphording and Otten (2013).

25. The literature has not yet determined the cause of the slowdown in economic assimilation documented in Table 2.2. Borjas (2013a) provides a more detailed discussion of the link between assimilation and group size that takes into account the geographic clustering of the group. Interestingly, a small part of the relative decline in assimilation experienced by the late 1990s cohort (relative to the late 1970s cohort) is explained by the group size variable, suggesting that the increasing number of ethnic compatriots may be playing a role in the slowdown.

3. Immigration and the Wage Structure: Theory

1. Hicks (1932) gives the classic derivation of Marshall's rules of derived demand. Ewerhart (2003) and Kennan (1998) provide much simpler and clearer derivations; see also Pemberton (1989).

2. Although the simple case of homogeneous labor may seem to have little empirical relevance, many of the attempts to incorporate different types of skills in the production function simplify the problem by "homogenizing" workers into efficiency units. As will be seen below, this approach turns the more complex heterogeneous labor case into a problem where key predictions of the homogeneous labor model continue to hold.

3. The elasticity of complementarity is the dual of the elasticity of substitution. Hamermesh (1993, chap. 2) presents a detailed discussion of the properties of the elasticity of complementarity; see also Hicks (1970) and Sato and Koizumi (1973).

4. The labor supply of the preexisting workforce in the receiving country is assumed to be perfectly inelastic. The immigration-induced supply shift can then be represented as an outward shift of a vertical supply curve.

5. Immigrants and natives in skill group i are assumed to be perfect substitutes. This assumption is relaxed in the next section.

6. The denominator of (3.15) equals the sum of the weights, $s_K c_{KK} = -\sum_{\ell} s_\ell c_{K\ell}$.

7. Other applications of the nested CES approach in related contexts in labor economics include Bowles (1970) and Card and Lemieux (2001). The mathematical properties of the nested CES emphasized in this section—and their role in producing estimates of the wage impact of immigration—were first noted in Borjas (2013b).

8. There is one minor caveat: the definition of the supply shift is slightly different. In the homogeneous labor context, the supply shift is measured by the percent increase in the size of the workforce, whereas in the nested CES framework it is measured by the percent increase in the number of standardized efficiency units.

9. The caveat noted earlier again applies: The variable m_i gives the percent shift in the number of efficiency units in skill group i when within-group complementarities exist, but the percent increase in the number of workers in the simpler model.

10. Although the presence of within-group complementarities does not play a role in determining how the supply shock affects the average wage calculated across *all* preexisting workers in a skill group, the average wage of preexisting native and immigrant workers in that particular skill group will be differentially affected if σ_{MN} is not equal to infinity.

11. The more general model in Borjas (2013b) relaxes the assumption that the price of the imported good is constant, allowing a more faithful representation of the open-economy assumption. Although the technical details are far more complex, the theoretical implications resemble those implied by the simpler model. The analysis is related to the standard 2×2×2 model in international trade (Dixit and Norman 1980). Trefler (1997) and Kennan (2013) present alternative approaches.

12. The definition of the goods implies that immigration and trade are complements, because there is complete specialization of goods production. If immigration and trade were substitutes, as in Mundell's (1957) classic analysis, there may then be factor price equalization across countries. Immigration would have no wage effects and would only alter the distribution of outputs as described by the Rybczynski Theorem. I do not address the long-running debate over whether immigration and trade are complements or substitutes. The model presented here is designed to depict an economic environment where international wage differences do exist and induce workers to migrate to other countries.

13. The issue of whether immigrants are "new" consumers can be approached in various ways. It could be that immigration substantially increases the number of domestic consumers (through the increase in C_L), and leads only to a trivial decline in the relative number of consumers from abroad. Alternatively, immigrants may change their preferences for the domestic good after arriving in the host country. Even though the increase in C_L may be completely offset by a decline in C_X, the weight determining the post-migration demand of the immigrants for the domestic good increases from g_X to g_L. Staehle (1934) gives a prescient discussion of the consumption behavior of immigrants.

14. The marginal productivity conditions suggest that it is straightforward to generalize the model to allow for heterogeneous labor in the context of the nested CES framework. In particular, the labor input L can be reinterpreted as the number of standardized efficiency units.

15. The source of the international wage differences that induce migration can be modeled in different ways in the context of an open-economy model. These modeling choices influence the theoretical implications. One could argue, for example, that workers gain a permanent productive advantage by moving to the developed countries. The characterization of the long run in this case is one that views the host country as having higher total factor productivity levels, and the readjustments that take place create sizable global gains as the various countries move to a global equilibrium (see Chapter 7). Alternatively, one can view the long run through the lens of the closed economy models presented earlier in this chapter: the host country's labor market was in a steady state equilibrium that was temporarily disturbed by the influx of immigrants.

The eventual reallocation of resources from other countries (where the capital flows presumably originate) to the host country hastens the move of the "rest of the world" toward equilibrium.

16. It is important to note that the assumed functional form of the utility function restricts the size of the scale effect. Borjas (2013b), for example, uses a functional form that allows for $\eta > 1$. Wagner (2010) and Özden and Wagner (2013) specifically attempt to estimate the scale effect arising from immigration-induced supply shifts.

17. Because immigration affects consumer demand, the model also has implications for product prices; see Borjas (2013b) for details. Recent empirical studies of the price effect of immigration include Cortes (2008), Lach (2007), and Saiz (2003, 2007).

18. Olney (2013b) provides an interesting exception. He examines the impact of remittances on wages in a host country (Germany), and confirms the theoretical prediction that outgoing remittances lower the wage of native workers.

4. The Wage Effects of Immigration: Descriptive Evidence

1. Hamermesh (1993) gives a detailed discussion of the properties of the translog and related production functions.

2. A large number of studies estimate spatial correlations in the United States and other immigrant receiving countries; see, for example, Addison and Worswick (2002), Altonji and Card (1991), Card (2001, 2005), De New and Zimmerman (1994), Dustmann et al. (2005), LaLonde and Topel (1991), Pischke and Velling (1997), Schoeni (1997a), and Zorlu and Hartog (2005). Other early studies that used a structural approach include Borjas (1987a) and Bean et al. (1988). Friedberg and Hunt (1995) and Longhi et al. (2009) survey the literature.

3. The regression specification typically estimates "own" effects, the impact of immigration on the wage of similarly skilled workers. A few studies have expanded the spatial correlation approach to estimate some of the potential cross-effects, the impact of immigrants in one skill group on the wage of native workers in other skill groups; see, for example, Altonji and Card (1991) and Pischke and Velling (1997).

4. The immigrant share $p_{exr}(t)$ is calculated using information on hours worked by all foreign- and native-born workers, including men and women, and both wage-and-salary and self-employed workers.

5. The five metropolitan areas with the largest contributions to immigrant labor supply were New York, Los Angeles, Chicago, San Francisco, and Washington, DC. The respective list for natives is New York, Chicago, Los Angeles, Dallas, and Washington, DC.

6. To better approximate the price of a skill unit, the empirical analysis reported in this chapter and in Chapter 5 excludes self-employed workers when calculating weekly earnings (defined as annual wage and salary income divided by weeks worked).

7. The MSA-level regressions reported in Table 4.2 use only the 1980–2010 cross-sections. The 1960 census does not provide any information on metropolitan area of residence, and the 1970 census provides limited information.

8. It might seem easier to specify the right-hand-side variable in equation (4.3) to be m, rather than the immigrant share p. I opt for the share specification because the relation between the log wage and m is highly nonlinear and the calculation of the marginal impact would require an even more meticulous calculation. It is interesting to note that the variable $\log m$ is approximately a linear transformation of the immigrant share; specifically, $\log m \approx 2(2p - 1)$.

9. The construction of the instrument uses the 60 largest national origin groups that can be consistently defined between 1980 and 2010. All other immigrants are classified into a residual "other" category. It is worth noting that the geographic sorting of natives is also not exogenous, but this problem has generally been ignored in the literature.

10. The standard error of the difference-in-differences point estimate, however, is quite large; see Donald and Lang (2007) for a discussion of the issues surrounding statistical inference in the Mariel context. Hunt (1992) and Carrington and Lima (1996) present related case studies of the impact of localized supply shocks in France and Portugal, respectively.

11. In fact, the result that supply shocks influence the price of labor is documented by many studies examining such disparate contexts as the Dust Bowl (Hornbeck 2012), the industrial mobilization of American women during World War II (Acemoglu et. al. 2004), the baby boom (Welch 1979), the Palestinian Intifada (Angrist 1996), the 1918 flu epidemic (Brainerd and Siegler 2003), and the internal migration of Americans during the Great Depression (Boustan et al. 2010). The empirical difficulty of finding a downward-sloping labor demand curve seems specific to the immigration context.

12. Early studies motivated by the incongruity include Borjas, Freeman, and Katz (1992, 1997). Related work by Friedberg (2001) and Card (2001) also does not rely on geographic variation in labor market outcomes to measure the impact of immigration (and instead rely on differences across occupations).

13. Borjas (2001) documents that regional variation in rates of return to schooling affects the geographic settlement of new immigrants. The new arrivals tend to settle in those states that offer the highest relative returns for their skills. Similarly, Cadena and Kovak (2013) show that the location decisions of low-skill Mexican immigrants during the Great Recession were strongly influenced by local labor-market conditions.

14. It is impossible for natives to suddenly become younger or older to avoid com-
    petition from an immigrant influx into particular age groups, and it is very
    costly (and would take some time) for natives to obtain additional education.

15. Specifically, the points in the scatter diagram are the residuals from a regres-
    sion of the log weekly wage of men (or the immigrant share) on a vector of
    interacted education-experience fixed effects and a vector of year fixed effects.
    The education-experience fixed effects effectively rescale the log weekly wage
    and immigrant shares relative to the mean value for the skill group.

16. In addition to the endogeneity in the immigrant share introduced by policy
    choices, it is also the case that foreign-born persons belonging to the skill cells
    that offer a relatively higher payoff are most motivated to migrate to the United
    States. This behavior would imply that the coefficients reported in Table 4.5
    understate the true wage impact. Similarly, only those persons who find it
    worthwhile to enter the workforce are included in the construction of the share
    variable. This problem can be easily addressed by using an instrument giving
    the immigrant share in the respective population. Borjas et al. (2010) show that
    using this instrument has a negligible effect on the estimated coefficients.

17. The MSA-level regressions use data beginning with the 1980 census and do
    not include workers who live outside a metropolitan area, so that the sample
    is not exactly identical to that used in the state, census division, and national-
    level analyses.

18. Raphael and Ronconi (2007, 2008) discuss the sensitivity of the national-level
    wage effects to the inclusion of other regressors in the model. They document,
    for example, that controlling for the native-born incarceration rate reduces
    the estimated wage impact of immigration. It is unclear, however, whether
    such a control should be included as a regressor. After all, the incarceration
    rate is endogenous, because it obviously depends on labor market conditions.

19. Although the point estimate is substantially larger for the earlier time period,
    the hypothesis that the two coefficients are the same cannot be rejected.

20. Many studies also use the framework to examine employment effects. Borjas
    et al. (2010), for example, find that immigration reduces the employment rate
    of competing black and white native workers. Smith (2012) offers the most
    detailed analysis of the employment effects of immigration and concludes
    that the supply shock had a particularly adverse effect on the employment of
    young workers in the United States.

21. Card (2009) first noted this similarity.

22. The OLS longitudinal coefficient estimated over this period is -0.022 (0.024).

23. To complicate matters further, long-term changes in the educational decisions
    of native workers could themselves be an endogenous response to the labor
    market impact of immigration.

24. Other studies of the German context, however, have not found the presumed
    negative correlation between immigration and wages. Related work by Glitz

(2012), for example, does not find any wage effect, but documents adverse employment effects, while D'Amuri et al. (2010) find neither wage nor employment effects. Similarly, Carrasco et al. (2008) apply the model in the Spanish context, where the immigrant share increased from 1 to 6 percent between 1991 and 2003, and find only a very weak correlation between employment propensities and immigration.

25. In related work, Bratsberg and Raaum (2012) examine the impact of immigration in the Norwegian construction industry and find even larger negative effects on wages, with an implied wage elasticity of around −0.6. Aydemir and Kirdar (2013) exploit a natural experiment in Turkey that resulted in the repatriation of a large number of ethnic Turks from Bulgaria in 1989 and find that the supply shock significantly increased Turkish unemployment rates.

26. Deaton (1985) examines a case where measurement error in the dependent variable may create problems in the longitudinal context. However, Aydemir and Borjas (2011) show that even though the log wage is also measured imperfectly, the sampling error in the dependent variable does not create any statistical problems in this context.

27. Cameron and Trivedi (2005, p. 904).

28. Each of these confidential files represents a 20 percent sample of the Canadian population (except for the 1971 file, which represents a 33.3 percent sample).

29. Aydemir and Borjas (2011) introduce several other correction methods, including split-sample IV and bootstrapping. The simplest back-of-the-envelope approach typically works as well as these alternative methods for relatively large cell sizes, and all methods break down when the mean cell size is small.

30. As noted earlier, many empirical studies use some transformation of a lagged immigrant share as an instrument to estimate the wage effect of immigration. This IV approach can correct for *classical* measurement error. However, Aydemir and Borjas (2011) show that the specific type of sampling error discussed in this section introduces nonclassical measurement error in the first-stage regressions and, in fact, the first-stage coefficient may turn negative (as was the case in some of the specifications reported in Table 4.3).

5. The Wage Effects of Immigration: Structural Estimates

1. It could be argued, in fact, that the descriptive approach does not even come close to estimating the own effect of an immigration-induced supply shift, because the regression models typically ignore all the cross-effects implied by factor demand theory. I return to this insight at the end of this chapter.

2. Of course, the shape of the production technology also depends on the relative productivity weights in each of the three levels (i.e., the parameter vectors λ, θ, and α).

3. If $\hat{\phi}_{ex}$ is the estimated coefficient of the fixed effect, then $\hat{\alpha}_{ex} = \exp(\hat{\phi}_{ex}) / \sum_x \exp(\hat{\phi}_{ex})$.

4. Consider the regression model given by $\log w = \beta \log L + u$. The IV estimator of β has the property:

$$\text{plim}\hat{\beta} = \beta + \frac{\text{cov}(\log M, u)}{\text{cov}(\log M, \log L)},$$

where $\log M$ is the instrument. The total number of workers in a skill group is, in fact, positively correlated with the number of immigrants in that group, so that $\text{cov}(\log M, \log L) > 0$. Further, $\text{cov}(\log M, u) > 0$, because skill cells with favorable demand conditions will attract larger numbers of immigrants. The IV regression coefficient then provides a lower bound for the wage reduction resulting from a supply increase.

5. In principle, the elasticity σ_{KL} could be estimated even without direct information on the aggregate capital stock by going up an additional level in the nested CES hierarchy. This exercise yields the marginal productivity condition for the average worker at time t. The log wage would then depend on a year fixed effect and on $\log L_t$, the total number of efficiency units in the workforce. The coefficient of $\log L_t$ identifies $-1/\sigma_{KL}$. However, this regression would have only one observation per year (or six observations in the decennial census data used in the empirical analysis), and one would need to make some assumption about the trend in the relative demand for labor over time (because the year fixed effects are perfectly collinear with L_t).

6. More precisely, in addition to the education-specific linear trends, the regression includes interactions between the education fixed effects and a dummy variable set to one in the 1990–2010 censuses.

7. The income shares used in the simulations reported in this chapter are calculated using the 2000 census, and are normalized so that labor's share of income is 0.7.

8. Alternatively, equation (5.8) follows directly from a simple differentiation of the marginal productivity condition giving the wage of education group e.

9. One minor caveat: The estimation of the elasticity of substitution σ_E requires the calculation of the size of the effective workforce in each education group, and this Armington aggregation, in turn, requires information on σ_X. As Table 5.1 shows, however, the estimated elasticity of substitution across education groups barely changes if one skips this step.

10. To define the supply shocks consistently throughout this chapter, I allow for the possibility that immigrants and natives are not perfect substitutes at the education-experience level. The introduction of a fourth level of the nesting implies that the supply shock for the (e, x) cell would be given by a weighted

average of the supply shifts for natives and immigrants in that cell. Let s_{ex}^M give the share of income accruing to immigrants in cell (e, x). By assumption, native supply is held fixed in the simulation. The supply shock m_{ex} is then defined by the product of the ratio s_{ex}^M / s_{ex} and $d \log M_{ex}$, where $d \log M_{ex} = \log(M_{ex,2010}/M_{ex,1990})$. The quantities m_e and $\bar{m}$ are calculated using the averaging formulas $m_e = \sum_x s_{ex} m_{ex}/s_e$ and $\bar{m} = \sum_e s_e m_e/s_L$.

11. It would be interesting to allow immigration to influence the labor supply of native-born workers, both in terms of the labor force participation decision and hours of work. Although this exercise would not be an easy task, it would be an important extension, particularly in markets characterized by inflexible wages.

12. The discussion presented in this section and the next is based on Borjas et al. (2012).

13. The within-group complementarities could arise, for example, due to differences in English-language fluency between immigrants and natives with the same education and experience. Peri and Sparber (2009) examine the question of how these differences can lead to differential "task specialization" by native- and foreign-born workers in the same skill group.

14. In their original work, Ottaviano and Peri (2006) estimated an inverse elasticity of -0.18 (0.06), implying that σ_{MN} equals 5.6. This elasticity was sufficiently low to imply that immigration increases the wage of almost all native workers. Borjas et al. (2008) showed that the value of this elasticity was attributable to a strange feature of the sample used in that study. In particular, Ottaviano and Peri used a sample of persons aged 17–65, but did *not* exclude persons who were enrolled in school. As a result, millions of native-born high school juniors and seniors were mistakenly classified as "high school dropouts" because they did not yet have a high school diploma. The exclusion of these students from the sample increases the estimate of σ_{MN} substantially.

15. None of the key studies in the wage structure literature use the log mean wage as the measure of earnings; see, for example, Katz and Murphy (1992), Card and Lemieux (2001), and Lemieux (2006). Borjas et al. (2012) also address the issue of how the data are weighted in the Ottaviano-Peri regressions. The motivation for weighting the regression arises from the concern that there may be differences across observations in the sampling error of the log wage difference used as the dependent variable. The appropriate weight is the inverse of the sampling variance for an observation, and this is the weight used in the regressions reported in Panels B and C of Table 5.3.

16. Ruist (2013) specifically examines the question of how the changing national origin mix of immigrants in a particular skill cell contaminates estimates of the elasticity σ_{MN}. He finds that the changing composition induces a substantial

bias, giving the impression of sizable within-group complementarities, when in fact none may exist. It is also worth noting that the existing studies uniformly ignore the potential endogeneity of the supply ratio in the right-hand side of equation (5.11). It is difficult to ascertain, however, how this endogeneity affects estimates of the elasticity σ_{MN}.

17. This assessment of the evidence in the modern U.S. context does not imply that within-group complementarities are universally absent. They may well be present in other labor markets or at different times; see, for example, Manacorda et al. (2012).

18. See Card (2009), Ottaviano and Peri (2012), and Manacorda et al. (2012).

19. The analysis could also allow for a separate "pooling" of workers who have more than a high school diploma. I ignore this extension in what follows because it plays a less important role in calculations of the wage impact of immigration in the United States.

20. In theory, the quantities L_{1t} and L_{2t} represent the number of "efficiency units" provided by all workers in each of these education groups. For example, if high school graduates in different experience groups were not perfect substitutes, the aggregation of the various groups into L_{2t} would make use of the estimated elasticity of substitution across experience groups (by performing the appropriate Armington aggregation). As noted by Ottaviano and Peri (2012), the results barely change if the regression uses the total number of hours worked by persons in the cell instead.

21. These are the data used in the regressions reported in Goldin and Katz (2010, p. 306). Borjas et al. (2012) restricted the analysis to the post-1963 period, when modern CPS data became available, and used the Goldin-Katz definition of the post-1992 spline: an additional linear trend variable initialized with a value of one in 1993. By including a few historical data points prior to 1963, Goldin and Katz also examined the possibility that there may have been a linear decline in the value of σ_{HS} over a century-long period. Specifically, they introduce a variable that interacts relative supply with the time trend, and the coefficient of this interaction is negative. Card (2009) extrapolates the negative interaction to argue that the value of the inverse elasticity is nearly zero for the post-1980 period. Table 5.5, however, shows that the post-1963 data imply an inverse elasticity that is significantly different from zero and numerically important.

22. Factor demand theory also implies that inverse labor demand functions are homogeneous of degree zero (if the production function has constant returns), and this restriction may also help in the interpretation of the descriptive regressions.

23. This estimator presumes that the regression model does not include any variables other than the own supply shift. In fact, the model typically includes

skill group and period fixed effects. This issue can be handled easily by redefining the variables in the model. For example, the inclusion of period fixed effects leads to a redefinition of the variables as being differenced from the mean observed in that period.

24. It is important to stress, however, that estimates of full-blown production technologies sometimes reject the symmetry predictions of factor demand theory (Hamermesh 1993).

6. Labor Market Adjustments to Immigration

1. Other studies include Frey (1995b), White and Liang (1998), Card (2001), and Kritz and Gurak (2001).

2. Specifically, the points in the scatter diagram are the residuals from a regression of the log native population (or the immigrant share) on a vector of skill-state fixed effects and a vector of year fixed effects. The skill-state fixed effects effectively rescale the log number of natives and immigrant shares relative to the mean value for the skill-state group.

3. The model extends the Blanchard and Katz (1992) framework that analyzes how local labor market conditions respond to demand shocks. The model presented in this section assumes that the labor market is in equilibrium prior to the entry of immigrants; the more general version in Borjas (2006) allows for the existence of internal migration flows prior to the immigrant supply shock. Hanson and McIntosh (2010) further extend the model to examine the dynamics of Mexican migration to the United States.

4. Bartel (1989) examines the internal migration decision of immigrants in the United States and finds that immigrants have relatively low internal migration rates.

5. The model assumes that the market clears and ignores the labor force participation and hours of work decisions of native workers. A labor supply response on the part of natives would help attenuate the wage effect and reduce the need for native internal migration; see Rowthorn and Glyn (2002) and Borjas et al. (2010) for related discussions.

6. More precisely, $\log \bar{w}_{ht} = \log w_h^* + \eta m_{ht}$, where $m_{ht} = (t+1)M_h / \bar{N}_h$. The model implicitly assumes that the native population is large enough (relative to the immigrant stock) to be able to equalize the wage across labor markets through internal migration.

7. The staggered native migration response in equation (6.4) can be justified in many ways. The labor market is in continual flux, with persons entering and leaving the market. Because migration is costly, workers may find it optimal to time the lumpy migration decision concurrently with these transitions. Workers may also face constraints that prevent them from taking immediate

advantage of regional wage differentials, including various forms of "job-lock" or short-term liquidity constraints.

8. The net migration rate, v, and the immigration-induced supply shift, m, both have the (fixed) native baseline as the denominator. The derivative $\partial v / \partial m$ is then equivalent to $\partial N / \partial M$.

9. It is important to emphasize that despite its empirical tractability, the model is very restrictive. For example, it assumes that native workers anticipate the future impact of immigration, but ignores the fact that firms have similar expectations and that the capital stock will adjust in an optimal fashion, likely dampening the adverse wage effects of immigration on the local labor market and reducing the need for native internal migration.

10. The information on lagged place of residence is only available for select censuses. The state-level analysis uses the 1970–2000 censuses, while the MSA-level analysis uses the 1990–2000 censuses.

11. The migration rates are calculated using the sample of all native men, regardless of their labor force status. I multiply all migration rates by 2—this adjustment converts the 5-year rates into decadal changes. As in Chapters 4 and 5, the immigrant share gives the fraction of work hours supplied by foreign-born workers in a particular cell, and the calculation includes all working men and women.

12. Wozniak and Murray (2012) estimate the impact of immigration on the growth of the native population, and allow the response to differ across skill groups. Their evidence is consistent with the results presented here for high-skill workers, but not for low-skill workers. The Wozniak-Murray study also attempts to differentiate between short-term and long-term responses, and finds that the long-term adjustments also differ by skill group.

13. Peri and Sparber (2011) simulate a related model and show that under some conditions there may be a spurious negative correlation between wage changes and the rate of growth in the local workforce. The regressions reported in this section potentially avoid this problem by estimating the correlation between wage changes and migration rates.

14. It is possible to conduct a more general exercise that adjusts the spatial correlation both for the native migration response and for the attenuation bias induced by sampling error (see Chapter 4). Even if the sampling error adjustment were to double the spatial correlation at the MSA level, however, the native internal migration correction would still predict a value of the elasticity η that is about half the value observed in national-level data.

15. It is worth reemphasizing that this analytical approach implicitly assumes that the host country was in steady state equilibrium prior to the immigration-induced supply shock, and that the capital flows simply speed up the process of reestablishing the preexisting equilibrium. Because both immigrants and capital have to come from somewhere, the analysis ignores the effects of these flows on other countries.

16. The model originates in the Autor et al. (2003) study of how the computer revolution affected relative demands for skills. Although the version of the model presented here represents a very special case, it captures the empirical relevance of the approach.

17. See also Hanson and Slaughter (2002), Dustmann and Glitz (2012), and Olney (2013a). Other studies that exploit geographic variation in the skill composition of the workforce to estimate related models include González and Ortega (2011), Peri (2012), and Peri and Sparber (2009). Lewis (2013) offers a critical appraisal of this literature.

18. For instance, if the production function were Cobb-Douglas, the inverse demand function would be given by $\log w = \alpha \log K - \alpha \log L$.

19. Hamermesh (1989) documents that adjustment costs are "lumpy." Firms tend to move quickly toward a new equilibrium when the supply shock is large and the economic benefits from a rapid adjustment exceed the substantial costs that would be incurred, but the firm will prefer to stay at the "wrong" equilibrium for some time if the supply shock is relatively small and the forgone earnings do not cover the adjustment costs.

20. Note also that the adjustments may involve native workers and firms making choices that they would otherwise not have made, that these choices are costly, and that these costs need to be incorporated into any cost-benefit analysis of immigration.

21. Greenaway-McGrevy and Hood (2011, p. 33) revisit the Blanchard-Katz evidence and find that it may take as long as two decades for the wage effects of a 1 percent local demand shock in employment to disappear.

22. Cohen-Goldner and Paserman (2011) provide a rare attempt to estimate the wage impact of a particular immigration-induced supply shock at different points in time. Their analysis "tracks" the impact of the Soviet Jews who migrated to Israel after the collapse of the Soviet Union. The Israeli data indicate that there is a negative short-run wage effect with an elasticity of around −0.1 to −0.3, but that this effect becomes negligible after 7 years.

7. The Economic Benefits from Immigration

1. Berry and Soligo (1969) present a very early discussion of the basic model in the context of emigration. Borjas (1995b) first applied the model to the calculation of economic benefits in the U.S. context.

2. The calculation of the gains from immigration would be more cumbersome if native labor supply was not inelastic, because one would then need to calculate the value of the change in utility experienced by native workers as they move between the market and nonmarket sectors.

3. It is easy to derive equation (7.2) by using the approximation $(w_0 - w_1) \approx (\partial w / \partial L) \times M$.

4. This implication is analogous to the result from international trade theory that cheap foreign imports, typically seen as having harmful and disruptive effects, often benefit the importing country.

5. The area of the rectangle DCLN in Figure 7.1 gives the total income accruing to the immigrant workforce. It is trivial to show that this quantity, as a fraction of GDP, is given by $s_L p$ (the product of labor's share of income and the immigrant share), so that immigrant earnings account for approximately 10.5 percent of GDP. The total increase in GDP caused by immigration is the sum of this quantity and the immigration surplus. Obviously, almost all of the increase in GDP (in fact, around 98 percent) accrues to immigrant workers.

6. Moreover, the theoretical implication of a positive immigration surplus depends crucially on the assumption of linear homogeneity in production. Rasmusen (2013) examines a number of cases where there are decreasing returns and shows that immigration can often lead to a reduction in native income.

7. The differentiation assumes that the immigrant supply shock is "small" and does not affect the values of π_S and π_U. Benhabib (1996) provides a related discussion of the political economy problem facing a social planner trying to maximize the gains from immigration.

8. The positive sign of the short-run immigration surplus follows from the fact that equation (7.12) is a quadratic form in the negative-definite matrix $\begin{bmatrix} c_{SS} & c_{SU} \\ c_{US} & c_{UU} \end{bmatrix}$.

9. Goldin and Katz (1998) offer a detailed discussion of the capital-skill complementarity hypothesis and summarize the supporting historical evidence.

10. See, for example, Borjas (1995b, 1999), Borjas, Freeman, and Katz (1997), and Johnson (1998).

11. Because the sum of factor price elasticities must equal zero, these assumptions uniquely determine all the other elasticities in the model.

12. All of these parameter values are drawn from the 2000 census. They also implicitly determine the value of b since $\pi_S = b(1 - p) + \beta p$.

13. Borjas (2001) notes another source of potential benefits that may arise within the canonical framework: Newly arrived immigrants tend to settle in high-wage states, arbitrage regional wage differences, and reduce the need for native internal flows. However, a back-of-the-envelope calculation suggests that these efficiency gains may be quite small. Cadena (2013, 2014) provides additional evidence that immigration helps to equalize regional wage differences in the United States.

14. In 2000, the fraction of hours supplied by foreign-born workers was 13.1 percent, and it declines to 12.3 percent when weighted by income shares. In 2010

the respective statistics are 16.6 and 15.7 percent. The calculation uses the 40 education-experience groups defined in previous chapters.

15. Recent applications include Lundborg and Segerstrom (2002), Moses and Letnes (2004), Benhabib and Jovanovic (2012), and Kennan (2013).

16. Di Giovanni et al. (2012) present an interesting generalization of the model that allows for imperfect competition and product variety. Their simulation also reveals substantial global gains from international migration.

17. Clemens et al. (2008) report that the adjusted wage gap for a low-skill worker between the United States and a large number of low-income countries is around 4.1. Ashenfelter (2012) provides a particularly fascinating study of the international wage gaps by using the price of a McDonald's Big Mac to deflate for wage differences across countries. He reports sizable differences in the number of Big Macs that can be purchased using the earnings resulting from a single hour of work: from 2.4 Big Macs in the United States, to 0.6 in China, to 0.4 in India and Latin America.

18. Hamilton and Whalley (1984), for example, present detailed estimates of the efficiency gains but fail to report the number of movers required to achieve those gains.

19. The more sophisticated approach in Benhabib and Jovanovic (2012) confirms that billions of persons need to move in order to maximize world welfare.

20. It is worth noting that a disproportionately large fraction of the global gains can be accrued even if only a fraction of the potential movers migrate to the North. For example, global GDP would increase by around 17 percent when 10 percent of the potential movers move (assuming $R = 4$).

21. See, for example, Clemens (2011), Clemens et al. (2008), Klein and Ventura (2007), Pritchett (2010), and Walmsley and Winters (2005).

22. This estimate of moving costs measures "the costs of hypothetical moves to arbitrary locations" (Kennan and Walker 2011, p. 232). Only a subset of persons in the data actually are observed to make a move, so that the subsample of movers may have moving costs that differ substantially from (and may be much lower than) these "average" estimates for hypothetical moves. They also estimate a model where a person is "forced" to move, but is allowed to choose his or her optimal destination; that move would still entail a cost of around $40,000. A recent study by Barrett and Mosca (2013) begins to examine the nature of some of these migration costs by specifically looking at behavioral problems in a sample of return migrants.

23. For expositional convenience, the calculation of the break-even costs reported in Table 7.3 ignores the fact that the presence of migration costs changes the number of migrants. A calculation that incorporates the behavioral response proceeds as follows. Suppose that migration costs are constant at C dollars per person, and that the migration of a single "worker migrant" leads to the

movement of n persons, including the related dependents. In the absence of immigration policy restrictions, a global equilibrium is attained when:

$$\alpha_N (L_N + M)^\eta - \alpha_S (L_S - M)^\eta = rnC,$$

where r is the rate of discount. The (annualized) global gains, net of migration costs, are given by:

$$\Delta Y = \int_{L_N}^{L_N + M} \alpha_N L^\eta \, dL - \int_{L_S - M}^{L_S} \alpha_S L^\eta \, dL - rnMC.$$

Breakeven migration costs, C^*, can be calculated by solving this system of nonlinear equations using the restriction that $\Delta Y = 0$. Assuming $r = 0.05$ and defining n as in the text leads to the following estimates (in thousands of dollars): $C^* = \$82.5$ if $R = 2$, $\$155.1$ if $R = 3$, $\$211.7$ if $R = 4$, $\$256.7$ if $R = 5$, and $\$293.1$ if $R = 6$. As in the simpler calculation reported in Table 7.3, much of the presumed gains from open borders would disappear if migration costs were roughly of the same magnitude as the estimates in the literature.

24. Docquier et al. (2012) examine the sensitivity of the estimates of the global gains to the presence of such factors as international differences in education quality, endogenous productivity, congestion effects, and migration costs. Their simulations show that accounting for these factors greatly reduces the estimate of the gains to less than 4 percent of world GDP.

8. High-Skill Immigration

1. The model is a special case of the framework presented in Borjas and Doran (2014).

2. The notion that high-skill labor supply is inelastic in the short run was a core assumption of the cobweb model used by Freeman (1975, 1976) to examine wage and employment adjustments in the markets for engineers and physicists.

3. Finn (2003) calculates the stay rate of foreign-born doctoral recipients. The proportion who remain in the United States after receiving their degree increased from 49 percent for the 1989 cohort to 71 percent for the 2001 cohort. Grogger and Hanson (2013) examine the factors that determine the postgraduation geographic settlement decisions of this group.

4. By 2000, immigration had increased the immigrant share in the stock of doctorates in the United States to 23.6 percent. Equation (4.4) shows that the elasticity $d \log w / d \log L$ is given by $\theta(1 - p)^2$, where p is the immigrant share. In this context, the elasticity estimate is -0.24 (or -0.409×0.584).

5. The adverse wage effects reported in Table 8.1 probably underestimate the "true" wage impact. After all, the flow of foreign immigrants into particular

disciplines will likely be greater when the labor market in those disciplines offers relatively favorable conditions. This behavioral response builds in a positive correlation between immigration and wages.

6. Sometimes the features of the two programs merge to allow the entry of a high-skill worker. For example, a doctoral student with a foreign student visa would not be allowed to stay in the United States after graduation. Some of these students, however, receive job offers from American employers, and these offers can include an H-1B visa.

7. The binding contract suggests that the employer has some market power over the visa holder. The implications of this institutional arrangement for the labor market outcomes of both immigrants and natives in the high-tech sector have not been explored carefully.

8. Paserman (2013) provides a related study of the impact of high-skill Soviet immigration to Israel. He uses firm-level data to estimate the correlation between productivity in manufacturing firms and the firm-specific immigrant share. If anything, there seems to be a *negative* relation between productivity and high-skill immigration in this context (although the correlation turns slightly positive for high-tech firms). Put differently, there is no evidence that this particular supply shock generated beneficial spillovers for the Israeli manufacturing sector.

9. Other studies that examine the impact of high-skill immigration using spatial correlations include Hunt and Gauthier-Loiselle (2010) and Peri et al. (2013). These studies generally find a positive correlation between the presence of high-skill immigrants and local area outcomes, although the use of spatial correlations, sometimes at the state level, clouds the interpretation of the findings.

10. A related literature in urban economics examines the spillovers arising from agglomeration effects; see, for example, Feldman (1999) and Combes et al. (2010). The urban economics literature tends to find much more robust evidence of human capital spillovers.

11. A department is defined to have "high-quality dismissals" if the mean quality of the dismissed professors was above the mean quality of the department.

12. Moser et al. (2013) revisit this natural experiment to examine the impact of the Jewish émigrés who settled in the United States on scientific innovation (as measured by the number of patents). They find that the arrival of the Jewish émigrés increased the rate of innovation by attracting new American scientists to their fields, but had no impact on the innovation rate of preexisting scientists.

13. The discussion in this section borrows from Borjas and Doran (2012).

14. A crucial factor behind this divergence is the randomness of where mathematical geniuses are born.

15. The different pre-1992 publication rate for the two groups reflects the fact that the annual rate of output differs among mathematicians specializing in

different mathematical fields. Borjas and Doran (2012) show that the difference-in-differences estimate is quite similar after controlling for the pre-1992 differences.

16. A dissertation is "Soviet-style" if it is in one of the top ten most popular fields of mathematical research in the Soviet Union prior to 1992; all other fields are classified as "American-style."

17. In closely related work, Azoulay, Zivin, and Wang (2010) show the importance of externalities in a collaborative network. They examined what happens to the colleagues of superstar scientists in biological labs after the superstars die, and find that the productivity of these colleagues declines dramatically after the event.

9. The Second Generation

1. The census stopped collecting information on parental birthplace in 1970, but the CPS began to collect the information in 1994. The sample size of the CPS data, however, is small compared to that of the decennial censuses, so that it is necessary to pool several years of the CPS in order to obtain relatively large samples of second-generation workers in specific national origin groups. The CPS data used in the analysis below consists of the pooled (March) Annual Social and Economic Supplements over the 1996–2005 period.

2. The adjusted wage differences are obtained by estimating (in each cross-section) a log weekly wage regression that includes age (introduced as a third-order polynomial) and fixed effects indicating the worker's generation. The regressions using the pooled Current Population Surveys also include a vector of dummy variables indicating the year of the survey. The choice of the third generation as the baseline is arbitrary, although it is probably preferable to using the mean wage in the workforce (which could introduce baseline wage changes over time due to compositional differences in the first and/or second generations).

3. This approach was introduced in Borjas (1993).

4. See also Perlmann and Waldinger (1997).

5. Park (1964) and Gordon (1964) provide the classic expositions of the melting pot hypothesis. The revisionist literature began with Glazer and Moynihan (1963); see also Lieberson and Waters (1988) and Portes and Zhou (1993).

6. See, for example, Becker and Tomes (1979, 1986) and Behrman and Taubman (1985).

7. See Couch and Dunn (1997), Björklund et al. (2007), Mazumder (2005), and Zimmerman (1992). Solon (1999) surveys the literature.

8. The figure provides information for 54 national origin groups. Each group satisfies the sample restriction that there were more than 30 observations in

both the 1970 and 2000 cross-sections to calculate the wage of the ethnic group in each respective generation. The ethnic background of second-generation Americans is determined by the mother's country of birth (unless only the father is foreign-born, in which case it is determined by the father's country of birth).

9. The intercept of the regression line in Figure 9.1, corresponding to the parameter α in equation (9.1), measures the "generalized" improvement in relative earnings between the first and second generations. The intercept (and standard error) is 0.089 (0.019) in the 1940–1970 regression and 0.084 (0.022) in the 1970–2000 regression, suggesting about an 8 percent improvement between the first and second generations that is common to all ethnic groups. Notably, this improvement is of roughly the same magnitude as that implied by the intergenerational tracking of generations in Table 9.1.

10. There are many precedents for introducing an ethnic externality into the human capital production function. For example, Coleman (1988), Loury (1977), and Wilson (1987) emphasize the concept of "social capital." In their view, the culture in which an individual is raised, which can be thought of as a form of human capital common to all members of that group, has significant effects on behavior, human capital formation, and labor market outcomes.

11. Other studies that attempt to measure the effect of ethnic capital in related contexts include Cutler et al. (2005), Darity et al. (2001), León (2005), and Philips and Fishman (2006).

12. The intergenerational transmission coefficients estimated in aggregate census data are known in the sociological literature as "ecological" correlations. Barro and Sala-i-Martin (1992) provide a related discussion of alternative concepts of convergence.

13. The discussion assumes that measurement error in parental skills is independent of ethnicity. In addition, I assume there is a sufficiently large sample size in each group so that the measurement error in parental skills "washes out" when averaging within the group. As a result, the random variable v_2 measures only how the skills of an individual parent deviate from the true group-specific mean. It can then be shown that $Corr(x, v_2) = -\sigma_2/\sigma_x$.

14. Put differently, the intergenerational correlation between parents and children is estimated properly because ethnic capital provides a valid instrument that can be used to correct for the measurement error problem.

15. A vast literature documents that neighborhoods matter and that "neighborhood effects" influence a person's economic outcomes; see, for example, Cutler and Glaeser (1997), Jencks and Mayer (1990), Katz et al. (2001), Kling et al. (2007), and Oreopoulos (2003).

16. To reduce sampling costs, the NLSY surveyed other persons in the randomly chosen household unit who were in the correct age range (i.e., 14–22 in 1979).

As a result, there are a large number of siblings in the data. To avoid the bias introduced by this sampling scheme, Borjas (1995c) calculated the segregation measures on the sample of nonrelated persons who reside outside the household unit. In addition, the NLSY also sampled households that resided geographically close to each other. This strategy suggests that the measures of residential segregation probably overstate the true extent of segregation.

17. Alba's (1990) study of social contacts among U.S.-born white ethnics indicates that half of all nonrelated childhood friends belong to the same ethnic group, while Holzer (1988) documents that friends are a key source of information about job opportunities, so that intragroup referrals play a major role in the job search process and might explain the concentration of some ethnic groups in narrowly defined occupations; see also the related work in Guiso et al. (2009).

References

Abramitzky, Ran. 2009. The effect of redistribution on migration: Evidence from the Israeli kibbutz. *Journal of Public Economics* 93: 498–511.

Abramitzky, Ran, Leah Platt Boustan, and Katherine Eriksson. 2012. Europe's tired, poor, huddled masses: Self-selection and economic outcomes in the age of mass migration. *American Economic Review* 102: 1832–1856.

———. 2013. A nation of immigrants: Assimilation and economic outcomes in the age of mass migration. Stanford University.

Acemoglu, Daron, David Autor, and David Lyle. 2004. Women, war and wages: The effect of female labor supply on the wage structure at mid-century. *Journal of Political Economy* 2012: 497–551.

Acemoglu, Daron, and James A. Robinson. 2012. *Why nations fail: The origins of power, prosperity, and poverty.* New York: Crown Business.

Addison, Thomas, and Christopher Worswick. 2002. The impact of immigration on the earnings of natives: Evidence from Australian micro data. *Economic Record* 78: 68–78.

Alba, Richard D. 1990. *Ethnic identity: The transformation of white America.* New Haven, CT: Yale University Press.

Altonji, Joseph G., and David Card. 1991. The effects of immigration on the labor market outcomes of less-skilled natives. In John M. Abowd and Richard B. Freeman, eds., *Immigration, trade, and the labor market,* 201–234. Chicago: University of Chicago Press.

Ambrosini, J. William, and Giovanni Peri. 2012. The determinants and the selection of Mexico-U.S. migrants. *World Economy* 35: 111–151.

Andridge, Rebbeca R., and Roderick J. A. Little. 2010. A review of hot deck imputation for survey non-response. *International Statistical Review* 78: 40–64.

Angrist, Joshua D. 1996. Short-run demand for Palestinian labor. *Journal of Labor Economics* 14: 425–453.

Angrist, Joshua D., and Alan B. Krueger. 1999. Empirical strategies in labor economics. In Orley Ashenfelter and David Card, eds., *Handbook of labor economics*, 3:1277–1366. Amsterdam: Elsevier.

Antecol, Heather, Peter J. Kuhn, and Stephen J. Trejo. 2006. Assimilation via prices or quantities? Sources of immigrant earnings growth in Australia, Canada, and the United States. *Journal of Human Resources* 41: 821–840.

Arnold, Barry C., Robert J. Beaver, Richard A. Groeneveld, and William Q. Meeker. 1993. The nontruncated marginal of a truncated bivariate normal. *Psychometrika* 58: 471–488.

Artuc, Erhan, Shubham Chaudhuri, and John McLaren. 2010. Trade shocks and labor adjustment: A structural empirical approach. *American Economic Review* 100: 1008–1045.

Ashenfelter, Orley. 2012. Comparing real wage rates: Presidential address. *American Economic Review* 102: 617–642.

Autor, David H., Lawrence F. Katz, and Melissa S. Kearney. 2008. Trends in U.S. wage inequality: Revisiting the revisionists. *Review of Economics and Statistics* 90: 300–323.

Autor, David H., Frank Levy, and Richard J. Murnane. 2003. The skill content of recent technological change: An empirical exploration. *Quarterly Journal of Economics* 118: 1279–1333.

Aydemir, Abdurrahman. 2011. Immigrant selection and short-term labour market outcomes by visa category. *Journal of Population Economics* 24: 451–475.

Aydemir, Abdurrahman, and George J. Borjas. 2007. Cross-country variation in the impact of international migration: Canada, Mexico, and the United States. *Journal of the European Economic Association* 5: 663–708.

———. 2011. Attenuation bias in measuring the wage impact of immigration. *Journal of Labor Economics* 29: 69–113.

Aydemir, Abdurrahman, and Murat G. Kirdar. 2013. Quasi-experimental impact estimates of immigrant labor supply shocks: The role of treatment and comparison group matching and relative skill composition. Sabancı University.

Aydemir, Abdurrahman, and Mikal Skuterud. 2005. Explaining the deteriorating entry earnings of Canada's immigrant cohorts, 1966–2000. *Canadian Journal of Economics* 38: 641–672.

Azoulay, Pierre, Joshua S. Graff Zivin, and Jialan Wang. 2010. Superstar extinction. *Quarterly Journal of Economics* 125: 549–589.

Baker, Michael, and Dwayne Benjamin. 1994. The performance of immigrants in the Canadian labor market. *Journal of Labor Economics* 12: 369–405.

Barrett, Alan, and Irene Mosca. 2013. The psychic costs of migration: Evidence from Irish return migrants. *Journal of Population Economics* 26: 483–506.

Barro, Robert J., and Xavier Sala-i-Martin. 1992. Convergence. *Journal of Political Economy* 100: 223–251.

Bartel, Ann P. 1989. Where do the new U.S. immigrants live? *Journal of Labor Economics* 7: 371–391.

Barth, Erling, Bernt Bratsberg, and Oddbjørn Raaum. 2004. Identifying earnings assimilation of immigrants under changing macroeconomic conditions. *Scandinavian Journal of Economics* 106: 1–22.

Bartolucci, Cristian, Claudia Villosio, and Mathis Wagner. 2013. Who migrates and why? Working paper, Boston College.

Bean, Frank D., B. Lindsay Lowell, and Lowell J. Taylor. 1988. Undocumented Mexican immigrants and the earnings of other workers in the United States. *Demography* 25: 35–52.

Beck, Audrey, Miles Corak, and Marta Tienda. 2012. Age at immigration and the adult attainments of child migrants to the United States. *Annals of the American Academy of Political and Social Science* 643: 134–159.

Becker, Gary S., and Nigel Tomes. 1979. An equilibrium theory of the distribution of income and intergenerational mobility. *Journal of Political Economy* 87: 1153–1189.

———. 1986. Human capital and the rise and fall of families. *Journal of Labor Economics* 4: S1–S39.

Beenstock, Michael, Barry R. Chiswick, and Ari Paltiel. 2010. Testing the immigrant assimilation hypothesis with longitudinal data. *Review of the Economics of the Household* 8: 7–27.

Behrman, Jere, and Paul Taubman. 1985. Intergenerational earnings mobility in the United States: Some estimates and a test of Becker's intergenerational endowments model. *Review of Economics and Statistics* 67: 144–151.

Belot, Michèle V. K., and Timothy J. Hatton. 2012. Immigrant selection in the OECD. *Scandinavian Journal of Economics* 114: 1105–1128.

Benhabib, Jess. 1996. On the political economy of immigration. *European Economic Review* 40: 1737–1744.

Benhabib, Jess, and Boyan Jovanovic. 2012. Optimal migration: A world perspective. *International Economic Review* 53: 321–348.

Ben-Porath, Yoram. 1967. The production of human capital and the life cycle of earnings. *Journal of Political Economy* 75: 352–365.

Berry, R. Albert, and Ronald Soligo. 1969. Some welfare aspects of international migration. *Journal of Political Economy* 77: 778–794.

Bertoli, Simone, Jesús Fernández-Huertas, and Francesc Ortega. 2013. Crossing the border: Self-selection, earnings, and individual migration decisions. *Journal of Development Economics* 101: 75–91.

Bhagwati, Jagdish N., and T. N. Srinivasan. 1983. *Lectures on international trade.* Cambridge, MA: MIT Press.

Björklund, Anders, Markus Jäntti, and Gary Solon. 2007. Nature and nurture in the intergenerational transmission of socioeconomic status: Evidence from Swedish children and their biological and rearing parents. *B.E. Journal of Economic Analysis and Policy* 7, no. 2.

Blanchard, Olivier Jean, and Lawrence F. Katz. 1992. Regional evolutions. *Brookings Papers on Economic Activity* 1:1–61.

Bollinger, Christopher R., and Barry T. Hirsch. 2013. Is earnings nonresponse ignorable? *Review of Economics and Statistics* 95: 407–416.

Bonin, Holger. 2005. Wage and employment effects of immigration to Germany: Evidence from a skill group approach. IZA Discussion Paper no. 1875.

Borjas, George J. 1985. Assimilation, changes in cohort quality, and the earnings of immigrants. *Journal of Labor Economics* 3: 463–489.

———. 1987a. Immigrants, minorities, and labor market competition. *Industrial and Labor Relations Review* 40: 382–392.

———. 1987b. Self-selection and the earnings of immigrants. *American Economic Review* 77: 531–553.

———. 1991. Immigration and self-selection. In John M. Abowd and Richard B. Freeman, eds., *Immigration, trade, and the labor market,* 29–76. Chicago: University of Chicago Press.

———. 1992. Ethnic capital and intergenerational mobility. *Quarterly Journal of Economics* 107: 123–150.

———. 1993. The intergenerational mobility of immigrants. *Journal of Labor Economics* 11: 113–135.

———. 1995a. Assimilation and changes in cohort quality revisited: What happened to immigrant earnings in the 1980s? *Journal of Labor Economics* 13: 201–245.

———. 1995b. The economic benefits from immigration. *Journal of Economic Perspectives* 9: 3–22.

———. 1995c. Ethnicity, neighborhoods, and human capital externalities. *American Economic Review* 85: 365–390.

———. 1999. The economic analysis of immigration. In Orley Ashenfelter and David Card, eds., *Handbook of labor economics,* 3:1697–1760. Amsterdam: Elsevier.

———. 2000. The economic progress of immigrants. In George J. Borjas, ed., *Issues in the economics of immigration,* 15–49. Chicago: University of Chicago Press.

———. 2001. Does immigration grease the wheels of the labor market? *Brookings Papers on Economic Activity* 1: 69–119.

———. 2003. The labor demand curve *is* downward sloping: Reexamining the impact of immigration on the labor market. *Quarterly Journal of Economics* 118: 1335–1374.

———. 2006. Native internal migration and the labor market impact of immigration. *Journal of Human Resources* 41: 221–258.

———. 2008. Labor outflows and labor inflows in Puerto Rico. *Journal of Human Capital* 2: 32–68.

———. 2009. Immigration in high-skill labor markets: The impact of foreign students on the earnings of doctorates. In Richard B. Freeman and Daniel L. Goroff, eds., *Science and engineering careers in the United States: An analysis of markets and employment,* 131–161. Chicago: University of Chicago Press.

———. 2013a. The slowdown in the economic assimilation of immigrants: Aging and cohort effects revisited again. NBER Working Paper no. 19116.

———. 2013b. The analytics of the wage effect of immigration. *IZA Journal of Migration* 2: 22.

Borjas, George J., and Bernt Bratsberg. 1996. Who Leaves? The outmigration of the foreign-born. *Review of Economics and Statistics* 78: 165–176.

Borjas, George J., Stephen G. Bronars, and Stephen J. Trejo. 1992. Self-selection and internal migration in the United States. *Journal of Urban Economics* 32: 159–185.

Borjas, George J., and Kirk B. Doran. 2012. The collapse of the Soviet Union and the productivity of American mathematicians. *Quarterly Journal of Economics* 127: 1143–1203.

———. 2014. Cognitive mobility: Labor market responses to supply shocks in the space of ideas. *Journal of Labor Economics,* forthcoming.

Borjas, George J., Richard B. Freeman, and Lawrence F. Katz. 1992. On the labor market effects of immigration and trade. In George J. Borjas and Richard B. Freeman, eds., *Immigration and the work force: Economic consequences for the United States and source areas,* 213–244. Chicago: University of Chicago Press.

———. 1996. Searching for the effect of immigration on the labor market. *American Economic Review* 86: 246–251.

———. 1997. How much do immigration and trade affect labor market outcomes? *Brookings Papers on Economic Activity* 1:1–67.

Borjas, George J., and Rachel M. Friedberg. 2009. Recent trends in the earnings of new immigrants to the United States. NBER Working Paper no. 15406.

Borjas, George J., Jeffrey Grogger, and Gordon H. Hanson. 2008. Imperfect substitution between immigrants and natives: A reappraisal. NBER Working Paper no. 13887.

———. 2010. Immigration and the economic status of black men. *Economica* 77: 255–282.

———. 2012. On estimating elasticities of substitution. *Journal of the European Economic Association* 10: 198–210.

Borjas, George J., Ilpo Kauppinen, and Panu Poutvaara. 2013. Self-selection of emigrants from a welfare state. Ifo Institute, in progress.

Boustan, Leah Platt, Price V. Fishback, and Shawn E. Kantor. 2010. The effect of internal migration on local labor markets: American cities during the Great Depression. *Journal of Labor Economics* 28: 719–746.

Bowles, Samuel. 1970. Aggregation of labor inputs in the economics of growth and planning: Experiments with a two-level CES function. *Journal of Political Economy* 78: 68–81.

Brainerd, Elizabeth, and Mark V. Siegler. 2003. The economic effects of the 1918 influenza epidemic. CEPR Discussion Paper no. 3791.

Bratsberg, Bernt. 1995. The incidence of non-return among foreign students in the United States. *Economics of Education Review* 14: 373–384.

Bratsberg, Bernt, and Oddbjørn Raaum. 2012. Immigration and wages: Evidence from construction. *Economic Journal* 122: 1177–1205.

Bratsberg, Bernt, Oddbjørn Raaum, Marianne Røed, and Pål Schøne. 2013. Immigration wage impacts by origin. *Scandinavian Journal of Economics,* forthcoming,

Butcher, Kristin F., and John DiNardo. 2002. The immigrant and native-born wage distributions: Evidence from United States censuses. *Industrial and Labor Relations Review* 56: 97–121.

Cadena, Brian C. 2013. Native competition and low-skilled immigrant inflows. *Journal of Human Resources* 48: 910–944.

———. 2014. Recent immigrants as labor market arbitrageurs: Evidence from the minimum wage. *Journal of Urban Economics,* forthcoming.

Cadena, Brian C., and Brian K. Kovak. 2013. Immigrants equilibrate local labor markets: Evidence from the Great Recession. NBER Working Paper no. 19272.

Calvin, Linda, and Philip Martin. 2010. The U.S. produce industry and labor: Facing the future in a global economy. Economic Research Report 106. Washington, DC: U.S. Department of Agriculture, Economic Research Service.

Cameron, A. Colin, and Pravin K. Trivedi. 2005. *Microeconometrics: Methods and applications.* New York: Cambridge University Press.

Caponi, Vincenzo. 2011. Intergenerational transmission of abilities and self-selection of Mexican immigrants. *International Economic Review* 58: 523–547.

Card, David. 1990. The impact of the Mariel boatlift on the Miami labor market. *Industrial and Labor Relations Review* 43: 245–257.

———. 2001. Immigrant inflows, native outflows, and the local labor market impacts of higher immigration. *Journal of Labor Economics* 19: 22–64.

———. 2005. Is the new immigration really so bad? *Economic Journal* 115: F300–F323.

———. 2009. Immigration and inequality. *American Economic Review* 99: 1–21.

Card, David, and John DiNardo. 2000. Do immigrant inflows lead to native outflows? *American Economic Review* 90: 360–367.

Card, David, John DiNardo, and Eugena Estes. 2000. The more things change: Immigrants and the children of immigrants in the 1940s, the 1970s, and the 1990s. In George J. Borjas, ed., *Issues in the economics of immigration,* 227–270. Chicago: University of Chicago Press.

Card, David, and Thomas Lemieux. 2001. Can falling supply explain the rising return to college for younger men? A cohort-based analysis. *Quarterly Journal of Economics* 116: 705–746.

Carliner, Geoffrey. 1980. Wages, earnings and hours of first, second, and third generation American males. *Economic Inquiry* 18: 87–102.

Carrasco, Raquel, Juan F. Jimeno, and A. Carolina Ortega. 2008. The effect of immigration on the labor market performance of native-born workers: Some evidence for Spain. *Journal of Population Economics* 21: 627–648.

Carrington, William J., and Pedro de Lima. 1996. The impact of 1970s repatriates from Africa on the Portuguese labor market. *Industrial and Labor Relations Review* 49: 330–347.

Chiquiar, Daniel, and Gordon H. Hanson. 2005. International migration, self-selection, and the distribution of wages: Evidence from Mexico and the United States. *Journal of Political Economy* 113: 239–281.

Chiswick, Barry R. 1977. Sons of immigrants: Are they at an earnings disadvantage? *American Economic Review* 67: 376–380.

———. 1978. The effect of Americanization on the earnings of foreign-born men. *Journal of Political Economy* 86: 897–921.

———. 1986. Is the new immigration less skilled than the old? *Journal of Labor Economics* 4:168–192.

Chiswick, Barry R., and Paul W. Miller. 1999. English language fluency among immigrants in the United States. *Research in Labor Economics* 17: 151–200.

———. 2005. Linguistic distance: A quantitative measure of the distance between English and other languages. *Journal of Multilingual and Multicultural Development* 26: 1–11.

Clemens, Michael A. 2011. Economics and emigration: Trillion-dollar bills on the sidewalk? *Journal of Economic Perspectives* 25: 83–106.

Clemens, Michael A., Claudio E. Montenegro, and Lant Pritchett. 2008. The place premium: Wage differences for identical workers across the U.S. border. Center for Global Development Working Paper no. 148.

Cobb-Clark, Deborah A. 1993. Immigrant selectivity and wages: The evidence for women. *American Economic Review* 83: 986–993.

Cohen-Goldner, Sarit, and M. Daniele Paserman. 2011. The dynamic impact of immigration on natives' labor market outcomes: Evidence from Israel. *European Economic Review* 55: 1027–1045.

Coleman, James. S. 1988. Social capital in the creation of human capital. *American Journal of Sociology* 94: S95–S120.

Combes, Pierre-Philippe, Gilles Duranton, Laurent Gobillon, and Sébastien Roux. 2010. Estimating agglomeration economies with history, geology, and worker effects. In Edward L. Glaeser, ed., *Agglomeration Economics,* 15–66. Chicago: University of Chicago Press.

Cortes, Patricia. 2008. The effect of low-skilled immigration on US prices: Evidence from CPI data. *Journal of Political Economy* 116: 381–422.

Couch, Kenneth A., and Thomas A. Dunn. 1997. Intergenerational correlations in labor market status. *Journal of Human Resources* 32: 210–232.

Cutler, David M., and Edward L. Glaeser. 1997. Are ghettos good or bad? *Quarterly Journal of Economics* 112: 827–872.

Cutler, David M., Edward L. Glaeser, and Jacob L. Vigdor. 2005. Ghettos and the transmission of ethnic capital. In Glenn Loury, Tariq Modood, and Steven M. Teles, eds., *Ethnicity, social mobility, and public policy: Comparing the US and UK,* 204–221. Cambridge: Cambridge University Press.

Dahl, Gordon B. 2002. Mobility and the return to education: Testing a Roy model with multiple markets. *Econometrica* 70: 2367–2420.

D'Amuri, Francesco, Gianmarco I. P. Ottaviano, and Giovanni Peri. 2010. The labor market impact of immigration in West Germany in the 1990s. *European Economic Review* 54: 550–570.

Darity, William, Jason Dietrich, and David K. Guilkey. 2001. Persistent advantage or disadvantage? Evidence in support of the intergenerational drag hypothesis. *American Journal of Economics and Sociology* 60: 435–470.

Deaton, Angus. 1985. Panel data from time series of cross-sections. *Journal of Econometrics* 30: 109–126.

Deininger, Klaus, and Lyn Squire. 1996. A new data set measuring income inequality. *World Bank Economic Review* 10: 565–591.

De New, John P., and Klaus F. Zimmermann. 1994. Native wage impacts of foreign labor: A random effects panel analysis. *Journal of Population Economics* 7: 177–192.

Di Giovanni, Julian, Andrei A. Levchenko, and Francesc Ortega. 2012. A global view of cross-border migration. IZA Discussion Paper No. 6584.

Dixit, Avinash, and Victor Norman. 1980. *The theory of international trade: A dual, general equilibrium approach.* New York: Cambridge University Press.

Docquier, Frédéric, and Abdeslam Marfouk. 2006. International migration by educational attainment, 1990–2000. In Caglar Özden and Maurice Schiff, eds., *International migration, remittances, and the brain drain,* 151–200. Washington, DC: The World Bank and Palgrave McMillan.

Docquier, Frédéric, Joël Machado, and Khalid Sekkat. 2012. Efficiency gains from liberalizing labor mobility. Discussion Paper no. 2012-23, Université Catholique de Louvain.

Donald, Stephen G., and Kevin Lang. 2007. Inference with difference-in-differences and other panel data. *Review of Economics and Statistics* 89: 221–233.

Douglas, Paul H. 1919. Is the new immigration more unskilled than the old? *Journal of the American Statistical Association* 16: 393–403.

Duleep, Harriet Orcutt, and Daniel J. Dowhan 2002. Insights from longitudinal data on the earnings growth of U.S. foreign-born men. *Demography* 39: 485–506.

Duleep, Harriet Orcutt, and Mark C. Regets. 1997. Immigrant entry earnings and human capital growth: Evidence from the 1960–1980 censuses. *Research in Labor Economics* 16: 297–317.

Duncan, Brian, and Stephen J. Trejo. 2011. Intermarriage and the intergenerational transmission of ethnic identity and human capital for Mexican Americans. *Journal of Labor Economics* 29: 195–227.

———. 2014. The complexity of immigrant generations: Implications for assessing the socioeconomic integration of Hispanics and Asians. *Industrial and Labor Relations Review,* forthcoming.

Dustmann, Christian, Francesca Fabbri, and Ian Preston. 2005. The impact of immigration on the British labour market. *Economic Journal* 115: F324–F341.

Dustmann, Christian, and Albrecht Glitz. 2012. How do industries and firms respond to changes in local labor supply? IZA Discussion Paper no. 6257.

Edin, Per Anders, Robert J. LaLonde, and Olof Åslund. 2000. Emigration of immigrants and measures of immigrant assimilation: Evidence from Sweden. *Swedish Economic Policy Review* 7: 163–204.

Edmonston, Barry, and Jeffrey S. Passel. 1992. Immigration and immigrant generations in population projections. *International Journal of Forecasting* 8: 459–476.

Ewerhart, Christian. 2003. A short and intuitive proof of Marshall's rule. *Economic Theory* 22: 415–418.

Feldman, Maryanne P. 1999. The new economics of innovation, spillovers and agglomeration: A review of empirical studies. *Economics of Innovation and New Technology* 8: 5–25.

Fernández-Huertas Moraga, Jesús. 2011. New evidence on emigrant selection. *Review of Economics and Statistics* 93: 72–96.

———. 2013. Understanding different migrant selection patterns in rural and urban Mexico. FEDEA and IAE.

Filer, Randall K. 1992. The impact of immigrant arrivals on migratory patterns of native workers. In George J. Borjas and Richard B. Freeman, eds., *Immigration and the work force: Economic consequences for the United States and source areas,* 245–269. Chicago: University of Chicago Press.

Finn, Michael G. 2003. Stay rates of foreign doctorate recipients from U.S. universities, 2001. Working Paper, Oak Ridge Institute for Science and Education, Oak Ridge, Tennessee.

Franz, Wolfgang, and Friedhelm Pfeiffer. 2006. Reasons for wage rigidity in Germany. *Labour* 20: 255–284.

Freedom House. 2011. *Freedom in the world, 2011: Tables, graphs, and other supporting documents.* Washington, DC: Freedom House.

Freeman, Richard B. 1975. Supply and salary adjustments to the changing science manpower market: Physics, 1948–1975. *American Economic Review* 65: 27–39.

———. 1976. A cobweb model of the supply and starting salary of new engineers. *Industrial and Labor Relations Review* 29: 236–248.

Frey, William. 1995a. Immigration impacts on internal migration of the poor: 1990 census evidence for U.S. states. *International Journal of Population Geography* 1: 51–67.

———. 1995b. Immigration and internal migration "flight" from US metropolitan areas: Toward a new demographic balkanization. *Urban Studies* 32:733–757.

Friedberg, Rachel. 1992. The labor market assimilation of immigrants in the United States: The role of age at arrival. Brown University.

———. 2000. You can't take it with you? Immigrant assimilation and the portability of human capital. *Journal of Labor Economics* 18: 221–251.

———. 2001. The impact of mass migration on the Israeli labor market. *Quarterly Journal of Economics* 116: 1373–1408.

Friedberg, Rachel, and Jennifer Hunt. 1995. The impact of immigration on host county wages, employment and growth. *Journal of Economic Perspectives* 9: 23–44.

Funkhouser, Edward, and Stephen J. Trejo. 1995. The labor market skills of recent male immigrants: Evidence from the Current Population Survey. *Industrial and Labor Relations Review* 48: 792–811.

Ganong, Peter, and Daniel Shoag. 2012. Why has regional income convergence in the U.S. stopped? Harvard Kennedy School Working Paper no. RWP12–028.

Gathmann, Christina. 2008. Effects of enforcement on illegal markets: Evidence from migrant smuggling at the southwestern border. *Journal of Public Economics:* 1926–1941.

Glazer, Nathan, and Daniel P. Moynihan. 1963. *Beyond the melting pot: The Negroes, Puerto Ricans, Jews, Italians, and Irish of New York City.* Cambridge, MA: MIT Press.

Glenn, Norval D. 1976. Cohort analysts' futile quest: Statistical attempts to separate age, period, and cohort effects. *American Sociological Review* 41: 900–904.

Glitz, Albrecht. 2012. The labor market impact of immigration: A quasi-experiment exploiting immigration location rules in Germany. *Journal of Labor Economics* 30: 175–213.

Goldin, Claudia, and Lawrence F. Katz. 1998. The origins of technology-skills complementarity. *Quarterly Journal of Economics* 1998: 693–732.

———. 2010. *The race between education and technology.* Cambridge, MA: Harvard University Press.

González Luna, Libertad, and Francesc Ortega. 2011. How do very open economies absorb large immigration flows? Evidence from Spanish regions. *Labour Economics* 18: 57–70.

Gordon, Milton. 1964. *Assimilation and American life.* New York: Oxford University Press.

Gould, Eric D., and Omer Moav. 2011. When is "too much" inequality not enough? The selection of Israel emigrants. Hebrew University Working Paper.

Green, David A. 1999. Immigrant occupational attainment: Assimilation and mobility over time. *Journal of Labor Economics* 17: 49–79.

Greenaway-McGrevy, Ryan, and Kyle Hood. 2011. Aggregate effects and measuring regional dynamics. Bureau of Economic Analysis, Washington, DC.

Greenwood, Michael J. 1997. Internal migration in developed countries. In Mark R. Rosenzweig and Oded Stark, eds., *Handbook of population and family economics,* 1:647–720. Amsterdam: Elsevier.

Greenwood, Michael J., and John M. McDowell. 1986. The factor market consequences of U.S. immigration. *Journal of Economic Literature* 24: 1738–1772.

Grogger, Jeffrey, and Gordon H. Hanson. 2011. Income maximization and the selection and sorting of international migrants. *Journal of Development Economics* 95: 42–57.

———. 2013. Attracting talent: Location choices of foreign-born PhDs in the US. NBER Working Paper no. 18780.

Grossman, Jean Baldwin. 1982. The substitutability of natives and immigrants in production. *Review of Economics and Statistics* 54: 596–603.

Guiso, Luigi, Paola Sapienza, and Luigi Zingales. 2009. Cultural biases in economic exchange. *Quarterly Journal of Economics* 124: 1095–1131.

Hamermesh, Daniel S. 1989. Labor demand and the structure of adjustment costs. *American Economic Review* 79: 674–689.

———. 1993. *Labor demand.* Princeton, NJ: Princeton University Press.

Hamilton, Bob, and John Whalley. 1984. Efficiency and distributional implications of global restrictions on labour mobility: Calculations and policy implications. *Journal of Development Economics* 14: 61–75.

Hanson, Gordon H. 2006. Illegal migration from Mexico to the United States. *Journal of Economic Literature* 44: 869–924.

Hanson, Gordon H., and Craig McIntosh. 2010. The great Mexican emigration. *Review of Economics and Statistics* 92: 798–810.

Hanson, Gordon H., and Matthew J. Slaughter. 2002. Labor-market adjustment in open economies: Evidence from US states. *Journal of International Economics* 57: 3–29.

Heckman, James J. 1979. Sample selection bias as a specification error. *Econometrica* 47: 153–161.

Heckman, James J., and Bo E. Honoré. 1990. The empirical content of the Roy model. *Econometrica* 58: 1121–1149.

Heckman, James J., Lance J. Lochner, and Petra E. Todd. 2006. Earnings functions, rates of return and treatment effects: The Mincer equation and beyond. In Eric Hanushek and Finis Welch, eds., *Handbook of the economics of education,* 1:307–458. Amsterdam: Elsevier.

Heckman, James J., and Richard Robb. 1985. Using longitudinal data to estimate age, period, and cohort effects in earnings equations. In William M. Mason and Stephen E. Fienberg, eds., *Cohort analysis in social research,* 137–150. New York: Springer-Verlag.

Heston, Alan, Robert Summers, and Bettina Aten. 2012. *Penn World Table version 7.1.* Philadelphia: University of Pennsylvania, Center for International Comparisons of Production, Income and Prices.

Hicks, John R. 1932. *The theory of wages.* New York: Macmillan.

———. 1970. Elasticity of substitution again: Substitutes and complements. *Oxford Economic Papers* 22: 289–296.

Holzer, Harry J. 1988. Search method use by unemployed youth. *Journal of Labor Economics* 6: 1–20.

Hoogeven, Johannes G., and Berk Özler. 2005. Not separate, not equal: Poverty and inequality in post-apartheid South Africa. William Davidson Institute Working Paper no. 739.

Hornbeck, Richard. 2012. The enduring impact of the American Dust Bowl: Short- and long-run adjustments to environmental catastrophe. *American Economic Review* 102: 1477–1507.

Hu, Wei-Yin. 2000. Immigrant earnings assimilation: Estimates from longitudinal data. *American Economic Review* 90: 368–372.

Hunt, Jennifer. 1992. The impact of the 1962 repatriates from Algeria on the French labor market. *Industrial and Labor Relations Review* 45: 556–572.

———. 2011. Which immigrants are most innovative and entrepreneurial? Distinctions by entry visa. *Journal of Labor Economics* 29: 417–457.

Hunt, Jennifer, and Marjolaine Gauthier-Loiselle. 2010. How much does immigration boost innovation? *American Economic Journal: Macroeconomics* 2: 31–56.

Ibarrarán, Pablo, and Darren Lubotsky. 2007. Immigration and self-selection: New evidence from the 2000 Mexican census. In George J. Borjas, ed., *Mexican immigration to the United States.* Chicago: University of Chicago Press.

Isphording, Ingo E., and Sebastian Otten. 2013. The costs of Babylon: Linguistic distance in applied economics. *Review of International Economics* 21: 354–369.

Jaeger, David. 1996. Skill differences and the effect of immigrants on the wages of natives. U.S. Bureau of Labor Statistics Working Paper (revised 2007).

Jasso, Guillermina, and Mark R. Rosenzweig. 1990. *The new chosen people: Immigrants in the United States.* New York: Russell Sage.

———. 1995. Do immigrants screened for skills do better than family reunification immigrants? *International Migration Review* 29: 85–111.

———. 2009. Selection criteria and the skill composition of immigrants: A comparative analysis of Australian and U.S. employment immigration. In Jagdish Bhagwati and Gordon H. Hanson, eds., *Skilled migration today: Phenomenon, prospects, problems, policies,* 153–183. New York: Oxford University Press.

Jencks, Christopher, and Susan E. Mayer. 1990. The social consequences of growing up in a poor neighborhood. In Laurence E. Lynn Jr., and Michael G. H. McGeary, eds., *Inner city poverty in the United States,* 111–186. Washington, DC: National Academy Press.

Johnson, George E. 1998. Estimation of the impact of immigration on the distribution of income among minorities and others. In Daniel S. Hamermesh and Frank D. Bean, eds., *Help or hindrance? The economic implications of immigration for African-Americans,* 17–50. New York: Russell Sage.

Johnson, Norman, and Samuel Kotz. 1970. *Continuous univariate distributions,* vol. 1. New York: John Wiley and Sons.

Jones, Charles I., and Paul M. Romer. 2010. The new Kaldor facts: Ideas, institutions, population, and human capital. *American Economic Journal: Macroeconomics* 2: 224–245.

Kaestner, Robert, and Ofer Malamud. 2014. Self-selection and international migration: New evidence from Mexico. *Review of Economics and Statistics,* forthcoming.

Kaplan, Greg, and Sam Schulhofer-Wohl. 2012. Interstate migration has fallen less than you think: Consequences of hot deck imputation in the Current Population Survey. *Demography* 49: 1061–1074.

Katz, Lawrence F., Jeffrey R. Kling, and Jeffrey B. Liebman. 2001. Moving to opportunity in Boston: Early results of a randomized mobility experiment. *Quarterly Journal of Economics* 116: 607–654.

Katz, Lawrence F., and Kevin M. Murphy. 1992. Changes in the wage structure, 1963–87: Supply and demand factors. *Quarterly Journal of Economics* 107: 35–78.

Kennan, John. 1998. The Hicks-Marshall rules of derived demand: An expository note. University of Wisconsin, Madison.

———. 2013. Open borders. *Review of Economic Dynamics* 16: L1–L13.

Kennan, John, and James R. Walker. 2011. The effect of expected income on individual migration decisions. *Econometrica* 79: 211–251.

Kerr, William R., and William F. Lincoln. 2010. The supply side of innovation: H-1B visa reforms and U.S. ethnic invention. *Journal of Labor Economics* 28: 473–508.

Klein, Paul, and Gustavo Ventura, 2004. Do migration restrictions matter? Paper presented at the Econometric Society 2004 North American Winter Meetings, Denver.

———. 2007. TFP differences and the aggregate effects of labor mobility in the long run. *B.E. Journal of Macroeconomics* 7, no. 1.

Kling, Jeffrey R., Jeffrey B. Liebman, and Lawrence F. Katz. 2007. Experimental analysis of neighborhood effects. *Econometrica* 75: 83–119.

Kritz, Mary M., and Douglas T. Gurak. 2001. The impact of immigration on the internal migration of natives and immigrants. *Demography* 38: 133–145.

Lach, Saul. 2007. Immigration and prices. *Journal of Political Economy* 115: 548–587.

LaLonde, Robert J., and Robert H. Topel. 1991. Labor market adjustments to increased immigration. In John M. Abowd and Richard B. Freeman, eds., *Immigration, trade, and the labor market,* 167–199. Chicago: University of Chicago Press.

———. 1992. The assimilation of immigrants in the U.S. labor market. In George J. Borjas and Richard B. Freeman, eds., *Immigration and the work force: Economic consequences for the United States and source areas,* 67–92. Chicago: University of Chicago Press.

Lazear, Edward P. 1999. Culture and language. *Journal of Political Economy* 107: S95–S126.

Lee, Chul-In, and Gary Solon. 2009. Trends in intergenerational income mobility. *Review of Economics and Statistics* 91: 766–772.

Lemieux, Thomas. 2006. Increasing residual wage inequality: Composition effects, noisy data, or rising demand for skill? *American Economic Review* 96: 461–498.

León, Alexis. 2005. Does "ethnic capital" matter? Identifying peer effects in the intergenerational transmission of ethnic differentials. University of Pittsburgh.

Levine, Ross, and David Renelt. 1992. A sensitivity analysis of cross-country growth regressions. *American Economic Review* 82: 942–963.

Lewis, Ethan. 2011. Immigration, skill mix, and capital skill complementarity. *Quarterly Journal of Economics* 126: 1029–1069.

———. 2013. Immigration and production technology. *Annual Review of Economics* 5: 165–191.

Lieberson, Stanley, and Mary C. Waters. 1988. *From many strands: Ethnic and racial groups in contemporary America.* New York: Russell Sage.

Lindstrom, David P., and Douglas S. Massey. 1994. Selective emigration, cohort quality, and models of immigrant assimilation. *Social Science Research* 23: 315–349.

Longhi, Simonetta, Peter Nijkamp, and Jacques Poot. 2009. Regional impacts of immigration: A review. Tinbergen Institute Discussion Paper 09–047/3.

Loury, Glenn C. 1977. A dynamic theory of racial income differences. In Phyllis A. Wallace and Annette A. LaMond, eds., *Women, minorities and employment discrimination*, 153–186. Lexington, MA: Lexington Books.

Lubotsky, Darren. 2007. Chutes or ladders? A longitudinal analysis of immigrant earnings. *Journal of Political Economy* 115: 820–867.

———. 2011. The effect of changes in the U.S. wage structure on recent immigrants' earnings. *Review of Economics and Statistics* 93: 59–71.

Lucas, Robert E. 1988. On the mechanics of economic development. *Journal of Monetary Economics* 22: 3–42.

Lundborg, Per, and Paul S. Segerstrom. 2002. The growth and welfare effects of international mass migration. *Journal of International Economics* 56: 177–204.

Manacorda, Marco, Alan Manning, and Jonathan Wadsworth. 2012. The impact of immigration on the structure of wages: Theory and evidence from Britain. *Journal of the European Economic Association* 10: 120–151.

Mattoo, Aaditya, Ileana Cristina Neagu, and Çağlar Özden. 2008. Brain waste? Educated immigrants in the U.S. labor market. *Journal of Development Economics* 87: 255–269.

Mazumder, Bhashkar. 2005. Fortunate sons: New estimates of intergenerational mobility in the U.S. using social security earnings data. *Review of Economics and Statistics* 87: 235–255.

McFadden, Daniel. 1974. The measurement of urban travel demand. *Journal of Public Economics* 3: 303–328.

McKenzie, David J., John Gibson, and Steven Stillman. 2010. How important is selection? Experimental vs. non-experimental measures of the income gains from migration. *Journal of the European Economic Association* 8: 913–945.

McKenzie, David J., and Hillel Rapoport. 2007. Network effects and the dynamics of migration and inequality: Theory and evidence from Mexico. *Journal of Development Economics* 84: 1–24.

———. 2010. Self-selection patterns in Mexico-U.S. migration: The role of migration networks. *Review of Economics and Statistics* 92: 811–821.

Mincer, Jacob. 1974. *Schooling, experience, and earnings.* New York: Columbia University Press.

———. 1978. Family migration decisions. *Journal of Political Economy* 86: 749–773.

Mincer, Jacob, and Solomon Polachek. 1974. Family investment in human capital: Earnings of women. *Journal of Political Economy* 82: S76–S108.

Mishra, Prachi. 2007. Emigration and wages in source countries: Evidence from Mexico. *Journal of Development Economics* 82: 180–199.

Moretti, Enrico. 2012. *The new geography of jobs.* Boston: Houghton Mifflin Harcourt.

Moser, Petra, Alessandra Voena, and Fabian Waldinger. 2013. German Jewish émigrés and U.S. invention. Working paper, Stanford University.

Moses, Jonathon W., and Bjørn Letnes. 2004. The economic costs to international labor restrictions: Revisiting the empirical discussion. *World Development* 32: 1609–1626.

Mundell, Robert A. 1957. International trade and factor mobility. *American Economic Review* 47: 321–335.

Munshi, Kaivan. 2003. Networks in the modern economy: Mexican migrants in the U.S. labor market. *Quarterly Journal of Economics* 118: 549–599.

Murphy, Kevin M., and Finis Welch. 1992. The structure of wages. *Quarterly Journal of Economics* 107: 215–326.

Olney, William W. 2013a. Immigration and firm expansion. *Journal of Regional Science* 53: 142–157.

———. 2013b. Remittances and the wage impact of immigration. Williams College.

Oreopoulos, Philip. 2003. The long-run consequences of growing up in a poor neighborhood. *Quarterly Journal of Economics* 118:1533–1575.

Ortega, Francesc, and Giovannia Peri. 2013. The effect of income and immigration policies on international migration. *Migration Studies* 1: 47–74.

Ottaviano, Gianmarco I. P., and Giovanni Peri. 2006. Rethinking the effect of immigration on wages. NBER Working Paper no. 12497 (original draft).

———. 2012. Rethinking the effect of immigration on wages. *Journal of the European Economic Association* 10: 152–197.

Özden, Çaglar, and Mathis Wagner. 2013. Immigrants versus natives? Displacement and job creation. Working paper, Boston College.

Park, Robert Ezra. 1964. *Race and Culture.* Glencoe, IL: Free Press.

Paserman, M. Daniele. 2013. Do high-skill immigrants raise productivity? Evidence from Israeli manufacturing firms, 1990–1999. *IZA Journal of Migration* 2: 6.

Pemberton, James. 1989. Marshall's rules for derived demand: A critique and generalisation. *Scottish Journal of Economics* 36: 396–405.

Peri, Giovanni. 2012. The effect of immigration on productivity: Evidence from U.S. states. *Review of Economics and Statistics* 94: 348–358.

Peri, Giovanni, and Chad Sparber. 2009. Task specialization, immigration, and wages. *American Economic Journal: Applied Economics* 1: 135–169.

———. 2011. Assessing inherent model bias: An application to native displacement in response to immigration. *Journal of Urban Economics* 69: 82–91.

Peri, Giovanni, Kevin Shih, and Chad Sparber. 2013. STEM workers, H-1B visas and productivity in U.S. cities. Working paper, University of California, Davis.

Perlmann, Joel, and Roger Waldinger. 1997. Second generation decline? Children of immigrants, past and present—a reconsideration. *International Migration Review* 31: 893–922.

Philips, Benjamin T., and Sylvia Barack Fishman. 2006. Ethnic capital and inter-marriage: A case study of American Jews. *Sociology of Religion* 67: 487–505.

Pischke, Jörn-Steffen, and Johannes Velling. 1997. Employment effects of immigration to Germany: An analysis based on local labor markets. *Review of Economics and Statistics* 79: 594–604.

Polachek, Solomon. 1975. Differences in expected post-school investments as a determinant of market wage differentials. *International Economic Review* 16: 451–470.

Portes, Alejandro, and Min Zhou. 1993. The new second generation: Segmented assimilation and its variants. *Annals of the American Academy of Political and Social Science* 530: 74–96.

Pritchett, Lant. 2010. The cliff at the border. In Ravi Kanbur and Michael Spence, eds., *Equity and growth in a globalizing world,* 263–286. Washington, DC: World Bank.

Ramos, Fernando. 1992. Out-migration and return migration of Puerto Ricans. In George J. Borjas and Richard B. Freeman, eds., *Immigration and the work force: Economic consequences for the United States and source areas,* 49–66. Chicago: University of Chicago Press.

Raphael, Steven, and Lucas Ronconi. 2007. The effects of labor market competition with immigrants on the wages and employment of natives. *DuBois Review: Social Science and Research on Race* 4: 413–432.

———. 2008. Reconciling national and regional estimates of the effects of immigration on U.S. labor markets: The confounding effects of native male incarceration trends. Working paper, University of California, Berkeley.

Rasmusen, Eric. 2013. How immigration can hurt a country. Working paper, University of Indiana.

Romer, Paul. 1986. Increasing returns and long-run growth. *Journal of Political Economy* 94: 1002–1037.

Rosen, Sherwin. 1972. Learning and experience in the labor market. *Journal of Human Resources* 7: 326–342.

Rowthorn, Robert, and Andrew Glyn. 2002. Convergence and stability in U.S. regional employment. Oxford University Department of Economics Discussion Paper Series, no. 92.

Roy, A. D. 1951. Some thoughts on the distribution of earnings. *Oxford Economic Papers* 3: 135–146.

Ruist, Joakim. 2013. Immigrant-native wage gaps in time series: Complementarities or composition effects? *Economics Letters* 119: 154–156.

Saiz, Albert. 2003. Room in the kitchen for the melting pot: Immigration and rental prices. *Review of Economics and Statistics* 85: 502–521.

———. 2007. Immigration and housing rents in American cities. *Journal of Urban Economics* 61: 345–371.

Sato, Ryuzo, and Tetsunori Koizumi. 1973. On the elasticities of substitution and complementarity. *Oxford Economic Papers* 25: 44–56.

Schaafsma, Joseph, and Arthur Sweetman. 2001. Immigrant earnings: Age at immigration matters. *Canadian Journal of Economics* 34: 1066–1099.

Schoeni, Robert F. 1997a. The effects of immigrants on the employment and wages of native workers: Evidence from the 1970s and 1980s. Rand Corporation Center for Research on Immigration Policy Working Paper no. DIU 1408-IF.

———. 1997b. New evidence on the economic progress of foreign-born men in the 1970s and 1980s. *Journal of Human Resources* 32: 683–740.

Sjaastad, Larry. 1962. The costs and returns of human migration. *Journal of Political Economy* 70: S80–S93.

Smith, Christopher L. 2012. The impact of low-skilled immigration on the youth labor market. *Journal of Labor Economics* 30: 55–89.

Smith, James P., and Barry Edmonston. 1997. *The new Americans: Economic, demographic, and fiscal effects of immigration.* Washington, DC: National Academy Press.

Solon, Gary R. 1992. Intergenerational income mobility in the United States. *American Economic Review* 82: 393–408.

———. 1999. Intergenerational mobility in the labor market. In Orley Ashenfelter and David Card, eds., *Handbook of labor economics,* vol. 3A, 1761–1800. Amsterdam: Elsevier.

Staehle, Hans. 1934. The reaction of consumers to changes in prices and income: A quantitative study in immigrants' behavior. *Econometrica* 2: 59–72.

Steinhardt, Max Friedrich. 2011. The wage impact of immigration in Germany: New evidence for skill groups and occupations. *The B.E. Journal of Economic Analysis and Policy* 11, no. 1.

Taylor, J. Edward. 1987. Undocumented Mexico-U.S. migration and the returns to households in rural Mexico. *American Journal of Agricultural Economics* 69: 626–638.

Thistle, Paul. D. 1993. Negative moments, risk aversion, and stochastic dominance. *Journal of Financial and Quantitative Analysis* 28: 301–311.

Trefler, Daniel. 1997. Immigrants and natives in general equilibrium trade models. NBER Working Paper no. 6209.

United Nations. 2011. *International migration report 2009: A global assessment.* New York: Department of Economic and Social Affairs, Population Division.

U.S. Bureau of Labor Statistics. 2012. *National occupational employment and wage estimates.* Washington, DC: Occupational Employment Statistics. Available at http://www.bls.gov/oes/tables.htm.

Wagner, Mathis. 2010. The heterogeneous labor market effects of immigration. Boston College.

Waldinger, Fabian. 2010. Quality matters: The expulsion of professors and the consequences for Ph.D. student outcomes in Nazi Germany. *Journal of Political Economy* 118: 787–831.

———. 2012. Peer effects in science: Evidence from the dismissal of scientists in Nazi Germany. *Review of Economic Studies* 79: 838–861.

Walmsley, Terrie, and L. Alain Winters. 2005. Relaxing the restrictions on the temporary movement of natural persons: A simulation analysis. *Journal of Economic Integration* 20: 688–726.

Welch, Finis. 1979. Effects of cohort size on earnings: The baby boom babies' financial bust. *Journal of Political Economy* 87: S65–S97.

White, Michael J., and Zai Liang. 1998. The effect of immigration on the internal migration of the native-born population, 1981–1990. *Population Research and Policy Review* 17: 141–166.

Wilson, William Julius. 1987. *The truly disadvantaged: The inner city, the underclass, and public policy.* Chicago: University of Chicago Press.

World Bank. 2013. *World development indicators, 2013.* Washington, DC: World Bank.

Wozniak, Abigail, and Thomas J. Murray. 2012. Timing is everything: Short-run population impacts of immigration in U.S. cities. *Journal of Urban Economics* 72: 60–78.

Wright, Richard A., Mark Ellis, and Michael Reibel. 1997. The linkage between immigration and internal migration in large metropolitan areas in the United States. *Economic Geography* 73: 234–254.

Yang, Dean. 2011. Migrant remittances. *Journal of Economic Perspectives* 25: 1–24.

Zimmermann, David J. 1992. Regression toward mediocrity in economic stature. *American Economic Review* 82: 409–429.

Zorlu, Aslap, and Joop Hartog. 2005. The effect of immigration on wages in three European countries. *Journal of Population Economics* 18: 113–151.

Acknowledgments

This book summarizes what I have learned about the economics of immigration. Since I began to work on immigration-related issues in the early 1980s, I have accumulated a long list of debts, almost all of which are impossible to repay. Nevertheless, this is as good an opportunity as will ever present itself to acknowledge some of those who made this exploration possible.

The debts started to accumulate at the beginning: I am very grateful to my teachers. I was one of those students who graduated from college quite uncertain of what to do with his future. In today's hypercompetitive admissions process to economics doctoral programs, where there seems to be a need to write an essay detailing exactly what one's interests are, evidence of research potential, and a description of the wonderful and influential career that one is expected to have a couple of decades into the future, I know my application would be one of the first to be thrown into the reject pile.

I decided to pursue a graduate education in economics for three reasons. First, I had to do something after college, and somehow the idea of getting a "real" job never occurred to me. Second, I was interested in social issues. And third, economics had equations, which I liked. To my good fortune, the very first class I took in graduate school at Columbia University was the first class taught by a very young Jim Heckman, who had just received his doctorate at Princeton. Jim was teaching the introductory yearlong econometrics sequence, and soon after the end of the first semester he asked me if I would like to be his research assistant. Needless to say, *that* was a life-changing moment.

In addition to studying with and working for Jim, who was just beginning his Nobel Prize–winning work on the economics of labor supply and self-selection, I was equally fortunate to study under the tutelage of two towering figures in modern labor economics, Jacob Mincer and Sherwin Rosen. After Jim left for the greener pastures at the University of Chicago, I became Jacob's research assistant, and that experience was about the best apprenticeship a young empirically minded labor economist could have, guided by a master practitioner. Similarly, Sherwin visited Columbia while I was a graduate student and taught his theory-oriented labor class. Sherwin believed that a small number of economic models could help us understand such diverse phenomena as selection, compensating wage differentials, and discrimination. That class radically changed the way I thought about the field. The combination of these influences made me very appreciative of the intellectual evolution of labor economics, of the intimate link between theory and data that characterized the best research, and of the importance of being careful. Although I quickly perceived back then that I could never reach the heights achieved by those three great economists, I have certainly tried to emulate their work and I know that their influence is stamped on every paper I have written.

I am also grateful to many generations of students. I have taught classes on the economics of immigration to graduate students at the Harvard Kennedy School, to undergraduates at Harvard College, and to many other students in various programs. The old adage that you never really learn something until you have to teach it is particularly true in my case. The preparation of lecture notes and the fact that I needed to present the material in the simplest way possible forced me to distill what was important and throw out what was not, to confront puzzles and problems that authors typically relegate to footnotes, and to answer questions that sometimes probed the validity of whole strands of research, including my own. I know that my work is much clearer and focused because of those interactions.

Over the years, I have been privileged to work with some extremely bright men and women trying to push forward the frontier of knowledge in immigration economics. These friendships and collaborations have been invaluable to my development. I have learned a lot from them, and I am certain that many of my coauthors can detect their influence in my subsequent work. I am particularly grateful to Abdurrahman Aydemir, Bernt Bratsberg, Steve Bronars, Kirk Doran, Richard Freeman, Rachel Friedberg, Jeff Grogger, Gordon Hanson, Lynette Hilton, Larry Katz, Valerie Ramey, Glenn Sueyoshi, Marta Tienda, and Steve Trejo. There is one other economist, with whom I never coauthored, but with whom I have talked to so often about our common interests that it feels like I have written several papers with him. Dan Hamermesh and I first met outside the seminar room just before he was to present a paper at the famed Columbia Labor Workshop. He was a young assistant professor and I was a graduate student. We have been friends since. He has commented frequently on my work-in-progress, and I have always learned something from his reactions.

I am also indebted to the many other colleagues who read some of the underlying research papers (usually at an early stage) and/or some of the chapters in this book and provided detailed comments. Although I was not able to pursue every suggestion, I know that many of their reactions percolated in my thinking for quite some time and often sparked new questions and opened new avenues for investigation. These colleagues include Alberto Abadie, Josh Angrist, Orley Ashenfelter, David Autor, Robert Barro, Gary Becker, Julian Betts, Fran Blau, Charlie Brown, John Conlisk, Sue Dynarski, Anthony Edo, Ron Ehrenberg, Ed Glaeser, George Johnson, Larry Kahn, Larry Kenny, Alan Krueger, Bob LaLonde, Ed Lazear, John Pencavel, Panu Poutvaara, Jim Rauch, Dani Rodrik, Mike Rothschild, Jim Smith, Joel Sobel, Petra Todd, Bob Topel, Mathis Wagner, and Finis Welch. In addition, over the years I presented early versions of the research papers that form the foundation for this book at countless seminars worldwide. I owe an enormous debt to the many seminar participants who chimed in with specific comments, criticisms, and suggestions. Often enough, those reactions helped guide the direction of my work and made me reshape and reformulate my approach to many specific issues and problems.

In fact, readers who are familiar with my academic papers on immigration may be surprised to find that the discussion here often differs in tone and approach, and sometimes even in the inferences drawn from the analysis. More often than not, these differences reflect the maturation in my thinking and my growing appreciation for the many subtleties and conceptual ambiguities inherent in the research.

Various government agencies and foundations funded my immigration-related research over the past three decades. They include the National Science Foundation, the U.S. Department of Labor, the Rockefeller Foundation, the Russell Sage Foundation, the Smith-Richardson Foundation, and the Sloan Foundation. The financial support provided by these institutions gave me a substantial amount of freedom with my time and allowed me to focus on my research for long stretches. I am particularly grateful to the MacArthur Foundation for providing financial support in the past two years so I could specifically work on and complete this book.

Further, this book could not have been produced without the encouragement and assistance of Michael Aronson, my editor at Harvard University Press. Although the book was "only" three years late, he waited patiently as I slowly tried to produce a coherent volume that attempted to summarize what immigration economics was about and knew exactly when to send a friendly email to ask how things were going. I am particularly grateful to two anonymous reviewers who provided detailed comments on the first draft of this manuscript. Their reactions, suggestions, and insights helped to improve the presentation and broaden the scope of the discussion. I am also indebted to Ran Abramitzky, Jesús Fernández-Huertas Moraga, Larry Katz, Bill Kerr, and Fabian Waldinger for generously sharing data and files they had used in their own research so that I could use them as inputs in some of the figures and tables reported in this book.

Finally, I am most grateful to my family: my wife, Jane, and my children, Sarah, Timothy, and Rebecca. Jane and I met soon after my first paper on immigration was published, and our three children came shortly thereafter in a very productive 18-month period. Jane is the glue that allowed all of us to have a normal family life. I know that her love, her support, and her steadiness allowed me to concentrate more fully on the work I was doing. As for my children, they are one of my greatest joys. If somebody were to ask me what my typical day was like over the past quarter-century, as much of the research summarized in this book was being shaped and as our children grew from toddlers into young adults, I know exactly what I would say: I worked on one of my papers and I played with my kids. I enjoyed both of these activities immensely, and I consider myself extremely lucky to have had the opportunity to do both.

I always found immigration to be a fascinating topic, dating back to my childhood when for a time, immigration issues were a daily concern in my family's life. It turned out that the study of the economics of immigration raised a multitude of interesting questions that drove many of my research interests during my professional career. It often felt as if I was putting together the pieces of an enormous jigsaw puzzle—the outline of which I could, at times, barely discern. It has been a most interesting and gratifying quest to try to find out what the puzzle is hiding.

Index